Self-Governance and Cooperation

Self-Governance and Cooperation

ROBERT H. MYERS

OXFORD
UNIVERSITY PRESS

OXFORD

UNIVERSITY PRESS

Great Clarendon Street, Oxford OX2 6DP

Oxford University Press is a department of the University of Oxford.
It furthers the University's objective of excellence in research, scholarship,
and education by publishing worldwide in

Oxford New York

Athens Auckland Bangkok Bogotá Buenos Aires Calcutta
Cape Town Chennai Dar es Salaam Delhi Florence Hong Kong Istanbul
Karachi Kuala Lumpur Madrid Melbourne Mexico City Mumbai
Nairobi Paris São Paulo Singapore Taipei Tokyo Toronto Warsaw

with associated companies in Berlin Ibadan

Oxford is a registered trade mark of Oxford University Press
in the UK and in certain other countries

Published in the United States
by Oxford University Press Inc., New York

© Robert H. Myers 1999

The moral rights of the author have been asserted
Database right Oxford University Press (maker)

First published 1999

British Library Cataloguing in Publication Data

Data available

Library of Congress Cataloging in Publication Data
Myers, Robert H.
Self-governance and cooperation/Robert H. Myers.
Includes bibliographical references and index.
1. Ethics. 2. Cooperation. 3. Consequentialism (Ethics.)
I. Title.
BJ1012.M94 1999 171—dc21 99–12991
ISBN 0–19–823839–8

1 3 5 7 9 10 8 6 4 2

Typeset in Times by
Cambrian Typesetters, Frimley, Surrey

Printed in Great Britain
on acid-free paper by
Biddles Ltd
Guildford and King's Lynn

*to my mother
and the memory of my father*

ACKNOWLEDGEMENTS

In writing this book, I have enjoyed the assistance and support of a number of colleagues and friends. My oldest and probably still deepest debts are owed to Samuel Scheffler, Donald Davidson, and Barry Stroud, who served as my thesis advisers at Berkeley and did much to shape my sense of philosophy. Since coming to New York ten years ago, I have learned a great deal from the community of moral philosophers here, especially from those who converge on the various colloquia and seminars at New York University, where I got my start, and perhaps most of all from Liam Murphy, who was just finishing his degree at Columbia when I moved uptown to Barnard. It was during some of our many conversations on the content and authority of morality that my own views on these subjects began to crystallize around the ideals of self-governance and cooperation. I would also like to thank my fellow members of the Barnard Philosophy Department, for providing such a congenial atmosphere in which to work, and Claudine Verheggen, kindred spirit in philosophy and out, for just about everything else.

On a more formal note, I would like to thank the following journals and publishers for permitting me to use here material that has already appeared elsewhere. Chapters 1 and 2 are based, in part, on 'Prerogatives and Restrictions from the Cooperative Point of View', *Ethics*, 105 (© 1994 by The University of Chicago); an earlier version of Chapter 3 appeared as 'On the Explanation, the Justification and the Interpretation of Action', *Nous*, 29 (© 1995 by Basil Blackwell); while Chapter 4 and the Conclusion draw heavily on 'The Inescapability of Moral Reasons', *Philosophy and Phenomenological Research*, 59.

Finally, thanks are owed to Barnard College, for granting me the Special Assistant Professor Leave during which most of this book was written, and to Nicole Couvreur and Dieter Koenig, for providing the remarkable Mediterranean setting in which much of the writing was done.

CONTENTS

Introduction: Two Problems in Moral Philosophy   I

1. Misgivings about Consequentialism and Contractualism   16

2. Cooperating to Promote the Good   48

3. Initial Counter-Arguments Supporting Value Monism   86

4. Self-Governance and Value Dualism   116

Conclusion: Implications for the Question of Morality's
     Authority   155

References   171

Index   177

Introduction

Two Problems in Moral Philosophy

MY aim in this book is to offer, at least in outline, solutions to two problems at the heart of moral philosophy. The first concerns the content of morality's demands; the second, the nature of reason's requirements (which I allow to be possibly different). As we shall see, not everybody shares my sense of these problems (they could hardly be philosophical problems if that weren't so). But let me for the moment just say what I think these two problems are and how I propose to approach them.

The first of these problems can be introduced by provisionally stipulating that there are at least three facts about morality's content that a general characterization of morality must account for if it is to have any chance of being correct.[1] First, there is the fact that morality includes a principle of *impartial beneficence*, a defeasible requirement on individuals to do everything they can in their circumstances to promote the overall good.[2] If by contributing £100 to Oxfam I could save the lives of ten children, there is surely some reason to think that morality requires me to do so. Second, there is the fact that impartial beneficence is significantly limited by *prerogatives*, principles which often have the effect of permitting individuals to refrain from bringing about the best available outcome.[3] Even if I could save the lives of thousands of children by contributing half my salary, it seems doubtful that morality requires as much of me as that. Third, there is the fact that impartial beneficence is also subject to *restrictions*, principles

---

[1] Compare Kagan 1992. Although these three facts about morality's content will be the exclusive focus of my attention here, I do not mean to be assuming that all others can necessarily be reduced to them. Perhaps, for example, morality also includes various special obligations or principles of desert that are similarly and equally fundamental. But this is not a possibility that I shall take time to explore in this book.

[2] In speaking of the 'overall' good, I mean to refer to the general good as it is measured from an impersonal point of view. There are of course many theories concerning the nature of this good, ranging from very simple hedonistic theories to much more elaborate pluralistic ones, but nothing in this discussion will turn on the differences among them. (I shall explain more clearly why this is so in Chap. 1.)

[3] Kagan calls these *options*; but I follow the usage in Scheffler 1982.

which sometimes have the effect of positively prohibiting individuals from performing the actions that promise optimal results.[4] Perhaps I could save the lives of even more children by embezzling funds from my college; but presumably that is something that morality strictly forbids me to do. These three stipulations present a problem because, as I shall argue in Chapter 1, none of the currently influential accounts of morality's content can accommodate all three principles without seriously jeopardizing their claim to be real determinants of individual morality.[5]

This is perhaps clearest in the case of act consequentialism, the view according to which morality always requires one to do everything that one can to promote the overall good, to bring about the best outcome available in the circumstances. For this theory seems at first sight to identify impartial beneficence with the whole of morality, leaving no room at all within which either prerogatives or restrictions might somehow be accommodated. Many act consequentialists admit as much, but try to make a virtue out of this necessity by arguing that prerogatives and restrictions cannot or should not be accommodated. Others, however, argue that there actually is room within their theory for prerogatives and restrictions, and that initial impressions to the contrary are the product of ungenerous interpretations of their approach. Some argue that room for prerogatives and restrictions can be found so long as we do not take an overly narrow view of the nature of impersonal value. Others think the crucial point is rather to remember that act consequentialism directs us to promote the overall good not just as individuals but also as members of larger social units. Still others argue that prerogatives and restrictions can be accommodated within act consequentialism if it is read as directing individuals to maximize not actual but rather expected utility. What we shall see, however, is that none of these suggestions succeed in showing that act consequentialism can accommodate either prerogatives or restrictions as I have here defined them—as principles limiting the importance of impartial beneficence within individual morality.

In what other theory might our three principles be accommodated? Some philosophers have been intrigued by the thought that our principles might be accommodated by replacing act consequentialism with

---

[4] Kagan calls these *constraints*; but my preference is again to follow Scheffler.

[5] Some take worries of these sorts to support a general scepticism about the prospects for moral theory (see Williams 1985); I take them rather to indicate that we need to do some fresh thinking about what morality really aims at. (As Williams quite rightly suggests on p. 117 of his book, what is needed in moral theory are new ideas. But we are hardly likely to generate these new ideas if we too quickly embrace a general scepticism about the subject.)

some other form of consequentialism that does not tie the justification of individual action so directly to the promotion of the overall good. Thus rule consequentialists argue that actions are justified if, and only if, they would be approved by an optimal set of rules—a set of rules which is such that, if everyone utilized them, the greatest amount of good would be brought about; and motive consequentialists argue that actions are justified if, and only if, they would be generated by an optimal set of motives—a set of motives which is such that, if one always had them, one would bring about the greatest possible amount of good.[6] Now these forms of consequentialism certainly look much more promising. For one can easily understand how it might turn out that the set of rules or motives that would be optimal from the consequentialist point of view would be one calling for people not to act contrary to our three principles. The worry, however, is that it is no less easy to understand how it might turn out that some people would produce more good overall if they were governed by rules or motives sanctioning actions of a very different sort. What we shall find, I believe, is that there is really no way for indirect consequentialists to make a case for prerogatives and restrictions that is reliable enough to save us from having to look elsewhere for a solution to our problem.

A more radical break from act consequentialism would seem advisable. Many philosophers have therefore concluded that we should abandon consequentialism in all its forms and replace it with some version of the contractualist idea that morality is a system of rules that reasonable people would agree should regulate their behaviour. Thus 'Hobbesians' argue that morality is a system of rules that would appeal to rational people who cared only for their own well-being and who were consequently concerned to push through rules that would work to their individual advantage, while 'Lockeans' argue that morality is a system of rules that would appeal to rational people who did not wish to profit at each others' expense and who were accordingly concerned to settle on rules that would work to their mutual advantage.[7] Now it is again unclear precisely what these rules would be. This time, however, the worry is not just that these conceptions of morality might not accommodate our three principles; one also has to wonder whether they are

[6] These are not the only possible formulations of these views; we shall have to consider some alternatives in Chap. 1.

[7] I speak of 'Hobbesian' and 'Lockean' views, rather than of Hobbes's and Locke's views, because I doubt that their own views can be as neatly and sharply distinguished as this.

going to be able to yield any sufficiently determinate results at all. If people shared nothing but a desire to honour rules in pursuit of either their individual or their mutual advantage, couldn't they find themselves forever in disagreement about what those rules should be and about how they should be applied? I shall argue that agreement on rules cannot be guaranteed unless the parties are assumed to share a substantive end; and I shall suggest that these rules will not be moral unless that end is of a significantly less self-interested sort.

Some have taken this simply as a challenge to devise a better version of contractualism, one that does not tie moral requirement so closely to either individual or mutual advantage. Thus T. M. Scanlon has suggested that moral rules are ones that could not reasonably be rejected by anyone concerned to reach agreement with others, while Thomas Nagel has suggested that they are rules that would appeal to reasonable people trying to strike a balance between an allegiance to the impersonal point of view and their own more personal concerns.[8] Though I believe these to be large steps in the right direction, I shall close Chapter i by arguing that neither of them can give us everything that we want. Scanlon's suggestion has the merit of linking moral rules to a single shared aim, the search for 'fair' or 'reasonable' rules with which people can regulate their interactions; but even if this aim could be shown to have some sufficiently substantive content, it seems unlikely to offer any firm support for a principle of impartial beneficence. By contrast, Nagel does not have any such difficulty accounting for a principle of impartial beneficence, since his view expressly assumes a shared commitment to the impersonal point of view; however, by asking people simply to balance this commitment against their own more personal concerns, without giving them any indication of the further aims such calculations should subserve, he leaves us without any clear sense of what the results of these calculations might be, and if anything with reason to be sceptical of the prospects for prerogatives and restrictions. What we seem to need, but contractualism fails to provide, is a way to make promoting the overall good *part* but not *all* of some *single* aim that morality subserves.

Obviously I am painting here with a very broad brush; a great many details will have to be filled in later on. But I think a certain possibility is already becoming visible, a possibility that promises to avoid the shortcomings of consequentialism and contractualism. What I have in mind here is the possibility of construing morality as a cooperative

---

[8]   See Scanlon 1982 and Nagel 1991.

undertaking that aims not at the fair pursuit of individual or mutual advantage but at the fair promotion of the overall good. In that case we could say that morality's rules are rules that no one could reasonably reject who wanted to work with others promoting the good on terms fair to everyone who might possibly be affected. This would seem to be a natural way to combine the consequentialists' claim that morality must be an undertaking primarily focused on the promotion of the overall good with the contractualists' insight that it must also be an undertaking tempered by considerations of basic fairness.[9] It would therefore seem to provide a way of thinking about morality that is in itself quite compelling, and moreover one that might finally prove capable of accommodating all three of impartial beneficence, prerogatives, and restrictions.

In Chapter 2, I shall argue that all three of our principles can indeed be accommodated within a theory of this sort. For imagine a group of people who want to work together promoting the good and who are seeking fair terms of cooperation. Given that a concern to help promote the overall good is a commitment that these people all share, it would surely be unreasonable for them not to adopt at least a defeasible principle of impartial beneficence. However, since each of them is bound to have commitments other than this concern to help promote the overall good, any rule requiring people always to contribute everything they can could surely be rejected as unreasonable.[10] Moreover, if limits are going to be set on the amount people are required to contribute, it would surely also be unreasonable not to place some restrictions on actions that would involve trespassing on such prerogatives. Thus the cooperative spirit of the undertaking would seem to require that people be given the prerogative sometimes to contribute less than they can to the overall good and that these prerogatives be protected by restrictions sometimes prohibiting other people from trespassing on them.

The idea here is not that, because unfettered beneficence would cost

---

[9] I suppose someone might argue that the view I am gesturing towards here is itself a contractualist one. But my own feeling is that it differs too much from traditional forms of contractualism to be accurately described in that way. (The same might even be said about Nagel's view, given its insistence on an allegiance to impersonal value. But in other important respects Nagel's view is still close enough to traditional forms of contractualism to merit inclusion in that group. For it does not give any sort of centrality or priority to the goal of promoting impersonal value; it simply insists that a concern for impersonal values is to be part of the profile of the people negotiating morality's requirements.)

[10] Also relevant here will be worries about the fairness of requiring people to take up the slack for those who fail to comply with morality's demands.

people too much, it should be rejected by self-interested agents who were seeking (individually or mutually) advantageous terms of cooperation. Nor is the claim here that, because single-minded pursuit of beneficence would be counter-productive, it would be more productive of utility in the long run if people abided by prerogatives and restrictions. Clearly claims of these sorts would not move us any distance beyond the contractualist and consequentialist arguments that I have already mentioned. The idea here is rather that unfettered beneficence should be rejected because it does not provide *fair* terms on which to cooperate. So one of the main goals of Chapter 2 will have to be to explain what fair terms of cooperation could amount to in the context of an undertaking to promote the overall good. If they are not terms that self-interested agents would find (individually or mutually) advantageous, nor terms that would in the long run prove to be especially productive of utility, then what are they? The challenge here is not simply to explain why fair terms on which to promote the overall good should be thought to incorporate an amalgam of impartial beneficence, prerogatives, and restrictions as opposed to something else. It is in the first instance to give content to the idea that an undertaking to promote the overall good might be tempered by considerations of fairness that are not reducible to considerations of advantage.[11]

My response to this challenge will turn largely on the claim that it is not just natural but also rational for people to act in ways that reflect the full range of their commitments. What I shall be arguing is that fair terms on which to promote the overall good cannot acknowledge this to be a fact about individual rationality without making some quite fundamental concessions to it. It is not enough, for example, simply to grant that the opportunity to achieve this rationality is another good to be promoted. For that, as I shall argue, does not do full justice to the nature of the requirements that rationality makes on individuals. What rationality requires is not simply that they concern themselves with the general promulgation of opportunities for people to act in ways that reflect the full range of their commitments. It requires them above all else to ensure that

---

[11]   A slightly different way to put the problem here would be to say that I need to explain how my view differs from Nagel's idea that morality is a matter of striking a reasonable balance between an allegiance to the impersonal point of view and one's own more personal concerns. My claim will be that by invoking the notions of fairness and cooperation my view is able to yield more palatable results than Nagel's is; the challenge will be to show how it can do this without reverting to the conception of morality as a compromise among self-interested agents.

they themselves are always acting in ways that reflect the full range of the commitments that they have at the moment in question.[12] The point at issue here is nowadays often put by saying that, while the requirements of impartial beneficence are purely *agent-neutral* in character, the requirements of individual rationality are for the most part *agent-relative*. My claim in Chapter 2 might therefore be put by saying that fair terms on which to promote the overall good can acknowledge the relativistic aspects of rationality's requirements only by embracing both prerogatives and restrictions.

As we shall see, there are a number of different views one might take about the nature of these prerogatives and restrictions. Different types of actions might be permitted or restricted and the strengths of these permissions and restrictions might be set at different levels. If my talk of cooperating to promote the good is to be given determinate content, I must therefore explain how reasonable people who were committed to this undertaking could reach agreement among those various possibilities. And of course I must check the prerogatives and restrictions that emerge here against the intuitions with which we began, in order to ensure that I am supplementing impartial beneficence in a way that seems sound. (In some cases, this will involve seeing whether my theory can validate judgements we already regard as correct; in other cases, it will involve seeing whether my theory can resolve disputes in ways that seem satisfactory.) All I have done here is point towards a path down which a compelling theoretical rationale for our three principles might be found; showing that we can traverse this path and arrive at that result is one of the two main concerns of this book.

But now, suppose we do succeed in traversing this path and that it does lead to a rationale for our three principles. Suppose my talk of cooperating to promote the good can be rendered sufficiently determinate and that it does yield the results we want. What I will then have established is that any person who accepts our original stipulations about morality's content has good grounds for accepting that reasons exist of

---

[12] As we shall see, what this means is not that they should necessarily be trying to minimize the number of times they will violate this requirement over the course of their lives but rather that they should be trying at every moment not to violate this requirement *then and there*. Strictly speaking, therefore, the requirements of individual rationality are relative not just to the agent in question but also to the moment of action. In spite of this, however, I shall follow the current fashion and describe these requirements by saying that they are *agent*-relative in nature.

both the agent-neutral and the agent-relative sorts.[13] But of course what this means is that any person who denies that reasons exist of both the agent-neutral and the agent-relative sorts has good grounds for rejecting our original stipulations about morality's content. Sceptics about agent-relative reasons will think it was a mistake to suppose that prerogatives and restrictions are real determinants of individual morality; sceptics about agent-neutral reasons will think the mistake was instead to suppose that this status could be conferred on impartial beneficence. Instead of taking my arguments so far as proof of the need for a dualistic conception of reason, many people will take them as proof of the need to revise our original stipulations about morality's content.

This brings us to the second of the two main concerns of this book—solving the problem of reason's nature. The problem here is to demonstrate that people have reasons of both the agent-neutral and the agent-relative sorts. If I am right, prerogatives and restrictions will not be accommodated so long as morality is characterized as an undertaking concerned solely with maximizing the satisfaction of agent-neutral reasons. By the same token, impartial beneficence is unlikely to be accommodated so long as morality is characterized as an undertaking concerned solely with striking a balance among agent-relative reasons. It is only if reasons of both these two sorts can be shown to exist that our three principles can be accommodated.[14] But reasons of both these two sorts can be shown to exist only if a number of daunting obstacles can be overcome. In the first place, there are some powerful arguments purporting to demonstrate either that all reasons are necessarily agent-relative or that all reasons are necessarily agent-neutral. And even if it can be established that reasons of both sorts are possible, it is no easy matter to establish that instances of both types actually exist.

[13] Some people might hold that morality could accurately be characterized as a matter of cooperating to promote the good even if no reasons of the agent-neutral sort actually exist. Although I shall not take time to argue against such views here, I should say that I do not find them at all plausible. I believe that morality must ultimately be characterized in terms of considerations that are guaranteed always to provide people with some reason to act. As we shall see, this is not to assume that reason and morality are one; it is, however, to assume that in some sense 'internalism' about morality is true.

[14] Strictly speaking, it is not enough to show that reasons of both sorts exist; both must also be shown to be relevant to questions about morality's content. Brink 1986, for example, allows that agent-relative reasons exist but denies that they pose any threat to unfettered beneficence. He insists that only agent-neutral reasons are relevant to questions about morality's content, seeking to confine the relevance of agent-relative reasons to questions about morality's authority. It seems to me, however, that a plausible characterization of morality is bound to make room for reasons of every sort.

How might it be argued that all reasons are necessarily agent-relative? The most powerful arguments draw on the connection between reasons and motives.[15] The claim, very roughly, is that a person could not have any reason to perform an action of some type if recognizing that an action was of that type could not move her to perform it. This is held to have important implications for the nature of reason because it is thought that a person's desires determine what she can in the relevant sense be moved to do. Given this, together with the seemingly plausible assumption that there are no desires that everyone must necessarily have, it follows that people's reasons for action turn crucially on the desires that they happen to have. In particular, if it is not necessary for people to have any desire to promote the overall good, it follows that they need not have any reason to cooperate in its promotion. But from here it is only a short step to the conclusion that many people *do* not have any (non-derivative) reason to cooperate in the promotion of the overall good. And this cannot but lend support to the contractualist idea that morality should be characterized as a set of rules that (even) self-interested agents could agree to be reasonable.[16]

As we shall see in Chapter 3, there are several points at which philosophers have tried to derail this train of thought. Some try to discredit the claim that reasons are necessarily linked to motives; some try to discredit the claim that motives are necessarily linked to desires; some try to discredit the claim that desires are fundamentally contingent in nature. As they are normally formulated, however, these responses are not persuasive enough to keep the relativistic argument from reaching its destination. There is no plausible way to deny the connection between reasons and motives, and no plausible way either to deny the connection between motives and desires, for these connections follow from simple truisms about what reasons and desires are. If the relativistic argument is successfully to be derailed, it can only be by taking a much deeper look at what desires are and finding that they are *not*, after all, as contingent as the relativistic argument seems to suppose. It is not enough simply to assert that some desires might be necessary; what must be explained is how this could in fact be the case. This I shall undertake to

---

[15] This is not the only form that such arguments might take; but it will be the primary object of my discussion here.

[16] Obviously it would not lend any support to Nagel's version of contractualism, given his insistence that people should have a concern for impersonal value. Throughout the remainder of this Introduction, therefore, my references to contractualism should be read as referring to contractualisms of the more traditional sort.

do in Chapter 3 by developing a broadly Davidsonian argument according to which the nature of desire is shaped by the demands of interpretation and attributions of desires are necessarily governed by views about reasons. My goal will be to show that people's reasons cannot be crucially dependent upon their desires because their desires are themselves importantly dependent upon their reasons.

Does this argument have positive implications concerning the nature of these reasons? There is a train of thought that might suggest that it does.[17] For, as we shall see in Chapter 3, what makes interpretation problematic is the worry that someone's history and circumstances might be so different from our own that we would have no idea where to begin. Unless we may assume that everyone should start with desires that are at bottom the same, it is difficult to see what principled strategy we could follow in interpreting such a person. On one possible reading of this assumption, however, it amounts to claiming not just that there are objective values determining what desires people should have but also that these values are exclusively agent-neutral in nature.[18] And if our understanding of each other presupposes some such claim about the nature of value, how plausible can it really be to suppose that the truth about value is radically different? Thus it might be thought that the only way to avoid the conclusion that reasons must be agent-relative is to embrace the conclusion that they must be agent-neutral. And this cannot but lend support to the consequentialist idea that morality should be characterized as a set of rules that in one way or another promote the overall good.

This also is a train of thought that philosophers have tried to derail at a number of different points. Some try to deny that conclusions concerning the epistemology of interpretation have any bearing on questions regarding the metaphysics of value; some try to deny that interpretation does in fact presuppose any claim about the desires that everyone should have. But what we shall find is that responses of these very dismissive sorts are once again not terribly reassuring. A better bet here is to look more closely at the claim about desires that *is* presupposed by the interpretative process, in the hope of giving a different twist to the claim that

---

[17] Once again, while there may be other arguments purporting to rule out the possibility of agent-relative reasons, I shall concentrate my discussion on the one argument that I think has the best chance of succeeding.

[18] Following Nagel 1986 and many others, I shall use the terms 'reason' and 'value' more or less interchangeably. To say that objective values exist is just to say that people have reasons independent of their desires.

everyone should have desires that are at bottom the same. When we do this, we shall find that we can distinguish the claim that everyone's desires should be at bottom of the same type from the claim that they should be at bottom directed towards the same outcomes. And while the first of these claims is indeed presupposed by the interpretative process, it is only the second of them that invokes the notion of agent-neutrality. My conclusion, therefore, will be that the process of interpretation does indeed presuppose that all reasons are at bottom universal but that it does not thereby presuppose that they are all at bottom agent-neutral as well. In fact, nothing about the process of interpretation rules out the possibility that the values determining what we should all desire are exclusively agent-relative in nature.

But of course neither is there anything about this process that requires that some of these values be agent-relative. All abstract ruminations about explanation and interpretation can teach us is that reasons of both these two sorts are possible.[19] Now it might be thought that this result nevertheless does remove the only serious obstacle in the way of our concluding that reasons of both these sorts really do exist. For it might be thought that the presumption in favour of their joint existence is such that both should be assumed to exist if each can be imagined to exist. Not everyone will agree that there is such a presumption, however, so rather than assuming it we must somehow *establish* it. And obviously the arguments that we contemplate cannot simply fall back on my claims about what the vindication of our three stipulations requires. For we have seen that many consequentialists and contractualists will question whether the vindication of our three stipulations can be worth the price that they feel value dualism exacts. I shall therefore turn in Chapter 4 to the general theory of practical reason, hoping to show that value dualism is actually a view with considerable independent appeal.

Just as morality might be characterized in terms of the notion of cooperation, with different theories of morality offering us different accounts of what cooperation involves, so too might reason be characterized in terms of the notion of *self-governance*, with different theories of reason offering us different accounts of what self-governance

---

[19] That is to say, they cannot by themselves yield any more substantive conclusions about which sorts of reasons actually exist. What they can do, however, is underwrite a *methodology* that explains how these more substantive conclusions might be uncovered. I shall explain how they do this in Chap. 3, and then apply the methodology in question in Chap. 4.

involves.[20] Now many philosophers would nowadays maintain that self-governance is to be understood as requiring people always to act in line with their 'higher-order' desires.[21] But just as I shall argue that interpretation requires the assumption that people's first-order desires answer to values that are in some important sense objective, so too shall I be arguing that it requires the assumption that their higher-order desires answer to 'commitments' that are in the same sense objective. As I see things, therefore, the task of developing a theory of practical reason is in large part one of explaining what these objective commitments might be.[22] It might seem to follow from this that a person can be objectively committed to a way of life only if it is one in which every universal value has a place. And this might in turn seem to suggest that there is some one way of life to which everyone must be objectively committed, the one in which every universal value is given its univocal due. But in fact what I shall be arguing is that the relative importance of even universal values can vary from person to person with certain differences in their histories and their circumstances. As a result, while the lives to which people can be objectively committed may all involve permutations of some one set of values, they can still differ from each other in many quite important respects.

This 'objective' view of self-governance will not by itself answer my opponents' worries about the credibility of value dualism. It might seem to, perhaps, for it might seem extremely likely that the set of universal values defining the possibilities of objective commitment will include values of both types, especially given that the relative importance that even the agent-neutral values would have for individuals could vary with their particular histories and circumstances. The trouble with this, however, is that values whose relative importance can vary from person to person cannot be agent-neutral in the sense presupposed by my moral theory, for what my moral theory presupposes is that the promotion of

---

[20] Although some people will no doubt find it odd to hear consequentialist theories described as accounts of what cooperation involves, I do not think very much needs to be said in order to see why this idea has real merit. Consequentialists may be regarded as explaining what cooperation would involve if the relevant values were all agent-neutral in character; contractualists may be regarded as explaining what it would involve on the assumption that all values are instead agent-relative.

[21] Many of these analyses take Frankfurt 1971 as their point of departure.

[22] The idea of an 'objective commitment' might seem too paradoxical to swallow; but all I mean by this is an objective higher-order value, a truth about how a particular person, in view of her own particular history and circumstances, should want her first-order desires to be.

the overall good has not just some but *the same* value for everyone. The problem here is the mirror image of the one that I shall be stressing in my discussion of morality's content. As I have mentioned, and we shall see, consequentialists can refine their accounts of impersonal value so as to acknowledge the value of things like family and friendship, but what they cannot do is acknowledge the special value that someone's *own* family and friends may have for her. They can acknowledge that family and friendship are among the impersonal goods to be generally promoted, but not that one may have special reasons to care for one's own family and friends. Similarly, in the case of self-governance, what I have described so far is a way of acknowledging that promoting the overall good may have some value, but it is not a way of acknowledging the especially agent-neutral value that promoting the overall good may have. Just as we need some way to acknowledge relative values from the impersonal point of view, so too we need some way to acknowledge neutral values from the personal point of view.

As I have already indicated, in the case of morality, I shall be arguing that agent-neutral and agent-relative values are to be balanced against each other under the auspices of fairness, the idea being to determine how agent-relative values might fairly be taken into account when the goal is to promote agent-neutral values. So the question before us now is how values of these two sorts are to be balanced against each other from the perspective afforded by reason. What stands to self-governance as fairness stands to cooperation? My suggestion in Chapter 4 will be that the concept we should be focusing on here is the concept of *integrity*, which I take to be a matter of acting in ways that fully and accurately reflect one's own values and commitments. The challenge confronting us is therefore to determine what integrity requires of people given that many of the values generating reasons for them are agent-neutral in character. If I am right, it cannot simply require them to act on the particular permutation of universal values that is embodied in the way of life to which they are objectively committed. For that would in no way reflect the supposition that two comprehensive systems of value are in play, one of which does not allow that the relative importance of things can vary from person to person. Following our earlier lead, my claim in Chapter 4 will therefore be that integrity must instead require that people moderate action on their own commitments by a concern for agent-neutral value. Instead of morality's prerogative, however, what this will yield is a requirement that people satisfy their own more personal concerns so far as that is possible without countenancing too much damage to the overall good.

Evidently much work will have to be done before we can assert that this dualistic conception of reason is credible. Some will worry that it makes self-governance implausibly demanding. Are we really to suppose that self-governance might require me to sacrifice my life to save the lives of many others? Or is the idea rather that in such cases forsaking others would not be countenancing too much damage to the overall good?[23] Others will worry more about the commensurability of these values. Even if we can measure the relative value that my life possesses and the neutral value that the lives of the others possess, can we really hope to compare these quantities so as to determine whether securing the one value would justify sacrificing the other?[24] But by far the gravest worry that people have here concerns the very relevance of *neutral* values to *self*-governance. If the neutral value of an outcome is by hypothesis something other than the value that it has for a particular person in consequence of the life she has led and the circumstances she now inhabits, then in what sense can it really be a value for her? But if there is no sense in which it can really be a value for her, why should she count it as a value at all and not just as an imposition? If a dualistic conception of reason is to be made truly credible, I must somehow overcome worries of this sort by explaining why a perfectly neutral and so immutable system of values should nevertheless be thought to have an important bearing on the life of each individual agent. I shall do this in Chapter 4 by considering how a conception of reason like mine might be defended against relativistic arguments of the sort that Bernard Williams has long been advancing.[25]

I shall conclude this book by considering where this leaves the vexed

---

[23] Either way, of course, trouble will lie in the offing. If we suppose that self-governance may on occasion require one to sacrifice one's life, some people will object that this shows our account of it to be implausibly demanding. But if we suppose instead that self-governance will never make such demands of people, then we surely have to wonder what substance there can really be to the injunction never to countenance too much damage to the overall good.

[24] The worry here does not simply concern the possibility of uncovering a theory by which to explain how values of such different sorts should be combined; it also concerns the plausibility of supposing that values of such different sorts both figure in the determination of what a self-governed person should do.

[25] Although Williams has long been advancing this line of argument, it is only fairly recently (in Williams 1995) that he has clearly distinguished his powerful arguments against neutrality from his less persuasive (but more famous) arguments against objectivity. The arguments against objectivity, or what he likes to call 'external' reasons, will be among my targets in Chap. 3. What I have in mind to discuss in Chap. 4 are more recent arguments that focus more narrowly on neutrality.

question of the relation between morality and reason. My verdict here
will be in many respects quite sceptical; for while I believe that reason
agrees with morality on the importance of not countenancing too much
damage to the overall good, I think it will on at least some occasions forbid people to make supererogatory sacrifices that morality would be
happy to permit. Nor is this the worst of the differences between them;
for while I believe that its defining concern for fairness requires morality's prerogatives to be backed up by correlative restrictions, I find no
argument indicating that its concern for integrity would generate an analo-
gous structure in the case of reason. Thus I see little prospect of linking
morality to reason in the very firm way that some philosophers have
desired. This is perfectly compatible, of course, with thinking that the
rewards to be won by honouring morality's demands and the penalties to
be paid for violating them are typically so great and so probable that most
people will normally have more reason to comply with them than not.[26]
But it is to concede that no guarantees can be made about reasons to act
morally; they cannot be guaranteed always to be overriding, nor even
never to be overridden themselves. What can be said, however, is that
cooperating in the promotion of the overall good may itself be an activity possessed of considerable agent-relative value, so much so that it may
be only very rarely and with great reluctance that reason's verdicts come
down against morality's. My parting suggestion will be that this is a
result that we should find quite reassuring; for while it does not make
morality overriding, it at least explains its feeling of inescapability.

Some people, of course, will complain that this is not enough, that we
must not settle for anything less than the conclusion that morality is
overriding. But that, I believe, is more than can be established—unless,
perhaps, we were to adopt an account of morality's content even more
sceptical than my claims about its authority. As we shall see, compromise is inevitable here. We cannot accommodate all three of impartial
beneficence, prerogatives, and restrictions while also confirming morality to be overriding. The question, therefore, is what we should settle for.
My claim will be that the least sceptical view on balance is the one that
I shall be developing here.

[26] Arguments of this view are of course familiar from Hobbes 1651 and, more
recently, Gauthier 1986. They become particularly compelling when developed in the
context of the view that values are objective; but that is not something that I shall undertake to demonstrate in any great detail here.

Misgivings about Consequentialism and Contractualism

My goal in this chapter is to demonstrate that neither consequentialism nor contractualism can succeed in accommodating all three of the facts that we stipulated about morality's content. But first I need to say something more about the point of this exercise. For contractualists often deny that morality includes even a defeasible principle of impartial beneficence; and consequentialists often deny that impartial beneficence is encumbered by prerogatives and/or restrictions. So what is to be gained by showing that their theories cannot accommodate these principles?

The first response to make here is that there are in fact a great many contractualists and consequentialists who would actually prefer *not* to deny that morality includes all three of impartial beneficence, prerogatives, and restrictions. Admittedly, consequentialists will usually deny that prerogatives and restrictions are as fundamental to morality as impartial beneficence is, while contractualists will usually deny that impartial beneficence is as fundamental to morality as prerogatives and restrictions are. On both sides of the aisle, however, it is easy to find people who would nonetheless like to believe that impartial beneficence, prerogatives, and restrictions are for all that equally secure features of morality's content. Therefore, by showing this to be unrealistic, by showing that they are bound to destabilize one or more of our three principles, we can give many consequentialists and contractualists good grounds to adopt a different approach.

Moreover, even when they do concede that they cannot recognize all three of impartial beneficence, prerogatives, and restrictions as equally secure features of morality's content, many consequentialists and contractualists would like to believe that they can at least explain why so many people find such principles so very attractive. They grant that many people feel strongly drawn to the sorts of verdicts that the triumvirate of impartial beneficence, prerogatives, and restrictions would hand down, and so they try very hard to show that their respective approaches to moral theory can replicate as many verdicts of these types as possible.[1] Obviously enough, this then leaves them vulnerable to the charge that their respective approaches to moral theory in fact fall far short of this intuitive standard—not only much farther short than they would themselves like to believe, but perhaps even farther short than they are themselves prepared to accept. So if we can demonstrate not just that consequentialist and contractualist theories fail to accommodate our three principles but also that they fail quite badly, we will have provided so many more proponents of these theories with grounds (as good as their replications are bad) to adopt a different approach.

Of course, there remains the possibility that some consequentialists and contractualists might be totally indifferent or positively hostile to verdicts of the sorts that our three principles would hand down. What are we to say, for example, to consequentialists who have no qualms at all about taking one innocent life in cases where that will save five equally innocent lives? Or again, to contractualists who have no qualms at all about declining to make any sacrifices for strangers in cases where those strangers will never be in a position to reciprocate? How can we expect to dislodge such people from their respective theories simply by demonstrating that neither consequentialism nor contractualism can accommodate all three of impartial beneficence, prerogatives, and restrictions?

Evidently that would be too much to expect—consequentialists and contractualists of these persuasions are going to have to be addressed in different terms. They tend to be moved almost exclusively by more general considerations about the nature of value, which will be my subject in later chapters.[2] For now, however, we can take some heart from the fact that consequentialists and contractualists of these persuasions are comparatively few in number. The majority are at least somewhat enamoured

---

[1] Although it is not entirely clear how concerned either of them is to replicate the fullest possible range of these verdicts, Scheffler and Kagan both give clear expression to this tendency. Thus Scheffler 1982 freely admits that impartial beneficence, prerogatives, and restrictions are all intuitively appealing, even though he thinks that only impartial beneficence and prerogatives have a compelling 'theoretical rationale'. Similarly, Kagan 1989 happily grants that impartial beneficence, prerogatives, and restrictions, are all part of 'commonsense morality', even as he maintains that only impartial beneficence can withstand theoretical scrutiny.

[2] Specifically, the contractualists tend to be moved by the thought that there could not be or in any event are not any agent-neutral values, whereas the consequentialists tend to be moved by the thought that there could not be or in any event are not any agent-relative values. In their different ways, they both reject the sort of value dualism that I shall be arguing for in the second half of this book.

of the sorts of verdicts that the triumvirate of impartial beneficence, prerogatives, and restrictions would hand down, and so at least somewhat
vulnerable to the charge that their respective approaches to moral theory
keep them from replicating these verdicts very well. How vulnerable they
are to this charge will of course depend on how concerned they are to
replicate the broadest range of these verdicts. But it seems fair to say that
enough of them will be concerned enough about this to make our efforts
in this chapter worthwhile. And of course the graver the difficulties we
create for them on this front, the larger our beachhead against consequentialism and contractualism will be.

One final remark before we set to work. Even if my assessment of the
situation is badly misguided, and there turn out to be very few consequentialists and contractualists who are very much concerned to replicate verdicts of the sorts that the triumvirate of impartial beneficence,
prerogatives, and restrictions would hand down, we will still have something quite important to gain by considering where and why their
approaches cannot replicate these verdicts. For so long as *we* are concerned to articulate a moral theory that can accommodate all three of our
principles, it evidently behoves us to get as clear as we possibly can
about where and why the available alternatives cannot succeed at this
task, as their failures may have much to tell us about the direction in
which what we want might be found. That in itself is reason enough to
proceed.

I. *Consequentialism, Prerogatives, and Restrictions*

Let us begin by considering a version of act consequentialism that
directs individuals to perform the actions (or, in case there is more than
one, *an* action) that will in their circumstances bring about the best (or,
in the event that there are ties, an *optimal*) available outcome.[3] It is easy
to see how this theory could accommodate impartial beneficence, but
much harder to see how it could accommodate prerogatives and restrictions; for it seems to identify impartial beneficence with the whole of
morality. Is there any reason to think this appearance is in fact illusory?

---

3   To keep things simple, I shall hereafter ignore such complexities and talk as if, for
any given person at any given time, there is one available outcome better than all the others. I shall also pass over various difficulties concerning the proper formulation of this
notion of 'availability', except to stress that I am at this stage talking about 'actual' rather
than 'expected' availability.

One possible reason for thinking this might stem from a common misunderstanding about what these prerogatives and restrictions really are. For example, it might be argued that act consequentialism cannot help but accommodate prerogatives because the theory of the good around which it is built cannot help but recognize the impersonal value of cultivating and implementing personal projects and commitments. Much of value would be lost if people were never to lay aside their commitment to promoting the overall good and act instead on their more personal concerns for the particular people and causes that they happen to hold dear. In fact, it might be argued that one of the principal factors determining the ranking of available outcomes is the extent to which people succeed in devoting themselves not to the overall good but to their own more personal concerns. And so it might be argued that act consequentialism cannot help but accommodate prerogatives because it cannot help but take seriously the importance of getting people to devote as much time as they can to their own projects and commitments.[4]

In a similar vein, it might be argued that act consequentialism cannot help but accommodate restrictions because the theory of the good around which it is built cannot help but recognize the impersonal value of avoiding and averting certain actions.[5] Murder and torture, enslavement and exploitation, corruption and degradation—actions such as these are evidently so terrible in nature that one hesitates to admit that the performance of them could ever be included as part of the best available outcome. At the very least, it might be argued that one of the principal factors determining the ranking of available outcomes is the extent to which people manage to refrain from performing any actions that are as intrinsically objectionable as these. And so it might be argued that act consequentialism cannot help but accommodate restrictions because it cannot help but take seriously the importance of getting people to refrain as much as they can from performing actions of various proscribed types. Why should we suppose that any of this presents a problem that act consequentialism will not be able to overcome?

The answer, of course, is to be found by looking more closely at our original stipulations. When we say that morality includes prerogatives permitting people on some occasions to refrain from bringing about the best available outcome, we are not simply saying that people's devoting themselves to their more personal concerns has some significant impersonal value (though it would be surprising if that were not implied). For

---

[4] See e.g. Sosa 1993.   [5] Here too, see Sosa 1993.

that, by itself, would leave each person free to devote time and energy to her more personal concerns only in so far as her doing so would promote the overall good. In so far as she could better promote the overall good by treating her personal concerns no differently from anybody else's, as just the personal concerns of one person among many other people whose well-being is of equal importance, that is still what act consequentialism would require of her.[6] But prerogatives, by contrast, are supposed to free people from always having to pay this strict sort of obedience to the impersonal point of view.[7] Their point is not to moderate the demands of impartial beneficence by modifying its theory of the good so that it will require less of people; it is to limit the authority of impartial beneficence by supplementing it so that people will not always have to do what it requires.

Pretty clearly, remarks of a very similar sort can be made in the case of restrictions. When we say that morality includes restrictions requiring people on some occasions to refrain from bringing about the best available outcome, we are not simply saying that certain sorts of actions are objectionable in the extreme (though it would once again be surprising if that were not at least implied). By itself, that would leave each person having to perform such actions whenever it did happen that her doing so would in the circumstances bring about the greatest possible amount of good. If, for example, the circumstances happen to be such that it is only by committing one murder that many other murders can be averted, then, all else being equal, one would be required to murder, no matter how objectionable murder might be when considered from the impersonal point of view. By contrast, restrictions are supposed to prohibit certain actions even on some occasions when performing them would generate the greatest possible amount of good.[8] Their point is not to alter the demands of impartial beneficence so that it will less frequently justify people in performing actions that seem quite objectionable; it is to constrain the authority of

---

[6] In particular, if she could enable other people to devote more extra time to their personal concerns by devoting no extra time to her own, then, everything else being equal, this is what act consequentialism would require her to do, no matter how important it took personal concerns to be.

[7] This point is very nicely (and more thoroughly) explained in Scheffler 1982, chap. 2. He puts it by saying that prerogatives conflict with act consequentialism's 'strict proportionality requirement'.

[8] To be more precise, this is a feature of restrictions as we have defined them. For a brief discussion of a rather different view of restrictions, see Chap. 2 below.

impartial beneficence so that on some occasions it will not bear on questions of justification at all.[9]

Once we are clearer about what prerogatives and restrictions are, it becomes even harder to see how act consequentialism could accommodate them. If it cannot accommodate them by adjusting its theory of the good, what form could its accommodation of these principles possibly take?

One possible answer to this question might be drawn from chapter 5 of Mill's *Utilitarianism*. There Mill argues, quite persuasively, that it would be in various ways counter-productive for us, as a society, to try to compel each one of our number in all circumstances to do everything she can to promote the overall good. Certainly it would be a mistake to bring the coercive power of the law to bear on every single case. While that might indeed lead many people to contribute more to the overall good than they otherwise would have done, those gains would surely be offset by the losses inevitably incurred when so much power is placed in bureaucratic hands. I take it that these losses would be of a sort too familiar to need cataloguing. Perhaps it is true, for example, that the overall good would be marginally enhanced if I were required by the law to give up my career in philosophy and devote my energies instead to the study of mathematics or economics. But a society in which decisions of this sort were made by bureaucrats seems certain to be an unhappy one—not only because, as a group, we would lose the many benefits that individual initiative and experimentation alone make possible, but also because, as individuals, we would lose the special good that comes of making important decisions oneself.[10]

Now of course, as Mill is fond of pointing out, the law is by no means the only mechanism through which society could try to compel its individual members to do everything they possibly can to promote

---

[9]   More precisely, so that on some occasions the mere fact that a certain action would bring about the best available outcome would not serve to make it even permissible, let alone required. (In other respects, of course, impartial beneficence may always be relevant to questions of justification, for the amount of good at stake may help determine whether an action is restricted at all.)

[10]   It is worth stressing that Mill is at all times worried about losses of these two different kinds—not just the losses incurred to the overall good when the law (because imperfectly written, or imperfectly applied) obliges people to make choices less productive of overall utility than the choices they otherwise would have made, but also the losses incurred to the individual's good (and thereby, of course, to the overall good) whenever a person is forced to compromise her capacity for autonomous decision and act simply as someone else decrees. For a helpful discussion of this point and some important questions it raises for Mill, see Brink 1992.

the overall good. There is also the mechanism Mill refers to when he speaks of 'public opinion'. Some expectations may be enforced not by the law but by tacit conventions governing expressions of society's favour or disfavour. (A closely related mechanism, which Mill also mentions, involves the shaping of individual conscience through the practice of moral education—a practice that Mill believes should be regulated by society but otherwise left so far as possible to individual families.[11]) Suppose, for example, that I have led you to believe you will have my rent-controlled apartment when I leave but that, when the time comes, I am inclined to accept a substantial bribe and give it to somebody else. Depending on the details, this might once again be the sort of case where the law should fear to tread.[12] But it might yet be a case where public opinion could usefully be brought to bear. It may very well be true that society would produce the greatest amount of good overall if it were to express its strong displeasure at all those who lead others to have legitimate expectations which they then fail to meet.

But Mill's familiar point is that even the exercise of public opinion can be counter-productive.[13] It is only, he thinks, in cases where the contribution a person could be making to the overall good is of an assignable and enforceable type that society should attempt to compel maximal contributions via the law or public opinion. The second of our examples might be of this type, if indeed my actions have clearly created a legitimate expectation. But in our first example, and in examples like it, where no one has any especially salient claim on me, the chances are, Mill thinks, that society would do best in the long run leaving me to my own devices. This is not to say that it should never express its views about such cases. Mill's point is rather that, while society may usefully try to persuade people to act in certain ways in such cases, it cannot usefully try to compel them to do so, whether by the law or by public opinion. On the contrary, it will do better to compel others to leave them free to decide such cases for themselves. Whenever the contribution a person could be making to the overall good is not of an assignable and enforceable type, society should employ either the law or public opinion to ensure that that person is left to her own devices.

Summary and schematic though these remarks obviously are, I

---

[11] To keep things simple, I shall focus in what follows on the two mechanisms of the law and public opinion.

[12] Of course, if an agreement has been signed, or if certain other conditions have been met, things might be different.

[13] This point is of course especially familiar from Mill 1859.

believe they suffice to indicate how Mill thought he could accommodate rights within his consequentialism, and how this in turn might be thought to make accommodation of prerogatives and restrictions possible. Rights, for Mill, are things 'which society ought to defend me in the possession of'.[14] They are in essence prerogatives to decide certain matters oneself, prerogatives that society should protect by restricting interference from others. (If the right were to something like gainful employment or adequate housing, it would presumably not be enough simply to restrict interference from others, but the protection of a prerogative by correlative restrictions would still figure prominently in the analysis.) Mill clearly believes, for example, that sane adults typically have the prerogative to choose for themselves the particular careers that they will try to pursue, even though, in exercising this prerogative, they don't always produce as much good as they could. What this means for him is that society should try to ensure that people are not coerced in such matters. And this it should do by trying to enforce certain restrictions on everybody else's behaviour. All of this is held to be consonant with his consequentialism, of course, because, if an objector were to ask why society should try to enforce these restrictions, we 'can [and need] give him no other reason than general utility'.[15]

Does this argument succeed in showing that prerogatives and restrictions can be accommodated within consequentialism? I doubt very much that it does. No doubt it does show that something rather like prerogatives and restrictions can be so accommodated. But what of prerogatives and restrictions themselves?

To see what I have in mind here, we need only imagine one of those scenarios, of the sort so often discussed in philosophy, where circumstances are such that it is only by maltreating one person that another person can make her maximal contribution to the overall good. Let us suppose it is a scapegoat case, so that we can call the one person 'the scapegoat' and the other person 'the sheriff'. Let us also suppose it is well constructed, so that convicting the scapegoat really would enable the sheriff to produce the most good overall. (In order to secure this result, we might have to suppose that nobody would ever learn that an innocent person had knowingly been convicted, that convicting this innocent person would not cause the sheriff to convict other innocent

---

[14] See Mill 1861, chap. 5, para. 25. For a more recent account along strikingly similar lines, see Waldron 1994.
[15] See Mill 1861, chap. 5, para. 25.

people in the future, and so on and so forth.) And let us finally suppose the case is one instance of a general sort of case about which the following can truly be said: we as a society would produce the most good overall if we were to try to enforce a restriction against acting in such ways.[16] What in these circumstances should our sheriff do? The consequentialism we have so far considered would seem to require that she convict the scapegoat. No restrictions have been placed on individual conduct; the issue has so far been what policies it would be productive for society to pursue. Her society may try to restrict such actions, either through the law or through public opinion; but what has that to do with her? She herself can produce the most good overall by convicting the scapegoat; so why should we suppose that consequentialism requires anything else of her?[17]

What these reflections reveal is that Mill's argument (or anyway my retelling of it) succeeds in accommodating prerogatives and restrictions only by treating them as matters of social policy rather than as principles governing individual action. But this is pretty clearly not what we originally had in mind. Regarding restrictions, for example, what we stipulated at the beginning was that morality itself sometimes prohibits individuals from performing actions that promise optimal results. This is not at all the same as saying that morality sometimes requires society to try to coerce its members into eschewing such actions. And of course precisely the same point can be made regarding prerogatives. It is one thing for morality to permit individuals to refrain from performing actions that promise optimal results, but quite another thing for society to ensure that they will in fact be free to do so. Now it is easy to imagine how Mill would respond to this. He would want to insist that, if these were our original stipulations, then we slightly missed the mark, for prerogatives and restrictions actually exist as right-making features not of individual conduct but of social policy.[18] He would allow that they also have an extremely important role to play as 'secondary principles' by

---

[16]   It is important that the claim be about the utility of *society's* enforcing the restriction. If the Millian account held that rights exist wherever *somebody* could usefully enforce a restriction, it would generate many results that are extremely implausible—a point that surfaces in Kagan's (1994) response to Waldron.

[17]   Compare Kagan 1994: 345, and (especially) Lyons 1994, chap. 6, pp. 164 ff.

[18]   An alternative reading of Mill, nicely elaborated in Lyons 1994, makes him out to be a kind of indirect consequentialist, one for whom principles governing individual action are determined by precisely the questions concerning social policy that we have been considering. I briefly comment on this reading of Mill, and on this version of consequentialism, on p. 27 below.

which individuals should guide their practical deliberations; for he holds that the record of human experience clearly indicates that individuals normally produce the most good by exercising prerogatives and honouring restrictions.[19] He might even go so far as to recommend that individuals always base their decisions on these principles, even when they feel certain more good lies elsewhere, since the record shows such feelings to be unreliable. But that wouldn't alter his view about what makes individual conduct right.

If consequentialists are to accommodate the claim that prerogatives and restrictions really exist as right-making features of individual conduct, and not simply as secondary principles helpful in directing individuals towards actions that are right, then they must abandon the simple act consequentialist idea that the right action for a person to perform at any moment is one that will in actual fact produce the greatest amount of good overall. Hoping to remain act consequentialists, they might try to replace this with the idea that the right action for a person to perform at any moment is one that can be *expected* to produce the greatest amount of good overall.[20] For as we have seen, it might be held that the record of human experience speaks so overwhelmingly in favour of prerogatives and restrictions that no one could reasonably expect to promote more good by acting in some other way. But surely the plain fact of the matter is that the record of human experience does not speak overwhelmingly in favour of prerogatives and restrictions but instead reveals their neglect often to have good consequences. And surely it is possible to say something about when their neglect has good consequences, enough to ensure that people sometimes could reasonably expect to promote more good overall by acting in some other way.

Act consequentialists of this 'decision-theoretic' sort might respond by arguing that people can reasonably expect neglect of prerogatives and restrictions to have optimal consequences only when the amount of good at stake is very great—great enough to ensure that neglect of these principles would in any case be justified. After all, they might say, plausible

---

[19] See Mill 1861, chap. 2, para. 24. For an account of rights that treats them simply as guides to decision-making (both individual and social), and not as right-making features of individual conduct, see Sumner 1987, chap. 6. For a similar treatment of prerogatives, see Railton 1984.

[20] More precisely: one that will (in actual fact) maximize not actual overall utility but rather *expected* overall utility. See Jackson 1991. (I should stress that Jackson himself does *not* argue that decision-theoretic consequentialism would accommodate prerogatives and restrictions. See p. 482.)

prerogatives and restrictions are bound to have thresholds beyond which they no longer apply. When we stipulated that morality sometimes permits or even requires people to refrain from performing actions that promise optimal results, we presumably did not mean to deny that performing such actions could become required if enough good was at stake. But even if this is correct (a question I shall return to) it is difficult to believe that these thresholds will correspond with the points at which people can reasonably expect neglect of prerogatives and restrictions to have optimal consequences. Surely there could be circumstances in which neglect of prerogatives or restrictions could reasonably be expected to have optimal consequences, but in which the amount of good at stake seems not sufficient to override them. And in any case it is difficult to understand how this strategy could accommodate prerogatives; for if it works at all it seems to make their exercise required rather than optional as we have stipulated.[21]

This last is a point of some importance. While shifting their focus from actual utility to expected utility may enable act consequentialists to avoid identifying morality with impartial beneficence, they are still going to be thinking of morality as a set of requirements governing individual action and social policy. But prerogatives involve permissions and not (just) requirements.[22] Perhaps a requirement to refrain from certain actions could be derived from a more general requirement to maximize expected utility; but a permission to refrain from certain actions is surely going to have to be generated in some other way.

Thus it seems safe to say that consequentialists who wish to accommodate prerogatives and restrictions will have to abandon act consequentialisms in favour of some 'indirect' version of the theory such as

[21] I suppose it might be argued that on some occasions what would maximize expected utility is a spontaneous choice from among a list of possibilities, ranging from the action that would in fact bring about the best available outcome to actions that would have consequences somewhat more favourable to oneself. If that were true, one wouldn't be required on such occasions to make less than one's maximal contribution to the overall good, one would simply be permitted to do so. But I doubt that there are very many cases of this sort or that the ones there are line up very well with the prerogatives we believe actually to exist. More importantly, I doubt that even this more sophisticated argument would yield permissions of precisely the sort that prerogatives involve. For clearly one can have a prerogative to do less and yet legitimately resolve always to do everything one can.

[22] They do involve requirements in the sense that there are limits to when and how far one is permitted to stray from the action that would bring about the best available outcome, and one is required always to stay within those limits. But the point, once again, is that, within these limits, the prerogative gives one the permission to perform whatever action one likes.

rule or motive consequentialism. Even Mill is sometimes read as a consequentialist of this indirect sort. I myself am inclined to think that his reliance on 'secondary principles' in chapter 2 of *Utilitarianism* preempts this interpretation.[23] But the distinction he draws in chapter 5 between mere expediency and moral requirement clearly does lend it considerable support.[24] Be that as it may, however, the idea, on this reading, is that an action is not required by morality, no matter how productive of utility it would be, unless it would be prompted by a conscience that would in the long run produce an optimal amount of good. (For an action to be required not simply by morality but also by justice, it must in addition conform with rules that society would do well to enforce, if not through the mechanism of the law, then at least through the mechanisms of public opinion and moral education.) Now this version of consequentialism has the distinct advantage of making it clear how prerogatives might be included within morality. For a *conscience* that would be optimally productive of utility might very well be silent when *actions* are less so. Perhaps the ideal conscience from the consequentialist point of view would be one that remains silent so long as people contribute 'enough' to the promotion of the overall good without performing actions of various 'prohibited' sorts. If so, then this version of consequentialism would accommodate prerogatives and restrictions.

But is this the form that people's conscience should take? One worry that is standardly expressed here is that, while it is easy to say that such

---

[23] I say this because the need for secondary principles is obviously going to be greatest if consequentialism is understood as requiring individuals to maximize actual or expected utility. If consequentialism is instead understood as requiring people to act as an ideal conscience would have them act, then it is not principles that they need but that conscience. I suppose it might be replied that an ideal conscience is best acquired through the inculcation of such secondary principles; but it seems to me that this would take us some distance from Mill's discussion as we actually have it.

[24] The point here is obviously that, if the merely expedient action is the one in the circumstances that would bring about the best available outcome, and moral requirement sometimes differs from that, then morality cannot always require one to perform the action that would bring about the best available outcome. My own view of the matter is that Mill is trading here on an ambiguity in talk of 'moral requirement', on the difference between what society can morally require of one and what one is oneself morally required to do. For Mill, what morality requires of one is that one maximize (actual or expected) utility. However, not all the judgements that we make about moral requirement fit this analysis. Mill tries to account for these judgements by showing how we can take up society's point of view and ask, from that vantage point, what morality would require us to do. Certain judgements about what morality requires of individuals turn out, on this analysis, really to be judgements about what inducements and protections morality requires their society to provide them with.

a conscience would be ideal from the consequentialist point of view, it is much harder to prove that this would be so. Is it not possible that some people's capacities and circumstances might be such that they would produce more good in the long run if their conscience made them exclusively concerned with considerations of impartial beneficence? And might there not be other people whose capacities and circumstances were such that they would produce more good in the long run if their conscience left them utterly indifferent to considerations of impartial beneficence? It is not clear how these possibilities can be dismissed. The problem of interpersonal variation could of course be avoided by stipulating that everyone is to have the same conscience and then identifying morality with the promptings of the conscience that would be ideal in the circumstances granted this stipulation.[25] But there would still be the problem of demonstrating that the conscience that would be ideal in this special collective sense would speak as if reading from some amalgam of impartial beneficence, prerogatives, and restrictions. And even if that could be managed there would be the problem of demonstrating that the prerogatives and restrictions thereby accommodated would be sufficiently like the prerogatives and restrictions to which we are intuitively attracted.

And why should everyone be governed by the same conscience? Thus suppose it could be shown that the best conscience for everyone to share would be one that accommodates impartial beneficence, prerogatives, and restrictions, and that these prerogatives and restrictions would be very like the ones we find intuitively attractive. Pretty clearly, when considered by itself, this would not rule out the possibility that some individuals would contribute much more to the overall good if they were governed by a conscience of a radically different sort. If that is possible, however, it is difficult to see how a consequentialist could avoid conceding that people of whom it is true should be governed by the conscience that is for them the best. The worry here resembles one that we have already canvassed. It is easy to see why *society*, in its efforts to shape individual conscience, might find it best to try to instil the same conscience in everybody, the conscience that would be ideal

---

[25] Notice, however, that this would blur the distinction between justice and the rest of morality; for the suggestion a moment ago was that something is required by justice if society would do well to enforce it through one of its mechanisms of coercion and control, one of which is the shaping of individual conscience through the regulation of moral education.

given the stipulation that it be shared.[26] For any attempt by society to tailor its teachings to different audiences is likely to be counter-productive, given how blunt the instruments of social policy are and how frequently people from different categories must interact.[27] But even if it is true that this collective morality would ideally incorporate impartial beneficence, prerogatives, and restrictions, why should we suppose that this settles the question of the form that *individual* morality would ideally take?

In response to this, someone might ask why we should *not* allow this collective morality to determine the form that individual morality should take. If doing so finally enables us to explain why individual morality incorporates all three of impartial beneficence, prerogatives, and restrictions, why not go ahead? As I said before, however, it is far from clear to me that this would be the result. More importantly, even if it were, I think this characterization of morality's content would still suffer from a grievous failing. To count as satisfactory a characterization of morality's content must do more than generate verdicts that square with our considered judgements about particular cases; it must also generate those verdicts by appealing to a vision of what morality is about that is both independently compelling and internally coherent.[28] And while I believe there is something compelling about the claim that morality has in some fashion to do with promoting the overall good, I can make no good sense at all of the suggestion that *individual* conduct should therefore be judged according to standards of *collective* efficacy. Surely it makes more sense to suppose that individual conduct should be judged according to standards of individual efficacy. I shall not try here to settle whether similar considerations would show that all consequentialists should really be act consequentialists. But I would submit that indirect versions of consequentialism have a chance to succeed only if they keep themselves focused on the individual agent, say by requiring each person to follow the promptings of the

[26] Of course, as Mill points out, it would probably be counter-productive for society to try to shape individual consciences in very fine detail. It would probably do much better simply to regulate the general form that moral education is to take, leaving the details to individual families. Even in that case, however, the point remains that it would probably do best to impose the same regulations on everybody's moral education.

[27] A great many utilitarians in the 19th century would have denied that this was true of colonial India. They thought that the British administrators and the Indian populace would best be governed by quite different consciences. But it seems obvious that this application of their theory was grounded less in fact than in prejudice.

[28] Compare Rawls 1971 and Daniels 1979 on the difference between narrow and wide reflective equilibrium.

conscience that would maximize her contributions to the promotion of the overall good.

So far as I can see, therefore, something like this 'individual conscience' consequentialism offers consequentialists the only chance that they have to accommodate all three of impartial beneficence, prerogatives, and restrictions. Other versions of consequentialism seem either internally incoherent or woefully inadequate to the task at hand. The question we must return to, therefore, is whether it is really plausible to suppose that every person's capacities and circumstances are such that some one conscience would suit them best—a conscience that speaks as if reading from an amalgam of impartial beneficence, prerogatives, and restrictions.

I have already expressed grave doubts about this. When discussing decision-theoretic consequentialism, I insisted that cases do arise where secondary principles codifying the record of human experience could safely be set aside and a person could reasonably expect to promote more good overall by acting contrary to the triumvirate of impartial beneficence, prerogatives, and restrictions. But once this is granted, it becomes difficult to deny that some people's capacities and circumstances will be such that they would produce more good overall if they were guided by a conscience that prompted them to take advantage of such opportunities whenever they seem to present themselves. Now of course some consequentialists *will* deny this. And their denials will not be entirely baseless. For one does have to worry that a person whose conscience prompted her to act contrary to the triumvirate of impartial beneficence, prerogatives, and restrictions whenever that seemed to her likely to promote more good overall would too often misjudge her situation and end up making things worse.[29] But surely we can grant that this would be true of most people and yet still insist that some people are capable of developing a conscience that would prompt them to contravene our three principles only in cases where their doing so would in fact promote more good overall.[30] How is this possibility to be ruled out?

Clearly it cannot be dismissed on 'logical' grounds. There is nothing incoherent in the idea that a person's capacities and circumstances might be such that she would produce more good overall if she were governed

---

[29] This could of course happen for any number of reasons—because she tends to overestimate the effects that her actions will have on herself and her friends, because she tends to underestimate the precedent that her actions will set for the future actions of others, and so on and so forth.

[30] Or anyway, only in cases where this would be the result more often than not.

by a conscience that on some occasions prompted her to act contrary to the triumvirate of impartial beneficence, prerogatives, and restrictions. What consequentialists might suggest, therefore, is that this possibility can nevertheless be dismissed on 'empirical' grounds because it could be realized only by someone who was either preternaturally lucky or inhumanly prescient in her decisions about when she could produce more good overall by contravening these principles.[31] Now I doubt that this can be established. But I have no *proof* to this effect. All such a proof would require is the presentation of a single case where a person possessed neither of preternatural luck nor of inhuman prescience would contribute most to the overall good if she were governed by a conscience that sometimes prompted her to contravene our three principles. However, while this sounds simple, the unfortunate fact of the matter is that it is extremely difficult both to assess the long-term consequences of possessing particular dispositions to act and to determine which of those consequences should in the circumstances be put down to luck.[32] Presenting a clear counter-example may not be possible.

Nor is this by any means the end of our difficulties here. For as we saw at the beginning of this chapter, while most consequentialists are concerned to replicate a broad range of the verdicts that our three principles would hand down, they are not necessarily concerned to replicate all of them. So even if we could find cases where people possessed of neither preternatural luck nor inhuman prescience would contribute most to the overall good if they were governed by consciences that sometimes prompted them to contravene our three principles, the force

---

[31]   The reference to luck is necessary because the laws of psychology cannot by themselves be expected to rule out the possibility that a person might just happen to contravene our three principles only in cases where that would in fact promote more good overall. Thus a full statement of individual conscience consequentialism would have to include some qualification to the effect that morality requires people to follow the promptings of the conscience that it would be best for them to have *given only a normal allotment of luck*. Just how this qualification would be unpacked is far from obvious. One might even wonder whether consequentialists have the resources they need to unpack it in a way that is not simply ad hoc. But that is not a worry that I shall pursue here.

[32]   Some of these difficulties can be traced to certain obscurities in the notion of a conscience as it has been developed and deployed by consequentialists of this stripe. (These obscurities are also in large part to blame for the uncertainty I feel about whether individual conscience consequentialism really does provide a coherent alternative to act consequentialism.) But even if we were clearer than we are about what a conscience is, assessing the long-term consequences of possessing different such consciences would be extremely difficult. For some relevant discussion, consider the various doubts that are raised by Frey 1984 regarding the distinction between levels of moral thinking that is drawn in Hare 1981.

of this point would depend very much on how widespread those cases were and on how radically the deliverances of those consciences would depart from the verdicts that the triumvirate of impartial beneficence, prerogatives, and restrictions would hand down. Thus we mustn't suppose that we are anywhere near a *refutation* of consequentialism. But of course the consequentialists are in a similar predicament, for they too need to establish not just the conceivability but also the truth of their claims about optimal consciences, and that is no easier for them than it is for us.[33] What they need to show is that the overall good would in a sufficiently broad range of cases benefit most from consciences that would come sufficiently close to replicating the verdicts that impartial beneficence, prerogatives, and restrictions would hand down; and unless the standard of sufficiency here is set extremely low there is no good reason to think it is going to be any easier for them to establish their claim than it will be for us to establish ours.

My own view is that most consequentialists are inclined to claim more here than the facts will actually bear out; but of course this is just speculation on my part, not a conclusion that I can claim to have established. All I can claim to have established to this point is that it will be no easy matter for us to accommodate all three of our stipulations about morality's content if we insist on characterizing morality exclusively in consequentialist terms. But this gives us all the reason we need to look for a different way of accommodating these three stipulations, one not so dependent on calculations of the different consequences that the possession of different consciences is likely to have. So let us leave the consequentialists to the side for a while. Once we have succeeded in uncovering a conception of morality that can more easily or reliably accommodate our three stipulations, we can always return to the consequentialist approach and consider just how much less easy or reliable its accommodations are. If our rival conception of the subject should turn out to fare less well than consequentialism on some other score, an accurate assessment of how well consequentialism can accommodate our three stipulations might be something that we cannot do without.[34] But until we reach the point where a comparative assessment of the overall advantages of some rival approach is necessary, it is enough for us to have shown that consequentialist theories may not accommodate our

---

[33]   As is often noted, this is something many indirect consequentialists conveniently forget.

[34]   I shall be considering whether this is so in the concluding chapter.

three stipulations all that well. That is all the reason we need to proceed to the contractualist approach.

2. *Contractualism and Impartial Beneficence*

The problem with consequentialist theories is that they assess moral principles by a standard, the promotion of the overall good, which prevents them from offering any direct or reliable support for prerogatives and restrictions. Contractualists invoke a quite different standard. Let us begin by considering 'Hobbesian' forms of contractualism, according to which moral principles are those that would emerge from a bargaining procedure in which each person was solely concerned to push through rules that would maximize her own advantage.[35] Would such theories make possible a less perilous accommodation of impartial beneficence, prerogatives, and restrictions? This seems far from clear. As the insistence on individual advantage might seem to create special difficulties for impartial beneficence, let us focus on that.

It is easy to see why a defeasible principle of impartial beneficence would have some real appeal for many people. Although no plausible prerogative could be expected to shield one from all the sacrifices and compromises that impartial beneficence requires, one could normally expect those sacrifices and compromises to be more than offset by the sacrifices and compromises of others.[36] Certainly an equal part of the benefits would exceed an equal part of the costs. But even if one expected to pay a greater share of the costs for a smaller share of the benefits, the sheer magnitude of the benefits guarantees that one could normally expect to come out a winner in the end. And of course the fact that certain sorts of actions were restricted would enhance many people's grounds for confidence here. For even if one feared that other people

[35] Whether or not the historical Hobbes held such an extreme view is not an issue I shall enter into here. It might be argued that his view was in fact closer to the one that I later describe as 'Lockean'. But my interest here is not with the correct attribution of these positions but rather with the differences between them.

[36] There are some good questions to be asked about the vantage point from which these expectations are to be gauged; but our purposes do not require that we answer them here. More pressing are questions about what counts as a sacrifice; so let us be clear that Hobbesian forms of contractualism employ a very restricted conception of what individual advantage is. (Just how restricted is of course itself a good question, but perhaps not one that we need enter into here. For some helpful discussion, see Gauthier 1986, chap. 2.)

could best promote the overall good by doing tremendous damage to oneself, the presence of a plausible set of restrictions could normally be expected to ensure that such activity would be prohibited. Realistically limited and carefully constrained, a principle of impartial beneficence clearly could benefit many people. If morality is construed as a set of principles that would emerge as a compromise among individually self-interested agents, there would seem to be some very good reasons to suppose that it includes a defeasible principle of impartial beneficence.

But even if a defeasible principle of impartial beneficence could be expected to benefit many people, might there not be some people who could expect to do a lot better without it, and who should therefore insist on its rejection? One difficulty Hobbesians face is that of explaining when and how far self-interested bargainers would be prepared to compromise. Thus the super-rich might speculate that they would do better in a system without any principle of impartial beneficence, since such a system would inevitably leave them much freer to devote their inordinate wealth to advancing their own ends. Of course, they might then lose some benefits that a principle of impartial beneficence would bring. But they might quite plausibly point out that those benefits were in their case never likely to be very great, as their wealth puts them among the last people that a principle of impartial beneficence would normally be concerned with. Moreover, what they stand to gain from a greater freedom to focus on their own ends is evidently enormous. Weighing these self-interested calculations against each other, the super-rich might rightly conclude that they would probably fare better under a different system, perhaps a system that includes various restrictions but no principle of impartial beneficence at all.[37] The difficulty facing Hobbesians is therefore to explain why such people should settle for anything less.

Now of course Hobbesians might try to overcome this difficulty by arguing that self-interested bargainers must compromise if they are to have any hope of reaching an agreement.[38] For the super-poor, after all, might rightly insist that they stand to do very much better under a system that includes a principle of impartial beneficence than under one

---

[37] I shall hereafter refer to this as a 'libertarian' system, although some might argue that this name is better reserved for systems that do include a principle of impartial beneficence, but one that is limited by prerogatives of exceptional strength.

[38] The assumption here, obviously enough, is that the bargainers are all motivated by a desire to reach an agreement. As we shall see, however, the implications of this assumption for the bargaining procedure are not nearly so obvious.

that does not.[39] In fact, they might very well conclude that their prospects would be better still under a system that includes a principle of impartial beneficence that is unencumbered by either prerogatives or restrictions. For then there would be no limits placed on the efforts that the better-off might be required to make to improve the plight of people like them. Admittedly, they would then run some risk of being called upon to make heavy sacrifices themselves; however, they might decide that their prospective gains would make this a risk well worth running. Thus the super-poor might be inclined to hold out not just for the endorsement of impartial beneficence but also for the rejection of both prerogatives and restrictions. And this might be taken to indicate that a compromise could be reached among self-interested bargainers only if the parties involved were prepared to split their differences. The super-rich would have to give up their objections to a principle of impartial beneficence; the super-poor would have to give up their objections to any limitations on that principle.

The trouble with this reply, however, is that it says nothing about the abilities that these bargainers have either to influence the other parties or to hold out for better terms.[40] Thus the super-rich might reason that their greater resources should enable them to wear down the super-poor and win an agreement much more favourable to themselves; if they steadfastly refuse to accept an amalgam of impartial beneficence, prerogatives, and restrictions, won't the super-poor eventually reach a point where they have to give in? The super-rich might also reason that by threatening in the meantime to use their greater resources against the super-poor they could give them an additional incentive to reduce their demands. Of course, on the other side, the super-poor might reason that their greater numbers and greater desperation should actually give them the upper hand in any negotiations. Precisely because they have so very little without the agreement, they might feel more capable of steeling themselves to the thrust and parry of the negotiating process and holding out for better terms. And if they use their greater numbers to good effect, don't they have the capacity to make trouble and so to give the super-rich an additional incentive to reduce their demands? But the difficulty is to see why this difference in perceptions

---

[39] This talk of the 'super-rich' and the 'super-poor' is obviously terribly schematic. But so, in a sense, is the point I am trying to make here—that what self-interested bargainers would be prepared to agree upon is bound to depend a great deal on the circumstances and the psychologies of the parties involved.

[40] For a helpful and extremely thorough discussion of such matters, see Barry 1989, part I.

would lead these bargainers to a happy compromise on the amalgam of impartial beneficence, prerogatives, and restrictions.[41]

It might, of course; but why should it? It seems safe to say that the results of any such bargaining procedure would depend a great deal on the circumstances and the psychologies of the parties involved. There simply is no particular compromise that rational and self-interested bargainers could always be expected to reach. But what this means is that contractualism cannot provide a determinate account of the content of morality unless stronger assumptions are made about the people doing the bargaining.[42] Hobbesian versions of contractualism have to be abandoned. The bargainers cannot be assumed to care solely about pushing through rules that would maximize their individual advantage.

This assumption is somewhat modified in 'Lockean' versions of contractualism, according to which moral principles are those that would emerge from a bargaining procedure in which people were concerned to settle on rules that would work to their *mutual* advantage.[43] The idea is that people concerned about mutual advantage would bargain in better faith, that they would not be trying at every opportunity to win an agreement that was more favourable to themselves. Thus they would not be tempted to drag out the negotiations in the hope that the other parties would eventually wear down and begin to look more and more favourably on agreements that would do them less and less good. Nor would they feel any temptation to threaten the other parties with various kinds of mischief in the hope of giving them an additional incentive to look with ever greater favour on agreements that would do them increasingly little good. Instead of trying to maximize their own prospective gains at the possible expense of the other parties to the negotiations, these people would be looking for an agreement from which everyone could expect to benefit. And the claim might be that this search would inevitably lead to the amalgam of impartial beneficence, prerogatives,

[41] The point here is that, because this is a difference in perceptions, and moreover perceptions of how the other parties would be likely to react to one's own possible choices, what it would be just to 'split the difference' becomes increasingly unclear.

[42] See Gibbard 1991. (Alternatively, contractualists might shift their focus from ideal to actual bargainers, but then the worry would be that impartial beneficence would too rarely figure in the result.)

[43] As before, I choose this label because I think it will be understood as referring to a particular strand of contractualist thought, not because I think it picks out a position that is in every respect identical to Locke's own. (If nothing else, Locke pretty clearly held that some part of morality's content derives directly from our status as creatures of the deity, and not from any contractualist search for principles that everyone would find either individually or mutually advantageous.)

and restrictions, since such an agreement would give both the super-rich and the super-poor at least something that they want.

But would everyone stand to gain, no matter what their desires and interests, no matter what their capabilities and circumstances? One difficulty Lockeans face is that of casting the net of mutual advantage wide enough to bring everyone within morality. The worry here is not that an individual might sometimes stand to gain more from her non-compliance than from her compliance; it is that some individuals might not stand to gain anything even from general compliance.[44] Thus the super-rich might worry that plausible prerogatives would still leave them highly exposed to the demands of beneficence, obliging them to spend enormous amounts of time and money promoting the good of others. They might also worry that plausible restrictions would not protect them from theft or confiscation, either because activity of that sort would not be restricted or because the restrictions would in their case be overridden.[45] Now of course it might be replied that the benefits would still offset such costs, given how terrible would be the world in which people's actions were not governed by any moral requirements at all. It is far from obvious, however, that this is anything but a bluff, one that the super-rich should call. Might they not expect to do better in a world without requirements than in one that requires impartial beneficence?

This of course depends on how other people would behave in the world without requirements. Yet that is hard to predict. They might threaten to perform actions that would make impartial beneficence seem comparatively advantageous. But would they actually carry through? That seems likely to depend on a wide range of factors too complicated to forecast. The worry here is not simply that people are imperfectly rational; even assuming perfect rationality it is not clear what to expect. For reasons in many ways similar to the ones we considered just a moment ago, it seems safe to say that a lot would depend on the circumstances and the psychologies of the parties involved.[46] And problems would remain even

---

[44]   This would be true of many people if the 'circumstances of justice' did not obtain. The worry here is that it could continue to prove true of some people even though those circumstances do obtain.

[45]   Of course, the super-poor are likely to have parallel worries about any set of principles that excludes impartial beneficence. That is precisely the point: the idea of mutual advantage seems much too indeterminate to capture any aspect of morality's content.

[46]   Gibbard 1991 is again useful here. (And, again, switching the focus from ideal to actual bargainers would only transform our worry from one about the determinacy of Lockean contractualism to one about the reliability of its support for impartial beneficence.)

if there were an identifiable baseline against which to measure the advantages of impartial beneficence. For any plausible baseline would surely reveal many packages of principles to be mutually advantageous. So the case for impartial beneficence would turn on establishing that it is part of the most mutually advantageous package. But what is meant by saying that a package of principles is most mutually advantageous? Is the idea that each person can expect to profit to the maximum degree compatible with like expectations for others? Or is it that the overall good is increased to the maximum degree compatible with each person's profiting somewhat?

This suggests that contractualists of the Lockean sort might face a kind of dilemma. What is the baseline above which every person is to be raised? Either it makes impartial beneficence mutually advantageous or it makes it disadvantageous for some. If the baseline is not such as to make impartial beneficence advantageous for everyone involved, then I think we really must ask ourselves why moral principles should have to be mutually advantageous in that sense. In as much as we are looking for a theory that can accommodate impartial beneficence, prerogatives, and restrictions, this will give us all the reason we need to abandon Lockean contractualism and start looking for some alternative approach.[47] But if the baseline does make impartial beneficence mutually advantageous, it seems certain to do the same for other principles, in which case some further criterion of selection is needed, and the idea of mutual advantage loses any real interest. This second horn of the dilemma could be avoided only by specifying a notion of the most mutually advantageous principles; but that is not a notion that I believe can be given sufficiently determinate content. Of course we can always import some notion of fairness to do the work, in the hope that it will help us narrow down the field, but this is effectively to abandon mutual advantage and take up some other view.[48]

Some Lockeans try to slip this punch by insisting that principles cannot be mutually advantageous unless they are recognizably fair, the idea

[47] Of course, as I have continually acknowledged, this may not be a source of great embarrassment to the Lockean contractualists themselves; they may not be much concerned to accommodate impartial beneficence, in which case different arguments must be addressed against them.

[48] This is perhaps a little bit too quick, as it might be argued that the notion of mutual advantage remains important in so far as it limits the possibilities from among which the notion of fairness is then to choose. How much force this rejoinder has would obviously depend on how many principles the appeal to mutual advantage lets through. My worry is that so many principles will get through that appeals to fairness will have to do almost everything.

being that unfair principles would be too often contested to be really advantageous. This makes appeals to fairness internal to the Lockean approach, rather than something that supplements and threatens to supplant it.[49] But in view of all the difficulties one encounters trying to specify a baseline against which effects can be measured, I think contractualists will do better to give up the Lockean insistence on mutual advantage. This is in fact what a great many contractualists do. So let us briefly consider two suggestions along these lines.

The first suggestion I want to consider is owed to T. M. Scanlon. He maintains that 'an act is wrong if its performance under the circumstances would be disallowed by any system of rules for the general regulation of behaviour which no one could reasonably reject as a basis for informed, unforced general agreement'.[50] Now one's first thought here might be that a system of rules could reasonably be rejected if it were not mutually advantageous. For why should anyone endorse rules from which she stands to lose? But Scanlon makes it quite clear that this is not his idea. He takes pains to insist, for example, that it would not be reasonable for a person to reject a system of rules that imposes certain burdens on her if the alternative systems would all impose much greater burdens on others.[51] The implication is clearly that moral principles can require sacrifices of people that will not be offset by the sacrifices of others. Does this make it easier to accommodate a principle of impartial beneficence?

Scanlon's own view of the matter seems to be that his version of contractualism would *not* accommodate a principle of impartial beneficence.[52] And it is not difficult to see why he might think this. For the super-rich may well exhibit no interest at all in promoting the overall

[49]   This is the approach that Gauthier 1986 takes to worries about indeterminateness.

[50]   Scanlon 1982: 110.

[51]   See ibid. 111. (I suppose it might be argued that Scanlon's intention here is not to distance himself from the idea that moral principles must be mutually advantageous but rather to enrich our understanding of what it is for a principle to be mutually advantageous. I doubt very much that this is what he has in mind; but the question is not one that we need to settle here. The important point for our purposes is to consider how contractualists might introduce more substantive appeals to fairness. Whether they are intended to refine or supplant their appeals to advantage is a question of less importance.)

[52]   While this is surely suggested by some of his remarks ibid. (e.g. at p. 115 and p. 119), I do not believe Scanlon intends to have taken a firm stand on such matters yet. He has so far been mainly concerned to establish the merits of his version of contractualism as a meta-ethical view, expressly leaving most of its substantive implications to be worked out at a later date. (For someone who claims that this sort of contractualism *would* accommodate not just a principle of beneficence but a right to welfare, see Sterba 1994.)

good; and in view of their lack of interest it would seem perfectly reasonable for them to reject even a defeasible principle of impartial beneficence. Would any system of rules eschewing impartial beneficence impose much greater burdens on the poor than impartial beneficence would impose on them? Would, for example, a libertarian system, which demanded some restraint of people but no positive assistance, impose even greater burdens on the poor? I think it is hard to see why the rich should accept this. Surely their inclination is rather going to be to make the contrary case against impartial beneficence, by insisting that any system of rules embracing impartial beneficence would impose much greater burdens on them than (say) libertarianism would impose on others. One again has to wonder how people are going to agree on a way of comparing these burdens and resolving such disputes.

Where before we needed to give some content to the idea of maximizing mutual advantage, the problem here is to give some content to the idea of minimizing individual sacrifice. Now, at first sight, this might seem an easier problem to overcome. Unless we are sceptics about interpersonal comparisons, which I am not, we must concede that some (at least ordinal) ranking of individual utilities will be possible. By contrast with this, as I suggested some paragraphs ago, the idea that one arrangement might be more mutually advantageous than another seems decidedly unclear. Noting this difference might prompt one to conclude, as it perhaps prompts Scanlon to conclude, that comparing individual gains or losses avoids difficulties that comparing mutual gains or losses invites.[53] Upon closer inspection, however, I think this advantage would prove illusory. For even comparisons of individual gains or losses are possible only relative to some baseline, and where exactly is that baseline to be set? If we take it to be the status quo, the rich would sacrifice more under impartial beneficence than the poor would under (say) libertarianism.[54] Yet this result would seem to be precisely reversed if we instead took the baseline to be an imaginary state of affairs in which everyone has everything she could desire. Then libertarianism would cost the poor more than beneficence would the

---

[53] See Scanlon 1982: 123.

[54] I say this because the status quo seems to me to be much closer to a libertarian system than to a system founded on impartial beneficence. Thus the move to impartial beneficence would appear to impose greater changes on the rich than the move to complete libertarianism would impose on the poor. (I have benefited here from a number of very helpful discussions with Liam Murphy, as well as from reading some unpublished writings of his on costs and demands.)

rich. My worry, therefore, is that simply appealing to reasonableness will not oblige the rich and the poor to agree on a single baseline—which suggests, of course, that Scanlon's version of contractualism fails not only to accommodate impartial beneficence but also to avoid the problem of indeterminateness.

Now it might be objected that such comparisons of burdens are unnecessary. Perhaps the super-rich could not reasonably reject some principles even though they would impose much greater burdens on them; perhaps the much greater burdens they would impose on them would be irreproachable in view of their much greater wealth. Certainly Scanlon nowhere suggests that the *only* way to show a person that she could not reasonably reject a certain principle would be to show that it minimizes individual sacrifice. On the contrary, he quite explicitly denies this.[55] So it remains possible that he could flesh out his account and escape the charge of indeterminateness. But the crucial question here is whether he could do so in a way that provides very firm or reliable support for impartial beneficence. I would be very surprised to learn that he could, notwithstanding the fact that his version of contractualism departs from its Hobbesian and Lockean predecessors by assuming that people are willing to entertain principles from which they stand to lose. Perhaps a rich person indifferent to the overall good could not reasonably refuse to make sacrifices greater than the average; but wouldn't her indifference at least make it reasonable for her to reject the particular burdens impartial beneficence would impose? I think it is hard to see how we can deny this.

In response to this, however, it might be objected that the rich person's possible indifference to the overall good is totally irrelevant to the question of whether the principle of impartial beneficence is one that she could reasonably reject. The claim might be that I am still tying Scanlon's version of contractualism too closely to its Hobbesian and Lockean predecessors by assuming that what it would be reasonable for a person to reject depends on the interests that are peculiarly hers. But in that case, of course, we need to be told how the notion of reasonableness is to be understood so that it will not depend in any way on the different and often conflicting interests of the parties involved.

The issue here closely resembles one to which John Rawls devotes considerable attention in his celebrated discussions of distributive justice. His suggestion, very roughly, is that we should imagine the relevant

---

[55] See Scanlon 1982: 123.

parties to be deliberating behind a 'veil of ignorance' that denies them access to certain important kinds of information both about their actual circumstances and about their actual motivations.[56] Thus the rich person of our example is to be imagined as lacking access to information about many things, not least of which is the fact that she is rich and that she is indifferent to the overall good. Rawls then sets out to show how a carefully crafted description of this 'initial situation' can explain why a person who was in this situation and who was deliberating rationally would choose his favoured theory of justice over its main rivals. The claim here might therefore be that we should apply a similar strategy to our broader puzzle about morality's content. If we want to know what it would be reasonable for people to choose in the circumstances they actually inhabit, perhaps we should be asking what it would be rational for them to choose in an appropriately described initial situation. If this is right, then of course the fact that a person who knows herself to be rich and indifferent to the overall good might be inclined to choose against impartial beneficence would indeed be not obviously to the point. Everything will turn on whether the initial situation is described as one in which people have knowledge of this sort, or whether it is instead described as one in which knowledge of this sort is systematically denied to people.

One worry that is often raised about this Rawlsian strategy is that, taken on its own, it has no real justificatory force.[57] After all, there are any number of ways in which the initial situation might be described, each leading to quite different conclusions. What does it matter whether a particular set of principles would be chosen by rational people who occupied a certain initial situation, if a different set of principles would be chosen by rational people who occupied a different initial situation? Even if there is a situation from which it would be rational to choose an amalgam of impartial beneficence, prerogatives, and restrictions, why should we take that as providing any justification for our belief that morality incorporates these three principles? Here, however, it is important to recall that we are *not* in these early chapters seeking a *justification* of this belief. For now, we are assuming it to be justified and asking what

---

[56] See Rawls 1971, esp. sect. 24. (The veil of ignorance is of course only the most familiar part of Rawls's 'original position'. Also important are his various stipulations about the information and motivations that the parties *do* have. But these points need not concern us here.)

[57] For some examples, see Daniels 1978.

this tells us about the nature of the moral undertaking.[58] So if we can describe an initial situation from which it would be rational to choose an amalgam of impartial beneficence, prerogatives, and restrictions, that would take us some considerable way towards a solution to our puzzle about morality's content. For the problem is to uncover a general characterization of morality's content that can satisfactorily accommodate all three of impartial beneficence, prerogatives, and restrictions, not to provide some proof to the effect that these principles are principles of morality.

Matters are not quite as simple as this suggests, however, because, as we saw when discussing indirect versions of consequentialism, a general characterization of morality's content will not be satisfactory if it is not both independently compelling and internally coherent. Of course, there is bound to be more than one general characterization of morality that can meet these two conditions, and some of them are bound to lead to principles different from the amalgam of impartial beneficence, prerogatives, and restrictions. So it would be pointless to insist that the characterization we seek must *prove* that our three principles are principles of morality. But it was something of an overstatement to say that it need not provide *any* support for our belief that they are.[59] In light of this, the worry we should be raising about the Rawlsian strategy is whether anything resembling his description of the initial situation could both accommodate our three principles and offer a compelling vision of what morality is about. As we have seen, our three principles will not be satisfactorily accommodated so long as the initial situation is described as one in which Hobbesian people bargain for individual advantage or Lockean people bargain for mutual advantage. Each of these descriptions offers a somewhat compelling vision of what morality is about, but neither of them yields the desired verdicts. The question is therefore whether a veil of ignorance can really improve matters here, or whether what is needed is a fresh start.

I do not myself believe that a veil of ignorance can contribute very much to our understanding of morality's content. There is of course something appealing in the idea that a self-interested person who is to

---

58 To some extent, this is true of Rawls as well. Certainly he does not mean to suggest that his two principles are justified *only* by the fact that they would be chosen from his original position. On the contrary, he believes they have some independent credibility. And so he takes the fact that they would be chosen from his original position as a partial vindication of his decision to privilege that situation.

59 For a nicely nuanced account of the possibilities here, see Scheffler 1979.

decide how certain goods will be distributed should be made to do so without knowing which of the resulting allocations will be hers. As Rawls rightly stresses, such ignorance would oblige even the most amoral of people to act *as if* they were moved by a genuine concern to promote the well-being of others or treat others in ways that are fair.[60] But what is appealing here is not the idea that people should be acting in ignorance but rather the idea that they should be trying to promote the well-being of others or treat others in ways that are fair. The veil of ignorance is appealing only in so far as it moves self-interested people to mimic moral behaviour. So even if we could describe a veil of ignorance from behind which it would be rational for self-interested people to choose impartial beneficence, prerogatives, and restrictions, this would not contribute very much to a solution to our problem. We would still have to provide a positive characterization of the sort of behaviour that this construction was successfully mimicking and then establish that this positive characterization constitutes a satisfactorily compelling and coherent vision of what morality is ultimately about. But if this is what it would take to solve our problem, it seems best to pass over discussions of the veil of ignorance and turn directly to the task of articulating and defending a positive characterization of morality's content.[61]

Looking as we are for a version of contractualism that can accommodate at least a defeasible principle of impartial beneficence, I think we must finally consider the possibility of a theory that assumes an unshakeable commitment to the overall good. Perhaps moral principles are those that could not reasonably be rejected by anyone seeking to balance this commitment against more personal concerns. This brings us to a version of contractualism very much like the one recently proposed by Thomas Nagel.[62] And is it not clear that this version of contractualism would accommodate at least a defeasible principle of impartial beneficence? For how could it be reasonable to reject such a principle when one is so firmly committed to that end?

---

[60]　See Rawls 1971, sect. 4 and sect. 25.

[61]　Compare Scanlon 1982, esp. sect. 4. (As Scanlon notes, Rawls's strategy may still have considerable value as a heuristic device, but only if we are already clear about how morality is to be characterized.)

[62]　See Nagel 1991. He talks of impartiality *tout court* where I talk of impartial beneficence; but in other respects the views are the same. Certainly he makes it clear (for example, on p. 70) that he intends the commitment to impartiality to inoculate contractualism against worries about indeterminateness.

The problem with this suggestion is that it succeeds in accommodating impartial beneficence only by putting prerogatives and restrictions at grave risk. A serious commitment to impersonal value, once assumed, is not easily curbed. Samuel Scheffler, for example, has recently speculated that a group of people who were seeking to balance such a commitment against more personal concerns could not reasonably reject a system of rules that includes certain prerogatives but excludes all restrictions.[63] Prerogatives would strike them as reasonable, he feels, in view of the fact that the personal concerns that they each have are naturally independent of their shared commitment to the overall good. It is not as if they develop concerns for such things as their selves, their friends, or their families simply because they believe that, by doing so, they will become better promoters of the overall good. Nor is it the case that the strengths of such concerns naturally fall into line with the strengths that they should have if the people possessing them are to be ideal promoters of the overall good. Given all of this, Scheffler feels that people would find it reasonable to 'reflect' the 'natural independence of the personal point of view' by adopting a prerogative that assigns it some moral independence as well. As we shall see in just a moment, it is actually not so clear why assigning moral independence to the personal point of view should be thought to call for a prerogative and not some more straightforward moderation of beneficence. But we can at least agree with Scheffler that restrictions seem at grave risk. Why should their possession of personal concerns suggest that people sometimes be prohibited from acting on their concern for the overall good?

Nagel once tried to meet worries of this sort by arguing that people's more personal concerns will inevitably include a strong interest in avoiding actions that have them aiming at others' harm.[64] Torturing an innocent child, he insisted, is evidently an action of this kind and so should not be done even if, in unusual cases, it would bring about the best available outcome. At first sight, perhaps, this might seem simply to miss Scheffler's point; for why should the agent's interest in avoiding such actions justify anything more than a prerogative? However, upon closer inspection, matters begin to look a little more promising; a lot seems to depend on how literally one takes the talk of balancing

---

[63] This, in any event, is how I read his remarks about 'rule hybrid' theories in Scheffler 1992*b*: 179 ff.

[64] See Nagel 1980 and 1986, chap. 9. For some discussion, see Scheffler 1982, chap. 4, and Kagan 1989, chap. 1.

competing concerns. For of course the image of balancing might suggest that people are required not to countenance too much damage to their more personal concerns in their endeavours to promote the overall good, in which case the existence of a very strong interest in not aiming at others' harm would on at least some occasions set real limits to the actions that people may perform. Still, this would amount to a restriction against aiming at others' harm only if people never stand to gain more from such activity than they stand to lose; and it is difficult to believe that our interest in avoiding actions that have us aiming at others' harm is for each of us always of paramount importance.

It is also worth noting that literally balancing competing concerns would improve the prospects for restrictions only by undercutting the case for prerogatives; so it cannot provide a satisfactory way of dealing with the problems we face. As I have already pointed out, prerogatives permit people to refrain from bringing about the best available outcome but do not require them to do so; they leave people free to sacrifice everything for the overall good if they wish. We have just seen, however, that literally striking a balance between a commitment to the overall good and one's own more personal concerns would require one always to give some weight to both sides.[65] If Nagel hopes to provide a rationale for both prerogatives and restrictions, therefore, he is going to have to provide us with some much less literal way of taking his talk of balancing competing concerns. And indeed, this is precisely what we find him doing in more recent work; instead of literally balancing competing concerns he tries to determine what principles could reasonably be rejected by people who had such motivations. However, having made this correction, Nagel then neglects to give us any clear or useful sense of the substantive aims or considerations that are supposed to shape our understanding of reasonableness in such contexts. And in the absence of this, it is difficult to see how we can avoid reverting to the more literal reading of his talk about balancing, despite the fact that it will not give us the results we want.[66] Another way of putting the worry here is to

[65] Kagan 1984 raises a similar worry about the Nagelian case for prerogatives. The metaphor of balancing seems to support not the complex conjunction of impartial beneficence and a prerogative but a principle much simpler in structure—one I shall later be referring to as a principle of moderated beneficence.

[66] Consider, for example, Nagel's defence of restrictions in 1991. Following Kamm 1989, he argues that it would be unreasonable for people to reject all restrictions because moral systems lacking restrictions fail to treat people with a sufficient degree of respect. As Lippert-Rasmussen 1996 demonstrates, however, there are bound to be other kinds of value that moral systems could confer on people and that the presence of restrictions

note that some aims might make a literal balancing of concerns perfectly reasonable; so we need to be told why the relevant aim in fact would
not.

In the end, then, I think our verdict has to be that Nagelian contractualism is no more able than its predecessors to accommodate the full
package of impartial beneficence, prerogatives, and restrictions. By
eschewing any commitment to maximizing mutual advantage or minimizing individual sacrifice, it does avoid the problem of identifying a
neutral baseline against which assessments of burdens and benefits can
be made. But in its own way it leaves us without the resources that we
need to provide all three of impartial beneficence, prerogatives, and
restrictions with a compelling rationale. If we take its talk of balancing
too literally, we get the wrong results; if we do not take such talk literally enough, we are left without direction. The problem here seems perfectly obvious; talk of balancing competing concerns is just too simple
and straightforward to yield a structure as complex as the one we are
assuming morality to exhibit. Such talk need not be jettisoned, but something needs to be said about the substantive aims that morality subserves, the aims in light of which some balances appear reasonable and
others not.[67] Only by balancing personal and impersonal concerns with
some more substantive aims in view can we plausibly expect to vindicate all three of the stipulations we began with. The challenge that
confronts us is therefore to shake off the discredited blinkers of consequentialism and contractualism so that we might finally see what that
aim really is.[68]

---

might impede. And why should the system be our sole concern? Thus it is far from clear
how strong this new case for restrictions could be. It still remains hostage to facts about
value, albeit facts of a rather more complicated sort. And as it says nothing about how
competing values are to be weighed against each other, it leaves us with no obvious alternative to the picture of striking a literal balance.

[67] Of course, by linking morality's content to some aim that it subserves, we risk
making it harder to account for its authority, since some people may lack the relevant aim.
One of the sources of contractualism's appeal has always been its promise to account for
morality's content while relying only on aims that most people can be assumed to have.
Hence the initial attempts to appeal only to individual advantage, and subsequent attempts
to appeal only to motives that few people would happily disavow, like those of fairness
and reasonableness. My own view is that the advantages of this strategy have often been
overstated; but these are questions that I shall return to in later chapters of this book.

[68] Some might think that the nature of this aim is already clear, that the aim of morality is obviously to facilitate cooperation among people. But still it remains to be determined why cooperation should require people to pay allegiance to the triumvirate of
impartial beneficence, prerogatives, and restrictions.

2

Cooperating to Promote the Good

THE following three (characteristically inflammatory!) claims about moral development can be culled from Rousseau's *Émile*: (1) Compromising for mutual advantage may be a morality suitable for children, incapable as they typically are of taking a sustained interest in others; (2) promoting the overall good may be a morality suitable for adolescents, preoccupied as they often are by feelings of pity and compassion; (3) but a mature person is capable of actually *cooperating* with others, and so a mature moral philosophy should somehow reflect this fact. Now there is (and was no doubt meant to be) some question about how claims like these should be understood. Famously, as Rousseau tells Émile's story, such claims seem to be offered as an account of the stages through which individual moral agents sometimes do, and ideally should, develop. But that appearance may be misleading; perhaps the narrative here is no more meant to be real psychology than Rousseau's other narratives are meant to be real history.[1] Be that as it may, however, Rousseau's claims are at the very least intended to map out the path along which moral *theorizing* generally is, or should be, developing.

We have already found some reason to trust in the accuracy of this map. We have seen how difficult it would be to accommodate a principle of impartial beneficence without allowing that morality is in some sense concerned with promoting the overall good. But we have also seen that the idea of promoting the overall good is not by itself capable of offering any direct or reliable support to prerogatives and restrictions. It does therefore look like neither the idea of compromising for mutual advantage nor the idea of promoting the overall good will lead to a satisfactory understanding of morality's content. But what of Rousseau's claim that the understanding we seek is to be found by exploring the idea of cooperation? That does not at first sight seem a very helpful suggestion, for it does not distinguish itself very clearly from the others.

---

[1] On the other hand, however, his developmental view does exhibit several striking similarities to some recent work in moral psychology—for example, to Kholberg 1981.

Compromising for mutual advantage is after all a kind of cooperating; and surely the same is true of promoting the overall good. If Rousseau's suggestion is to be of any help to us, more must be said about the ideal of cooperation it involves.

What Rousseau has in mind is evidently a form of cooperation that transcends and in some sense synthesizes the kinds of cooperation involved in compromising for mutual advantage or promoting the overall good. I think this is precisely what we should be looking for; but Rousseau's own solution is not the one that I favour. Whereas he seems content to identify moral principles with whatever results from a carefully contrived voting procedure, I think we must try to articulate the substantive aims that such procedures are intended to further.[2] What I shall argue is that morality directs people to promote the overall good on terms that are fair to everyone involved.

This is meant to be a suggestion different from the ones we have canvassed so far. The reference to promoting the overall good is intended to distance it from both the Lockean and the Scanlonian versions of contractualism. Thus I won't be arguing that fair terms on which to promote the overall good are terms from which everyone can expect to profit. Nor will I be arguing that such terms could not be rejected as unreasonable even by people indifferent to the overall good. On the contrary, the assumption of a shared commitment to the overall good will be centrally important to this view. But this does not make the view a consequentialist one, for the assumption is that people are committed to promoting the overall good on terms that are fair. So, for example, they are not looking for a set of rules general attempted adherence to which would in the circumstances be as productive of utility as possible. What they are looking for is rather a set of rules that would generate as much utility as can be generated while still being fair to everyone concerned.

Nagel's version of contractualism comes closest to the view I shall be defending here. His idea, remember, is that people are to ask themselves how they could strike a reasonable balance between a shared commitment to the overall good and their own more personal concerns.[3] I complained at the time that this talk of 'balancing' is too simplistic to generate a structure as complex as the triumvirate of impartial beneficence,

---

[2] Notice that the complaint here is similar to the one I directed towards Rawlsian contractualism in Chap. 1.

[3] To be more precise: this is what his idea comes to if we substitute for his talk of impartiality *tout court* our talk of impartial beneficence. (Recall Chap. 1, n. 54.)

prerogatives, and restrictions. Here, in effect, I shall be arguing that we can make such talk more fecund by linking it to the aim of promoting the good on terms that are fair. Refusing to temper impartial beneficence by acknowledging prerogatives and restrictions will be shown to be unreasonable in light of this aim. Prerogatives must be acknowledged because the people with whom one is dealing have values other than their commitment to the overall good. But one wouldn't really be treating people fairly if one granted them prerogatives yet regarded oneself as free to trespass on them. Their undertaking will be a truly fair one only if the prerogatives people grant each other are backed up by correlative restrictions.

In order to make good on these claims, I evidently need to explain what fair terms of cooperation can amount to in the context of an undertaking to promote the overall good. If they are not terms from which everyone can expect to profit, or terms that no one can reasonably reject, then what are they? I shall begin this chapter by sketching the preliminary case for thinking that promoting the overall good on terms that are fair requires that impartial beneficence be tempered by prerogatives and restrictions. The rest of the chapter will then be spent showing how these preliminary claims about fairness can be sharpened to deal with particular objections.

1. *The Case for Prerogatives*

Imagine a group of people who want to work together promoting the good and who are seeking fair terms of cooperation. Why might they be reluctant to accept that they are always required to do everything they can to promote that end?

One worry they might have about unfettered beneficence is that, in cases of partial compliance, it would require each person to do everything she can in the circumstances to take up the slack for anyone who was failing to comply. For example, given the fact that large numbers of people are contributing much less than they should to charitable organizations, unfettered beneficence seems likely to require much greater contributions from a person like me than it would otherwise have done.[4]

---

[4] The force of such worries was first brought home to me by Murphy 1993— though, for the reasons I go on to reject, he does not himself regard them as worries about fairness.

Now it is true that the principle doesn't single me out in this regard—if I were to join the non-compliers, it would with equal gusto require other people to do what they can to take up the slack for me. But surely this doesn't make unfettered beneficence immune to worries about fairness—it may treat everybody in the same way, but surely the fact of the matter is that the way in which unfettered beneficence treats people is decidedly unfair. The worry here is not that people can never fairly be required to take up the slack for those who fail to comply with morality's demands. Perhaps I should increase my contributions to charities in view of other people's non-compliance. The worry here is rather that unfettered beneficence seems to take this too far, requiring me not simply to make somewhat greater contributions but actually to do everything I possibly can to make up for other people's failures to comply. Surely what one wants to say is that, while such strenuous efforts on my part would of course be welcome, they are not in most cases required of me but fall rather into the category of the supererogatory. But of course that is to say that impartial beneficence, far from being unfettered, is in fact limited by a prerogative to make less than one's optimal contributions to the overall good in at least some cases of partial compliance.

Cases of partial compliance are not the only ones in which worries might arise about the fairness of unfettered beneficence. Even under conditions of full compliance unfettered beneficence could make demands of individuals that our cooperators would surely find excessive. If you and I are thinking about writing a paper together, and we are in the process of trying to decide upon a fair division of the work that is going to be involved, it would be unreasonable for you to expect me to agree to ignore my other commitments and devote everything to that task. Given that people inevitably have other values in addition to whatever commitment they may share to the promotion of the overall good, and that it would be natural and indeed rational for them to give those values some independent weight when justifying their actions, it is not clear why our cooperators should decide any differently.[5] Surely fair terms on which to promote the good must make reasonable allowances

---

[5] I used to think that, while these claims about rationality strengthen the case for prerogatives, it might survive without them. (See Myers 1994, n. 27.) As I put it then, even if rationality did require people to subordinate all of their other commitments to the ideal of cooperating in the promotion of the overall good, it could be that cooperating in the promotion of the overall good would not itself require people to give themselves over entirely to that undertaking. Now I'm not so sure. It now seems to me that some competition from rationality is crucial to any view of morality that recognizes prerogatives.

for the sorts of creatures people are. They must in some way take reasonable account of the fact that promoting the good is never people's sole concern.[6] And surely the obvious way to do this is to limit impartial beneficence by a prerogative that has the effect of allowing people, in at least some circumstances and to at least some degree, to set aside their commitment to promoting the overall good and act in ways that are designed to satisfy their other concerns. People would always be free to forgo this prerogative and subordinate their other concerns to the goal of promoting the overall good, but the point is that such devotion wouldn't always be required; on at least some occasions they would be permitted to give their other concerns a freer rein than unfettered beneficence would allow.

These worries about unfettered beneficence are sometimes put by saying that it is too demanding—too demanding in that it always requires people to do everything they can to take up the slack for non-compliers, and also in that it always requires people to subordinate their other concerns to a concern for the overall good. Now the possibility of putting these worries in some such way is obviously very important; for even though the possibility of partial compliance and the existence of rival values are undeniable facts of human nature, it need not follow that the best way to take account of these facts is to make allowances for them. Someone might concede that such facts explain why people often fail to make their optimal contributions to the overall good, without feeling any inclination at all to allow that such facts ever justify people in falling short in this way.[7] But putting these worries in terms of demandingness may convey an impression that is misleading; for it may suggest that the only complaint against unfettered beneficence is that it would sometimes *cost* people too much, as if moral requirements were still being held to some contractualist standard of maximizing mutual advantage or minimizing individual sacrifice.[8] My talk of cooperating to promote the good is meant to invoke a different standard; so my defence of prerogatives requires that I find some way of explaining why unfettered

---

[6] The inevitable existence of rival values is of course also at the heart of Bernard Williams's (1973) worries about the requirements of unfettered beneficence. But whereas I see it as raising worries about fair terms of cooperation, he sees it as raising worries about the very possibility of moral theory.

[7] Brink 1986 explores a different possibility, allowing that such facts might often make these failures *rationally* justified, but denying that they ever make them *morally* justified.

[8] I have benefited here from reading some unpublished work by Liam Murphy.

beneficence would be too demanding, but one that does not refer to the costs that principle could be expected to impose upon individual agents.

But if it is not the costs they would inflict that make certain require-ments too demanding, then what is it? Some people, I suspect, will be inclined to reply that unfettered beneficence is too demanding because it is too *alienating*.[9] Their claim here will be that unfettered beneficence, by requiring people to subordinate all their other concerns to a concern for the overall good, would alienate people from those other concerns in a way that is destructive of their integrity. But here again I think we should try to avoid putting our worry in this way, for we don't want to assume that unfettered beneficence is anything more than it actually is, a simple claim about the rightness of actions. All unfettered beneficence says is that actions are right to the extent that they bring about the best available outcome. It does not say that actions are in every case to be motivated by a desire to achieve that result. On the contrary, most people may be more likely to perform the actions that unfettered benef-icence requires if they are, in 'normal' circumstances, motivated not by some shared commitment to the overall good but by their own more per-sonal concerns. Perhaps only in 'unusual' circumstances should their commitment to the overall good come to the fore and supply their moti-vation. Now I suppose someone might object that the very existence of this possibility shows that unfettered beneficence is too alienating. But such an objector would then be in the uncomfortable position of main-taining that every plausible principle is too alienating. For any plausible principle will on at least some occasions insist that people not be moti-vated by their rival concerns.[10] The charge, therefore, had instead better be that in the case of unfettered beneficence this would happen too fre-quently—and that, of course, would make this accommodation of pre-rogatives no more direct or reliable than others we have rejected.

But surely a more straightforward argument is available. After all, it is not simply a fact of human nature that people inevitably value things in addition to promoting the overall good; it is surely also an ideal of individual behaviour that people act in ways that are true to all those values. Fair terms on which to promote the overall good need not for that

---

[9] This is no doubt the most influential reading of Williams's original worry. The general line of response to it which I go on summarily to recommend is developed with great care and insight in Railton 1984.

[10] It is worth noting, however, that Williams himself does not seem to find this posi-tion so uncomfortable. For, as I have mentioned, he does seem willing to extend his criti-cisms to moral theory generally.

reason be tailored so as to match this ideal, but they can at least be expected to make concessions to this ideal more fundamental than anything unfettered beneficence contemplates. Unfettered beneficence, though it may allow people on many occasions to be motivated by their more personal concerns, and perhaps even counts their being so motivated as itself a good deserving to be promoted, seems not to treat this as an *ideal*. It does not make any fundamental concessions to the suggestion that people's actions should ideally reflect all the values that they possess, but instead tries to appropriate this suggestion by incorporating it into its account of the goods deserving of general promotion. That hardly sounds like a principle of cooperation.

So the complaint is not that it would be unfair to require people to comply with unfettered beneficence because such compliance would exact costs from them that are too high or alienate them too frequently from their more personal concerns. It is rather that unfettered beneficence does not acknowledge people as individuals whose behaviour may quite appropriately be judged by the light of an ideal that is different from the ideal of cooperating in the promotion of the overall good. This would be reasonable if people had no rival concerns, but seems hopelessly unfair on the supposition that they do. This unfairness is perhaps clearest in cases of partial compliance, for by insisting that we always do everything we can to plug the breach unfettered beneficence clearly treats us as if we had no other correspondingly important claim upon our activity. But matters are really no better when compliance is full, for there too unfettered beneficence issues its decrees as if there were no other ideal of individual behaviour by the light of which our activity may quite appropriately be judged.

Now of course my opponents are likely to point out that this rationale for prerogatives is not without its problems. By insisting that people have various personal concerns quite independent of whatever commitment they may share to the overall good, and that this introduces the possibility of a different ideal by the light of which their behaviour might be judged, we perhaps do ensure that fair terms of cooperation cannot require people always to be making contributions that are optimal. But precisely by introducing the possibility of a rival ideal, we also risk making morality's authority harder to explain. For we cannot introduce the possibility of a rival ideal without also introducing the possibility that it is ultimately authoritative, and hence the possibility that morality's authority will depend on the extent to which its verdicts receive the other's backing. And it might well be wondered whether this arrangement

could really be compatible with a credible account of morality's authority, or whether it will turn out that we have bought our rationale for prerogatives at a price that is not worth paying.

Such worries will eventually have to be addressed. And of course
these are very far from being the only worries that might be raised about
our rationale for prerogatives. We shall have to get much clearer about
what it is for a thing to have some value for a person, and much clearer
also about what it takes for a person's actions to reflect everything that
has some value for her. Otherwise we cannot be sure that a person's
being true to all her values really is an ideal of individual behaviour, nor
that this ideal of individual behaviour really is something to which fair
terms of cooperation should be making fundamental concessions. But
before going any farther we should first consider how a prerogative of
the sort we are discussing might be *formulated*. In what circumstances
and to what extent might such a prerogative permit people not to take up
the slack for others? In what circumstances and to what extent might
such a prerogative permit people to give their rival values a freer rein?
What might such a prerogative actually look like?

By far the most familiar answer that we have to this question is one
that we owe to Samuel Scheffler.[11] Scheffler's idea is that people should
be allowed to give their own interests and desires some 'proportionally
greater' weight when justifying their actions, so that they would not
always be required to bring about the best outcome available to them.
Provided that the loss to the overall good would not be too much greater
than the gain from their own point of view, people should be allowed to
contribute to the overall good in ways that favour their other commitments. The point here is not that such motivations must be tolerated
because they would in the long run be especially productive of utility; it
is not that certain wrong actions are the price to be paid for more right
ones. Scheffler's claim here is rather that actions failing to bring about
the best available outcome are in some cases not wrong at all; it is a
claim designed to limit the authority of beneficence given the existence
of rival values. It therefore speaks to one of the worries we have raised;
but what of the worry having to do with non-compliance? Scheffler
sometimes talks as if the 'factor' by which people should be allowed to
'multiply' their interests and desires is immutable. But no fixed multiplying factor is going to enable a prerogative to deal fairly with all cases

---

[11]   See Scheffler 1982: 17 ff.

of partial compliance.[12] Pretty clearly, a multiplying factor that might seem appropriate under conditions of full compliance could, under conditions of partial compliance, leave a person much less freedom to perform actions that are designed to satisfy the other values that she has. On some of these occasions, of course, we might feel that this narrowing of people's options would be perfectly reasonable, either because it would not last for so very long or because they would still have considerable room for manœuvre. But often a fixed multiplying factor would leave people having to take up too much of the slack for others. For there is scarcely any limit to the amount of good that can be left undone by widespread failures of compliance.

The obvious response to this worry would be to have the multiplying factor increase as the level of compliance decreases. This would put us in a better position to accommodate the thought that a person should not always be required to do everything she can to take up the slack for those who are failing to comply with morality's demands, but without obliging us to deny that a person might be required to take up some of the slack left by others if a comparatively small narrowing of her options would make a comparatively large difference to the overall good. If other people were doing much less than they should to promote the overall good, then she might have to do more than she otherwise would, for there might be a much greater amount of good for her to bring about; but her prerogative would in that case be stronger too, so if it did transpire that she had to do more than she otherwise would, it wouldn't be *just* because the others were failing to do all that they should. I believe a prerogative along these lines can be defended; but we should straightaway note that it does face difficulties. One difficulty, which I shall discuss later in this chapter, surfaces the moment one tries to say something a little more precise about what it would be for a person to give 'disproportionate weight' to her own interests and desires. For even under conditions of full compliance the aggregated needs of other people could conceivably increase to almost any size, and so could presumably reach a point where they would outstrip a single person's needs by any degree that was specified. This suggests that a Schefflerian prerogative could still leave some people having to give up everything for the overall good, not just tremendous amounts of time or money but perhaps even

---

[12] The point here is again Murphy's (see 1993: 275), though he would again deny that it is one about fairness.

their lives or the lives of people they love.[13] The difficulty this creates
for us is to determine whether fair terms on which to promote the overall good could really require people to perform actions of these sorts
and, if not, whether a Schefflerian prerogative could avoid doing so too.

A more pressing difficulty, deserving our immediate attention,
emerges when we consider cases where satisfying one's own interests
and desires would require one to harm others. As Shelly Kagan has forcefully argued, Scheffler's prerogative can seem appealing so long as we
focus on cases where advancing one's own ends simply prevents one
from giving aid to others; but it seems quite appalling as soon as we turn
to cases where advancing one's own ends actually requires one to inflict
harm on others.[14] And surely our cooperators would agree; just as they
would deny that a cooperative undertaking should leave people free to
favour their own interests and desires as much as they like, so too they
would deny that a cooperative undertaking should leave people free to
favour their own interests and desires *whenever* they like. Fair terms of
cooperation may well require that we grant people prerogatives; but they
surely also require that those prerogatives be kept within limits. I may not
have to sacrifice £10,000 to save a stranger's life; but no amount of
money would justify my taking a stranger's life. Unlike our previous
worry, which seemed genuinely contestable, it seems quite clear that fair
terms of cooperation would not allow actions of this sort. So the task we
must immediately undertake is to determine whether a Schefflerian prerogative could avoid permitting such actions. Now Scheffler has himself
shown that there is no difficulty in formulating a version of his prerogative that avoids this.[15] Whereas a 'pure-cost' version of the prerogative
would allow people to give their own interests and desires a disproportionate weight even in cases where advancing their own ends would actually require them to harm others, a 'no-harm' version of the prerogative
would instead allow people to give their own interests and desires a disproportionate weight *only* in cases where advancing their own ends
would simply prevent them from giving aid to others. The real difficulty

---

[13] Compare Murphy 1993: 275–7. Worries like this prompt Murphy to abandon
Scheffler's prerogative in favour of a quite different approach to the question of morality's demands. I myself will instead be proposing a way in which we might meet such
worries without abandoning the spirit of Scheffler's project.

[14] Kagan worries, for example, that a prerogative allowing me to keep £10,000
instead of saving a stranger's life would also allow me to take my uncle's life in order to
inherit £10,000. See Kagan 1984, and also 1989, chap. 1.

[15] See Scheffler 1992*b*, sect. 3.

here lies rather in justifying such a prerogative without also justifying some sort of restriction against harming—or else, failing that, in showing how it is that some sort of restriction against harming could itself be justified.

As we shall see in the next section, Scheffler doubts that such restrictions can be justified, so he himself concentrates on the first of these options. He points out that, from the point of view of promoting the overall good, much less is lost by granting people a no-harm version of the prerogative than would be lost if they were granted a pure-cost version. He also notes that, from the point of view of advancing their own ends, most people would not profit much more from having a pure-cost version of the prerogative than they would from having only a no-harm version.[16] Taken together, he thinks these points suggest that people might strike a reasonable balance between a commitment to promoting the overall good and their own more personal concerns if they were to adopt a no-harm version of the prerogative; what is more, he thinks they suggest this without in any way suggesting that striking such a reasonable balance would also require people to impose a restriction even on harmings that are necessary in the circumstances to promote the overall good. But I think we saw enough in the last chapter to wonder whether these calculations of costs could yield such particular verdicts with any real reliability. Couldn't it be just as reasonable to go ahead and embrace restrictions, on the ground that they would profit many individuals without costing the overall good very much? Or for that matter to refrain from adopting any prerogatives at all, on the ground that they would damage the overall good without profiting many people very much? In any event, the question on the table here is whether people looking for *fair* terms on which to promote the overall good could reasonably adopt a no-harm version of the prerogative without also adopting restrictions on inflicting harm; and to this question I think the answer will probably be *no*. If it would in no case be fair for me to harm a person in the exercise of my prerogative, must it not in at least some cases be unfair to harm a person in pursuit of the overall good? Are the differences between these cases necessarily as great as all that?[17]

I suspect, therefore, that our justification of prerogatives will not be

---

[16] For most people are such that, in most cases, when they harm other people for their own benefit, they fear retaliation and feel remorse to a point sufficient to outweigh whatever gains they might have made. See ibid., sect. 2.

[17] These claims may seem at this point a little lame; but I will come back and strengthen them later on.

complete unless restrictions can be justified too. The question, however, is why cooperating to promote the good should require a restriction against inflicting harm. Doesn't this end suffice to justify such means?

2. *The Case for Restrictions*

Clearly we cannot hope to justify restrictions simply by pointing to the existence of rival values and the possibility of partial compliance. Fairness may well demand that people not always be required to subordinate their other concerns to a concern for the overall good. It may also demand that people not always be required to do everything they can to take up the slack for non-compliers. But if a person chooses to forgo either of these prerogatives, why should we suppose that fairness might stand in her way?[18]

Having endorsed prerogatives, however, it is difficult to see why our cooperators would now reject restrictions. At the very least, they seem certain to endorse restrictions against actions that trespass on prerogatives. Suppose, for example, that I alone am in a position to bring about some extremely favourable outcome A but that it falls within my prerogative to bring about some less favourable outcome B, so that my bringing about outcome A would be supererogatory. Suppose, in addition, that other people are in a position to force me to bring about outcome A and that this is the best way that they have to promote the overall good, notwithstanding the fact that it involves trespassing on my prerogative. Should they be permitted to force me to bring about outcome A even though I am not required to bring about that outcome myself? Surely the cooperators we are imagining would find it easy to agree that such cases of 'forced supererogation' must be to some extent restricted. If enough was at stake, they might allow that this restriction would give way and that I could fairly be forced to bring about outcome A.[19] What they would deny, however, is that the prospect of securing a more modest increase in the overall good would suffice to justify such behaviour.

The reason for this is not that rules permitting people to engage in forced supererogation would somehow contradict rules permitting people

---

[18] Compare Scheffler 1982: 94–8.

[19] But in that case, of course, my prerogative might give way too, in which case forcing me to bring about outcome A would not be a case of forced supererogation. I briefly comment on the implications of this on p. 76 below.

to bring about suboptimal outcomes; it is simply not true that implementing rules permitting activity of the one sort would be equivalent to rescinding rules permitting activity of the other sort. Some people find this hard to accept because they wonder what it could mean to say that morality sometimes permits people to bring about suboptimal outcomes if not that it sometimes prohibits other people or society from interfering in their attempts to do so.[20] But if the idea of moral requirement makes any sense at all it surely must be conceivable that it applies to individuals in such a way as sometimes to permit one person to interfere with an action that it permits another person to perform. The problem with theories that include prerogatives but not restrictions is not that they are incoherent. It is rather that they would have people promoting the overall good on terms that are unfair. What our cooperators must recognize is that forced supererogation is ruled out by the cooperative spirit of the undertaking to which they are committed. Their undertaking will not be a cooperative one if people are not granted even a defeasible right to decide when they will act in a supererogatory way.

Is this the only restriction that fairness requires? I do not see how it could be. Surely fairness would also require restrictions against various kinds of action closely resembling forced supererogation. Suppose, for example, that my uncle could help me greatly by giving me £10,000 but that he would prefer to donate the money to charity, which would as a matter of fact bring about a greater amount of good overall. Suppose, in addition, that I could force my uncle to hand over the money and that it would fall within my prerogative to do so, even though this would wreak havoc with his plans and subtract from the overall good. Clearly a simple restriction against forced supererogation would not prohibit extortion in a case like this; for I would not be forcing my uncle to do something that was strictly speaking supererogatory.[21] But I would be forcing him to do something that he was not required to do; and it is difficult to see how that could be permitted if forced supererogation was prohibited. This suggests that our cooperators should pass over any simple restriction against

---

[20] The people I have in mind here should not be confused with the act consequentialists we discussed in Chap. I. Those people *denied* that prerogatives exist as principles governing individual action, insisting instead that they exist only as principles governing social policy. By contrast, the people under consideration here allow that prerogatives might exist as principles governing individual action but insist that, if they do exist, they must for reasons of 'logic' or 'meaning' be accompanied by or tantamount to restrictions against forced supererogation.

[21] For I would not be forcing him to do more good than morality requires, even though I would be forcing him to do something other than it requires.

forced supererogation and adopt a broader restriction against forcing people to do things that they are not required to do. But now consider a slightly different case where what would fall within my prerogative is not actually forcing my uncle to give me the £10,000 but simply taking the money from him. Presumably acts like these would not be prohibited by restrictions against forcing people to do things that they are not required to do; for in cases of this sort nobody would strictly speaking be forced to do anything at all.[22] But harms would be inflicted on people that they would not be required to bring upon themselves; and it is hard to see how that could be permitted if forcing these people to bring these harms upon themselves would be prohibited. So it seems that our cooperators should opt in the end for a still broader restriction, a restriction against inflicting on people harms that they are not required to bring upon themselves.

Of course, if in response to Kagan's worry we embraced a no-harm version of the prerogative, cases of these sorts would not arise. This might seem to indicate that we could after all make do with a restriction against forced supererogation, a simple restriction against forcing people to do more good than they are required to do. This appearance would in fact be misleading, however, for it ignores the reason why pure-cost versions of the prerogative should be rejected. Why is it fair to give one's interests and desires some disproportionate weight when contemplating helping others, but not when the question is one of harming others for one's personal gain? The answer, I believe, is that in the latter cases but not the former one violates a restriction against inflicting on people harms that they are not required to bring upon themselves. If one declines to provide £10,000 needed to save a stranger's life, one may thereby be allowing her to die but one is not oneself inflicting any sort of harm on her.[23] But if one chooses to kill somebody in order to make £10,000, one pretty clearly is inflicting on that person a harm that she would not be required to bring upon herself. That would be unfair; and I believe it is because it would be unfair that one should not be allowed to favour one's own interests and desires in cases of this sort. Far from

---

[22] They are not even forced to acquiesce in our doing these things to them; these are not cases where people end up doing something simply by doing nothing.

[23] Here and elsewhere I am evidently counting on the fact that a reasonably sharp distinction can be drawn between doings and omittings. This is of course a matter of great controversy within philosophy; but that controversy is not one I can enter into here. I shall also leave to the side a number of related questions having to do with the difference between intending and foreseeing. Important as all these questions are, I do not believe that they constitute the most forbidding obstacles to the justification of restrictions.

enabling us to avoid acknowledging the existence of restrictions broader than the restriction against forced supererogation, our earlier adoption of a no-harm version of the prerogative presupposes that such restrictions exist.[24] We might still usefully take restrictions against forced supererogation as the model or paradigm around which our understanding of restrictions is to be centred. Indeed, for want of a simple term that naturally covers the broader range of cases, I shall often refer to the restrictions being contemplated here as restrictions against actions 'too closely resembling' forced supererogation. But these should be understood to include any actions that involve inflicting harms on people that they are not required to bring upon themselves.

In response to all of this, I suppose someone might argue that pure-cost versions of the prerogative should be rejected only because they would sometimes permit one to inflict harms on others for the sake of one's *own* ends. The claim might be that inflicting harms on people that they are not required to bring upon themselves is unfair only when done for the sake of one's own ends, not when done for the sake of the overall good. And if that were a better diagnosis of the problem, there would of course be no reason to think that in rejecting pure-cost versions of the prerogative we are somehow committing ourselves to any sort of *restriction* against harming. A hybrid theory like Scheffler's, one containing a no-harm version of the prerogative but no restrictions of any kind, would after all be vindicated, though not in quite the way that Scheffler seems himself to have had in mind.

Others might prefer a broader diagnosis of the problem, though one that is still much narrower than mine, and so one that, while taking us some distance beyond Scheffler's hybrid theory, would not take us all the way to restrictions. Their claim might be that inflicting harms on people that they are not required to bring upon themselves is unfair *whenever* one is aiming at an outcome that is suboptimal, even if one is not oneself the person who will profit. Returning to the example of my uncle and his money, it might be said that forcing him to hand it over or taking it from him would be no less objectionable if I was helping somebody else exercise her prerogative. But still it might be thought that Scheffler is right in insisting that there is no rationale for *restrictions* here, for it might be thought that there need be nothing unfair about taking the money to promote the overall good.

---

[24] I take myself here to be making good on the promissory note that the reader was issued in n. 17.

It seems to me, however, that these narrower diagnoses of the problem in both cases fail either to accord with our intuitive sense of the matter or to explain *why* pure-cost versions of the prerogative would be unfair. What is unfair about harming other people with my own ends in view, or with a view to other suboptimal outcomes, if *not* the fact that I am inflicting on them harms that they are not required to bring upon themselves? I don't myself see how the unfairness of any harming can be established without considering the requirements on the victim, and so without setting the stage for a restriction against some harmings done for the sake of the overall good. As I see things, the real threat to my position lies not in these narrower diagnoses but in broader ones—that is to say, in diagnoses that would support restrictions much broader in scope than the ones I have defended.

I say this because it might be thought that the real problem here lies in encroachments on *autonomy*, and because of this, that fairness ultimately requires a broader (and perhaps less attractive) restriction against harmings *of any sort at all*. I myself do not believe this to be the case, but as this is in the first instance a worry about the precise nature of the restrictions that fairness requires, not about the need for some principles of this type, I propose that we set it aside for a moment, so that we can first respond to certain objections that might be raised against the general line I have been taking, against the very idea that fairness might involve acknowledging restrictions. Scheffler and others have expressed grave and influential reservations about the possibility of providing restrictions with a rationale; so let us next consider why it might be thought difficult or even impossible to do what I'm suggesting we have just done.

Scheffler worries about the possibility of justifying restrictions because of the paradoxical nature of the verdicts they sometimes generate. We might set out his line of reasoning as follows.[25] Restrictions, as we have defined them, would on at least some occasions forbid one to perform an action even though one's performing that action would produce a better outcome overall; for example, a restriction against murder might forbid me to kill an innocent person even though my doing so would prevent five other people from dying, and even though the outcome involving the deaths of the five might be worse overall

---

[25] This line of reasoning is at no point explicitly laid out in Scheffler's work; but something like it must be behind his claim that any restriction will generate some results of the sort he finds paradoxical. (See e.g. Scheffler 1982: 84–7.)

than the outcome involving my murder of the one.[26] But now, if the outcome involving the deaths of the five would indeed be worse overall than the outcome involving my murder of the one, that is presumably because it would be just as bad as an outcome involving somebody's murdering not just one person but some number of people greater than that—say, two. Averting the murder of two people would in that case be an outcome no greater in overall value than averting the deaths of five people, and so no more able to justify violations of restrictions. It would seem to follow, therefore, that I would be forbidden to kill one innocent person even when my doing so would prevent two equally innocent people from being killed; more generally, it would seem to follow that for any restriction R there must be some number N such that N is greater than I and such that I would be forbidden to violate R even though my single violation of that restriction would prevent N different violations of it. Yet this is a result that seems paradoxical. For how are we possibly to justify it? Surely, one wants to say, there would be no reason to restrict actions of some particular type if actions of that type were not especially horrible. At the same time, however, if actions of that type were so very horrible, what reason could there be to prevent us from minimizing their occurrence?

One way to respond to Scheffler's reasoning would be to reject the general characterization of restrictions upon which it depends. But this is not the tack that I shall take. It is true, of course, that the line of reasoning I just finished attributing to Scheffler depends on a quite particular and so inevitably contestable idea of what restrictions are; more precisely, it depends on the idea that restrictions prohibit certain kinds of actions in some cases where performing those actions would produce more good overall, indeed in *all* such cases except perhaps those where the increase in the overall good would be great enough to surpass some predetermined threshold. If, against this, restrictions were introduced simply by supplying a list of cases in which actions of the designated kinds were not to be performed, there might be no good reason to think that we could derive from them prohibitions against performing such actions even in order to prevent more such actions from being performed. The list might prohibit murders necessary to avert five deaths, without it following from this that murder would sometimes be prohibited where it was necessary to prevent more than one other murder from

---

[26] Throughout these paragraphs, when I speak of deaths I mean 'mere' deaths—in other words, deaths that are not themselves the results of murders.

taking place. The idea, on this approach, would be that the impersonal value of deaths and murders has no bearing on the question whether averting five deaths could justify committing one murder; averting five deaths does not fail to justify committing one murder because it fails to surpass it in impersonal value by a sufficiently wide margin, but rather because mere deaths are simply not the sorts of things the averting of which could justify a person in committing an actual murder.[27] More murders, on the other hand, might be. But surely this is just not very plausible. And in any event it would clearly cut the legs out from under the rationale for restrictions that I am in the process of constructing here. For I am building precisely on the idea that there are limits to the sacrifices that people can be required to make for the sake of the overall good.[28]

Thus it seems to me that, instead of looking for ways to deny that restrictions generate the verdicts that trouble Scheffler so much, we should concede that they do and set about trying to dispel their apparent air of paradox. I want to concede, for example, that there will be cases where fairness forbids us to engage in an act of forced supererogation even though that is in the circumstances the only way to prevent more such acts from occurring. Now, as Scheffler's challenge clearly illustrates, what this means is that the *rationale* for restricting forced supererogation cannot lie simply in the negative reviews it receives from the impersonal point of view; for obviously an outcome involving several such acts would receive worse reviews than an outcome involving only one. What I want to stress, however, is that my objection to forced supererogation does *not* lie principally in the fact that it is a bad thing to have happen to a person. There are worse things that could happen to a person the doing of which would not be restricted. For example, as I shall argue in the next section, I do not think there is any restriction against forcing people to do things that they *are* required to do; if forcing a person to do her share really would promote the overall good,

---

[27] Some people adopt this rival approach to restrictions because they doubt that the idea of ranking overall states of affairs makes any real sense. But even if one grants that this idea does make sense one might argue that it has no bearing on the rationale for restrictions.

[28] If it could be shown that morality never requires people to sacrifice their own lives to avert any number of mere deaths, but that it on occasion does require them to sacrifice their own lives to avert even a small number of actual murders, then an appeal to fairness might justify a restriction against murder in the one sort of case but not in the other. My complaint against this rival approach to restrictions is ultimately that I see no way of defending its views about moral requirement.

despite the various ill-effects that such compulsion typically has, then I think it would be perfectly permissible for us to go ahead and do so.[29] The difference between these two cases is not, however, that being forced to perform required actions is always a less bad thing than being forced to perform supererogatory ones; given how large the sacrifices required by morality sometimes are, and how small are the sacrifices sometimes involved in acts of supererogation, it seems in fact quite clear that the ranking of such outcomes will sometimes tilt the other way. The difference between these two cases is rather one of fairness; it seems to me perfectly fair to force a person to do something that she is anyway required to do, but unfair to force her to do more than that, except perhaps in cases where that provides the only way to make a sufficiently large difference to the overall good. I believe this gives us our answer to Scheffler's challenge; forced supererogation is sometimes wrong even where it is necessary to prevent more actions of the same type, not because a person's being used like this is necessarily such a bad thing, but because a person's being used like this is in at least some of these cases *not fair*.

It is of course obvious that, if we refrain from forcing one person to perform a supererogatory act in a situation where that is necessary to prevent more people from being forced to perform supererogatory acts, more instances of forced supererogation will result, so more instances of unfairness will result. One can easily imagine, therefore, that Scheffler might reassert his challenge here by saying that, in so far as we are concerned about fairness, we should be trying to maximize it, and so should be trying to minimize the number of people who will be forced to act in supererogatory ways. But a desire to cooperate with other people on terms that are fair is not, I take it, the same as a desire to minimize the number of instances in which people are treated unfairly; it is not even the same as a desire to minimize the number of instances in which one has or will treat people unfairly oneself.[30] The object of the desire is that

---

[29] This is not to deny that we as a society should very often provide protections against coercion of this sort. It is just to say that morality would allow individuals to decide these cases on the basis of the consequences. (Waldron 1981 argues that because society should very often recognize 'a right to do wrong' individuals should do so too; but that is again because he doesn't distinguish as I do between questions of social policy and questions of individual morality.)

[30] Thus, contrary to what Brook 1991 suggests, a restriction against actions of a certain type would not require one to perform an action of that type whenever that is necessary to minimize one's total performance of such actions. Of course, as Pettit 1987 reminds us, we might sometimes be required to perform an action of that type because that

one's *current* treatment of people should be fair, here and now, even if the result should somehow be that more people will be treated unfairly in the future; the concern is not to maximize the number of instances in which either oneself or other people will cooperate but purely and simply to cooperate. Now of course the rationality of giving primacy in one's actions to such an exclusive concern might well be questioned; it might well be argued that there is reason for one to seek to ensure the fairness of one's own current actions only because fair activity in general has an impersonal value and so is something that there is reason for one to try (all else being equal) to maximize. Such questions about morality's authority cannot simply be dismissed on the ground that we are here discussing only its content; for it goes without saying that a correct account of morality's content will not stand in the way of a correct account of its authority, and for all we know the correct account of morality's authority is one according to which moral activity is always (or anyway nearly always) rational. However, it may also turn out that morality's authority is much less than this, and in any event we are not yet in a position to say whether the alleged connection between practical reason and impersonal value is real. Accordingly, I propose that we leave discussion of all such questions for later chapters, and concentrate here on the question whether we have at least uncovered a possible way of construing morality so that it accommodates both prerogatives and restrictions.

This is in fact the point at which Scheffler would launch his final assault on the defence of restrictions I've been mounting. He takes care not to make his attack on restrictions dependent on any particular view of the relation between morality and rationality.[31] What he would charge instead is that any defence like mine is bound to suffer from a particularly virulent form of indeterminateness. So let us next consider how this

is necessary to minimize the total number of such actions that will be inflicted upon the victim. If so, however, this will only be because the victim is herself required to bring that harm upon herself in order to minimize the total amount of harm she will undergo. Cases like this therefore fall outside the scope of the restrictions I am defending and so do not demonstrate that a kind of maximizing reasoning must after all be at work here.

[31] This is not always made very clear in Scheffler 1982. Indeed, in that work, Scheffler often puts his worry about restrictions by saying that they seem irrational. A careful reading, however, indicates that what he really means by this is that they seem paradoxical. I think this is repeatedly confirmed in his subsequent writings. Restrictions continue to seem paradoxical to Scheffler because he finds no vantage point from which they make sense, no coherent and compelling 'ultimate moral attitude' in light of which adherence to them would be rational.

charge might be pressed, and how well my defence of restrictions might fare against it.

3. *More on Restrictions*

In order to see what grounds Scheffler might offer for this charge of indeterminateness, it helps to remember that he himself has sometimes adopted the language of contractualism. As we saw towards the end of Chapter 1, and again in the first section of this chapter, he has argued that a balance between commitment to the overall good and one's own more personal concerns might most reasonably be struck by adopting a no-harm version of the prerogative and rejecting restrictions of every sort.[32] Perhaps, then, the best place for us to start is by asking why Scheffler sticks with this broadly Nagelian approach despite the problems that we've seen it faces.

The answer, I believe, is that this approach takes us as far as we can go while still acknowledging the fact, as Scheffler sees it, that moral reasoning must be a kind of maximizing reasoning if it is to be sufficiently determinate.[33] Unlike consequentialism, which seeks to maximize only impersonal value, or egoism, which seeks to maximize only individual gain, Nagelian morality recognizes both as values that must be given their due. If not for the other, each value should be maximized, so the challenge for Nagel is to determine the precise part that each should be assigned in the moral equation. As we have seen, this proves highly problematic, for Nagel would like the moral equation to yield all three of impartial beneficence, prerogatives, and restrictions, yet a literal balancing of personal and impersonal values is incapable of generating such a complex structure. Now I don't believe that Scheffler would want to deny that Nagel's view faces difficulties here; on the contrary, it is almost certainly his recognition of these difficulties that leads Scheffler to develop this approach somewhat differently from Nagel. Instead of looking for principles that in a direct way balance personal against impersonal values, he essays a more indirect argument that focuses on the comparative costs of adopting alternative principles. He suggests

---

[32]   As I mentioned in Chap. 1, n. 63, this seems to me to be the natural way to read his remarks about 'rule hybrid' theories in Scheffler 1992*b*. As he himself takes pains to make clear, this relatively recent paper marks both a substantive and a methodological departure from the simpler views espoused in Scheffler 1982.

[33]   See Scheffler 1988*b* for a general discussion of the importance of maximization.

that by embracing a no-harm version of the prerogative but shunning all restrictions one might succeed over time in maximizing some appropriately weighted function of personal and impersonal values. We may well wonder whether such calculations could reliably yield the particular conclusions that Scheffler wants; but his rejoinder, I believe, would be that we have no choice but to try to understand morality along some such broadly maximizing lines.

Far from conceding this point, I have been insisting throughout this chapter that we can and should be looking to organize personal and impersonal values under the auspices of an ideal that is not in any sense a maximizing one.[34] My claim has not been that by embracing the triumvirate of impartial beneficence, prerogatives, and restrictions we can succeed over time in maximizing some appropriately weighted function of personal and impersonal values. I have instead been arguing that we must embrace principles of all three of these types because that is the only way to promote the overall good on terms that are fair. And in arguing for this, I have been talking as if we can see that the alternatives are all unsatisfactory simply by asking what our concept of fairness would demand of people who were trying to promote the overall good. But is it really so clear that our concept of fairness is up to the task of generating a determinate conclusion? I have already explained why I think fair terms on which to promote the good must include both prerogatives and restrictions. In the course of doing so, however, I did also note that various questions remain to be cleared up regarding the form that these prerogatives and restrictions should take. For example, while introducing the case for restrictions, I noted that there was room for some real and quite serious debate about the breadth of the restrictions that fairness requires. Perhaps, then, Scheffler's challenge here is best addressed by trying to show that headway in resolving such disputes can be made, that the avowedly general and preliminary arguments presented in the preceding sections can be sharpened to deal with more detailed worries.

Let us return, therefore, to the defence we were mounting for restrictions. What I argued in the previous section was that fair terms on which to promote the overall good must include not just narrower restrictions against forced supererogation but much broader restrictions against any

---

[34] Though the details of our positions differ enormously, this puts me in some agreement with Foot 1985. She too wants to allow that restrictions sometimes generate the results that Scheffler finds so paradoxical, but like me she wants to deny that the paradox is as real as Scheffler thinks.

actions that inflict on people harms that they are not required to bring upon themselves. Now the question is whether even these restrictions would be broad enough. For it might seem that somebody else could just as credibly argue that what fairness requires here is not merely these restrictions against inflicting on people harms that they are not required to bring upon themselves but even broader restrictions against inflicting harms of any sort at all. No doubt this disputant would want to allow that such restrictions are far from absolute; if forcing people to make their fair share of the sacrifices required to improve the plight of the homeless or some other equally unfortunate group would bring about a significant increase in the overall good, surely we should go ahead.[35] But marginal increases to the overall good might be held not to justify such measures. The claim might be that by forcing people to make their required contributions to the overall good in such comparatively trivial cases we treat them as less than fully autonomous participants in that undertaking, and so less than perfectly fairly.

Now I suppose the admission that such extremely broad restrictions would have to be easily overridden might give one pause. There are bound, after all, to be many good consequentialist reasons not to force people to do even those things that they are required to do, for of course such compulsion is not without costs.[36] If, in addition to this, we are going to postulate the existence of a restriction against such compulsion even where it does promote the overall good, the need for that further step should be clear. Yet how clear can it be if at the same time any such restriction would have to be easily overridden? But this is not an objection that I would want to press. It seems to me that the need for such restrictions would be clear enough if it would indeed be unfair to force people to make their required contributions to the overall good in cases where the difference that would make to the overall good would be only marginal. What concerns me more at this stage is the claim that this

---

[35] Consider also a closely related case: whatever we think about the importance of people's making their own choices, can't we agree that the automatic withholding of taxes is ultimately justified? But how could it be justified, if forcing people to make their required contributions to the overall good were subject to a restriction that could in no circumstances be overridden?

[36] Among these, of course, are the costs that we discussed in Chap. 1 while assessing Mill's attempt to accommodate prerogatives and restrictions within a version of act consequentialism. What we found, remember, was that such costs may well justify a social policy of respecting and protecting various rights, but that, by themselves, they are never going to suffice to establish the existence of actual *restrictions* on individual behaviour.

would be unfair because to force people to make their required contributions in such comparatively trivial cases would be to treat them as less than fully autonomous participants in the undertaking to promote the overall good. How are we to tell whether that claim is in fact true?

It is not difficult to understand why this claim can seem to have real appeal. For fair terms on which to promote the overall good must in some way acknowledge people's capacity for individual autonomy; and the exercise of this capacity must in some way involve people's governing their own actions by their own choices.[37] The difficulty lies rather in figuring out what the implication of these facts might be. Clearly the implication cannot be that people should never be forced to make their required contributions to the overall good; for we have already granted that people should be forced to make their required contributions when enough is at stake. So there must be more to say about the nature or importance of individual autonomy than these facts by themselves suggest. Either forcing people to make their required contributions to the overall good is not always incompatible with treating them as fully autonomous participants in that undertaking, or treating people as fully autonomous participants in the undertaking is not something that fair terms on which to promote the overall good would always require. The fact that at least one of these possibilities must actually obtain does not of course settle the question against broader restrictions.[38] But by allowing that for one reason or the other it sometimes is permissible to force people to make their required contributions to the overall good, we do at least open the door to the possibility that such activity is never actually restricted but always to be judged on straightforwardly consequentialist terms.

As I have indicated, my own view is that fairness requires nothing more than the narrower restrictions against anything too closely resembling forced supererogation; I see nothing unfair about principles allowing us to force people to do things they are anyway required to do. To say that morality is a matter of cooperating in the promotion of the overall

---

[37] Just what is involved in the exercise of this capacity is of course a good question. It is a question that must be answered if we are to distinguish persuasion from force, as surely we must if our restrictions against certain uses of force are to be credible. But these issues, though undoubtedly important, are not ones that I can pursue in this book.

[38] However, as I suggest below, I think it does count against them to some degree, for defeasible restrictions do generate complications that it would be better to be able to avoid. (In other words, while I would deny that the idea of a defeasible restriction is self-contradictory, I do agree that there is something to be said for restrictions that are absolute.)

good is not in my view to say that people's contributions to that undertaking should only in extreme cases be compelled. I think people are cooperating in the promotion of the overall good so long as the principles governing their interactions do not permit them to force each other to contribute more than they are required to contribute. Against this, however, it will be objected that there are any number of very different positions that could be taken on this matter, and that to this point we have no real understanding of how any particular choice among them might be justified. On the one side, some people will insist that we give short shrift to individual autonomy unless we embrace restrictions that at least sometimes prohibit us from forcing people to do everything they are required to do. On the other side, it might be argued that we do well enough by individual autonomy simply by embracing principles that prohibit us from imposing harms on people for the sake of outcomes that are not optimal. The challenge I confront, therefore, is to explain why my position on this matter is to be preferred over the others, without of course reverting either to compromises for mutual advantage or to calculations of overall good. The claim must be that the very notion of fairness singles out one of these positions as the one appropriate to people who are cooperating in the promotion of the overall good. But given that each of them provides a way of acknowledging the importance of individual autonomy, why should we suppose that one of them is fairer or more cooperative than the others?

It seems to me, however, that we should not let the fact that these different attitudes towards autonomy are equally articulatable mislead us into thinking that their initial credibility must for that reason be equal as well. On the contrary, as I have mentioned, I think we can quite confidently reject the suggestion that imposing harms on people is unfair only when the aim is to promote a suboptimal outcome. However coherent this suggestion may be, it is just not credible to suppose that we can take fair note of the importance of individual autonomy without going so far as to embrace restrictions. The question, as I see things, is whether such a straightforward appeal to the notion of fairness can in a similar way enable us to decide among broader and narrower views of what these restrictions should look like. It is tempting simply to assert that broader restrictions against all harmings lack any real credibility, that they obviously go much farther than they should in acknowledging the importance of individual autonomy. For we are obliged to draw a line somewhere along the broad spectrum of possible views, and the point at which people's contributions become required seems the most salient of the lot. As we shall see, restrictions against anything too closely resembling forced supererogation also have the advantage of not needing to be limited by thresholds, which makes them significantly more palatable to many people's intuitions and decidedly less problematic from a theoretical point of view. Taken together, these considerations seem to me to make a convincing case for concluding that fair terms on which to promote the overall good require nothing broader than restrictions against anything too closely resembling forced supererogation. However, I fear that a number of readers will find these considerations rather less persuasive, so we need to look for something more definitive to say in support of the line I am taking.

I think we can find what we need here by asking why our capacity for individual autonomy cannot be acknowledged more straightforwardly. If individual autonomy is so important, why not simply amend our theory of the good by assigning it a special place in the pantheon of value? Following our earlier discussion of prerogatives, we should evidently reply that individual autonomy is an ideal of individual behaviour and so deserving of more fundamental concessions. We should say that a person achieves this ideal to the extent that her own actions are governed by her own choices. And because this is an ideal, we should insist that at least some of people's opportunities for achieving it be at least to some extent protected. And how should they be protected? Evidently by supplementing impartial beneficence with principles prohibiting other people from interfering with their actions in certain kinds of cases.[39] Now I think we may assume that there is some such ideal of individual autonomy.[40] The question I think we should be focusing on here is whether individual autonomy is an ideal independent of personal integrity, by which I mean the ideal requiring people to be true to all of the values that apply to them. This was of course the ideal that I appealed to in my defence of prerogatives. So what I am in effect working us round to is the idea that we can settle questions about the proper scope of morality's

[39] Why would it not be enough to grant people the prerogative to insist on exercising their autonomy in some cases where relinquishing it would promote more good? Because *actually* exercising one's autonomy is something more than simply *insisting on* exercising it. A prerogative may protect the latter but it cannot by itself secure the former.

[40] As we shall see in a moment, this assumption could conceivably come under attack from somebody who doubts that there really are any personal values rivalling impersonal ones. But for now it seems safe enough. The more pressing matter is to determine what principles can be justified on the assumption that individual autonomy is an ideal.

restrictions by getting clearer about the precise relation between the two ideals of autonomy and integrity.

Suppose individual autonomy were an ideal independent of personal integrity. This would introduce the possibility that it might be the more important of the two ideals and so deserving of more fundamental concessions, deserving in fact of precisely some broad restrictions against inflicting on people even those harms that they are required to bring upon themselves.[41] But now consider some of the difficulties confronting this view. A person who succeeds in governing her actions by her choices achieves very little if those choices themselves aren't true to her values; nor is much gained by making choices that are true to one's values if one's actions aren't going to be governed by them. And even deeper connections are not very far to find. It seems clear, for example, that it is largely by exercising their capacity to govern their own actions by their own choices that people are led to develop the wide variety of more personal concerns that personal integrity then requires them to take proper account of. And if people no longer had any such personal concerns? In that case, I submit, their governing their own actions by their own choices would no longer be an ideal of individual behaviour but would at most be a valuable state of affairs ranking highly on the list of outcomes that are generally to be promoted.

These last two points are perhaps the ones to stress. If governing their own actions by their own choices naturally leads people to value things independently of their commitment to the overall good, how could fair terms on which to promote the overall good give importance to individual autonomy without giving personal integrity an equivalent importance? And if the fact that people have their own personal concerns naturally lends a special urgency to the question of whose choices are governing whose actions, how could fair terms on which to promote the overall good give importance to personal integrity without giving individual autonomy an equivalent importance? The more one thinks about the relations between these ideals, the harder it becomes to believe that they are distinct. My claim, therefore, is that the ideals of individual autonomy and personal integrity, though apparently distinguishable from each other, are in reality correlative aspects of a more comprehensive

---

[41] By the same token, of course, it would also introduce the possibility that individual autonomy might be the less important of the two and so deserving of less fundamental concessions. It does not really matter which possibility we focus on; the point is that all of these possibilities depend on the supposition that we are dealing here with two distinct ideals.

ideal of individual behaviour, an ideal that I shall later discuss under the heading of self-governance.[42] This is why fair terms of cooperation should treat them on a par, by matching prerogatives with correlative restrictions against anything too closely resembling forced supererogation, but allowing that the harms people are required to bring upon themselves may in some cases be inflicted upon them. It is really the same argument at work in both cases.

While I certainly would not want to preclude the possibility of further discussion of this matter, I do believe that these considerations are compelling enough to vindicate my appeals to fairness against the charge of indeterminateness, at least so far as the breadth of the restrictions is concerned. Fair terms on which to promote the overall good will include restrictions against inflicting on people harms that they are not required to bring upon themselves, but they will not include broader restrictions against inflicting on people even those harms that they are required to bring upon themselves, for that would be unduly to favour individual autonomy over personal integrity. Now what about the strength of the restrictions that fairness does require? How much would it take to override this narrower restriction against inflicting on people harms that they are not required to bring upon themselves? The fact that an almost endless variety of different answers are conceivable here might again seem to give rise to the spectre of indeterminateness.[43] But I believe that we have a plausible answer already at hand. For if fair terms on which to promote the overall good really would assign to individual autonomy and personal integrity an importance that is ultimately equivalent, then the threshold beyond which restrictions give way should surely be ultimately equivalent to the threshold beyond which prerogatives give way, whatever that latter threshold should turn out in the end to be. Whenever the prerogatives would permit a person to decline to bring a certain harm upon herself, the restrictions should forbid other people to inflict that harm upon her, for otherwise the terms on which people were promoting the overall good would be assigning personal integrity a greater importance.

Taken by itself, of course, this very schematic consideration does not

---

[42] See Chap. 4 below.

[43] Worries about the possibility of setting thresholds are in fact probably among the most familiar grounds that have been offered for abandoning restrictions in favour of more straightforwardly consequentialist principles. They are if anything even more familiar than the worries that Scheffler and others have raised about the paradoxical nature of the verdicts that restrictions generate.

tell us where the threshold governing prerogatives and restrictions would be; it therefore leaves open the possibility that a relatively small increase in the overall good might often be sufficient to override the restrictions that fairness requires. If fair terms of cooperation allowed people to give only a relatively little extra weight to their own interests and desires, then a prerogative that would in some cases permit a person to decline to bring a certain harm upon herself might in many cases be overridden, as might the restrictions prohibiting others from inflicting that harm on her. It remains to be seen whether this is in fact the case. Before taking up that question, however, it is worth noting that in another sense the restrictions that fairness requires cannot help but be absolute. For, once the prerogative gives way, the harm in question is no longer one that the person is not required to bring upon herself. So we have to be careful about how we describe such cases. The restriction that would then be overridden is not the restriction against inflicting on people harms that they are not required to bring upon themselves, but rather a quite specific restriction generated from that more basic one, a restriction prohibiting other people from inflicting on this person harms of the particular sort that are here in question.[44] The basic restriction, it seems, is one that remains in effect no matter what the circumstances and no matter what the consequences; nothing that fair terms of cooperation would permit would count as inflicting on a person a harm that she was not required to bring upon herself.

I think this development should strike us as an encouraging one because it helps account for the sense, which I believe many people share, that the restrictions morality includes are somehow absolute.[45] At the same time, however, it must be admitted that an absolute restriction against inflicting on people harms that they are not required to bring upon themselves will not be of much note if the harms that people *are* required to bring upon themselves are many and onerous. Whether our hope is to dismiss this possibility, or simply to clarify its status, the time

[44] Suppose, for example, that it would fall within my prerogative to refuse to give £10,000 just to save a stranger's life but that, if thousands of lives were at stake, my prerogative would give way and I would be required to pay. The idea is that the restriction against forcing me to pay would in that case give way too but that, since my paying would no longer be supererogatory, this is not to say that the restriction against forced supererogation would be overridden.

[45] Notice, however, that it does so without suggesting that any more specific action-type, like killing, is at all times and in all circumstances to be scrupulously avoided. This is another aspect of the view that I think we should find encouraging.

has evidently come to consider in more detail the nature of the prerogatives that fairness requires.

4. *More on Prerogatives*

One question, concerning the breadth of the prerogatives that fairness requires, we have already settled, in favour of no-harm versions of the prerogative. Pure-cost versions were rejected on the ground that, by sometimes allowing people to harm each other for their own personal gain, they inevitably come into conflict with the restriction against inflicting on people harms that they are not required to bring upon themselves. No-harm versions of the prerogative, by contrast, do not suffer from this fault, for they allow people to give disproportionate weight to their own interests and desires only in a more restricted range of cases— in cases where advancing their own individual ends would prevent them from giving aid to others, but precisely not in cases where it would actually require them to inflict harm on others.

The questions that remain to be discussed concern the strength of the prerogatives that fairness requires. How much extra weight are people allowed to give their own interests and desires? What indeed is it to give extra weight to one's own interests and desires? This much more basic question is the one that I believe we should focus on here.[46] And I believe the way we should approach it is by considering again a problem that we first broached earlier in this chapter while introducing Scheffler's formulation of the prerogative. The worry, remember, was prompted by Scheffler's idea that the prerogative allows people to give their own interests and desires disproportionate weight, when it does, in the sense that it allows them to multiply the importance of their satisfaction or non-satisfaction by some factor, call it F, so that, say, a person might be allowed to count her need for some resource as equivalent in importance to the aggregated needs of F other people each of whom stands in the same relation to that resource as she does, needing it no less than she, with the result that she might not be required to give up her chances of acquiring that resource even if her doing so would give those F other people a comparable chance of acquiring it for themselves. This struck us as troubling because, if giving disproportionate weight to one's own interests and desires is simply a matter of multiplying them by

---

[46] I shall return to the first of these questions in Chap. 4.

some such factor F, then it could conceivably happen even under conditions of full compliance that a person might be required to make terribly heavy sacrifices. However high the multiplying factor is, it will be easy to imagine cases where the aggregated needs of others would be more than great enough to overwhelm it, with the result that a person might be required to sacrifice her life or various other things she cares very deeply about. So we face the following choice: either we reconcile ourselves to the fact that morality can require people to bring upon themselves harms of the gravest imaginable sort, or we find a way to formulate the prerogative so that it is no longer capable of yielding such terribly troubling verdicts.

Now the first of these alternatives is not one that I find very appealing. If a person happens not to care very much about the preservation of her life, then there might be occasions where a requirement that she sacrifice it would not seem unfair.[47] But what of the person who does care very deeply about her own life? I must say that I find it difficult to believe that a straightforward appeal to the overall good could ever yield a requirement that such a person sacrifice her life. Perhaps there are situations in which a person who has voluntarily undertaken certain commitments—a bodyguard or professional soldier, for example—might be required by morality to sacrifice her life for the sake of others, or anyway to put it at grave risk. Perhaps indeed the mere fact of standing in certain special relations to other people—being a parent, to take the obvious example—can on certain occasions generate requirements that one make sacrifices of this sort, even if one entered into these relations non-voluntarily. These are not cases that I mean to be taking a stand on here, for they concern the existence of special obligations, whereas I mean to be focusing here on questions concerning the nature of prerogatives, and in particular on questions concerning their strength.[48] The sort

---

[47] Even this concession would have to be qualified, however, for, as we shall see later in this section, what matters is not whether someone does care little about her life but whether she *should* do so. But perhaps people sometimes should care little about their own lives and so should be prepared to sacrifice.

[48] For very interesting, in part because surprisingly sympathetic, discussions of special obligations, see Scheffler 1995a and 1995b. One might well wonder whether his sympathy for special obligations does not conflict with his hostility towards restrictions; for one might suspect that they too would sometimes generate verdicts of the sort that he finds troubling. For example, might I not have a special obligation not to betray my good friend even in those rare cases where my betraying her is necessary to prevent more other people from betraying their good friends? Now of course Scheffler might deny that special obligations of precisely this sort are deserving of any sympathy. In conversation, however, he has taken a different tack, granting that there might be special obligations of this

of case I have in mind here is rather one where a person, through no fault of her own, finds herself in a situation where the sacrifice of her life is necessary in order to save the lives of many others, each of whom is a stranger to her. And the stand that I am inclined to take on such cases is that, no matter what the numbers involved, a person who cares deeply about her own life cannot be required by morality to sacrifice it for the sake of others, that sacrifices of that size must be supererogatory. But of course in taking this stand I am simply appealing to an intuition, and a controversial one at that; the real question must be why fair terms of cooperation should always give people the prerogative to decline to make such sacrifices, and how such a prerogative might be formulated.

How might we set about answering this question? Let us begin by imagining one of those cases where the only way I have to save N other people from a certain death is to sacrifice my own life. And let us brusquely stipulate that nothing else matters so that the question is simply whether the number of lives at stake is great enough to require me to sacrifice. Clearly, from the point of view of promoting the overall good, the loss of my life would be just the loss of one life; a terrible outcome, no doubt, but N times less bad than the loss of N lives. From the point of view defined by my own values, however, the loss of my life might be the loss of just about everything; and so, in a sense, an outcome much worse even than the loss of N lives. Surely fair terms of cooperation must acknowledge this. But one feature of Scheffler's account of what it is to give disproportionate weight to one's own interests and desires, at least as I understand it, is that he does not provide us with any way to acknowledge this fact. He is willing to allow me to multiply my prospective loss by some factor, possibly a factor greater than N, but the *measure* of my prospective loss is still taken from the point of view of promoting the overall good. What I want to suggest is that this does not take fair account of the fact that I am bound to value many things other than promoting the overall good, and that the totality of my values might define a point of view from which the loss of my life would be the loss of something of near insuperable value.[49]

sort but insisting that the rationale existing for them would not support any general restriction against harming. This is obviously a position very congenial to my own; for general restrictions against harming may be grounded in general considerations about cooperation, even as special obligations give rise to whatever other restrictions there may be.

[49] Notice that this complaint, unlike Murphy's, is not one that Scheffler could hope to accommodate by adjusting the factor by which he allows people to 'multiply' their own interests and desires. For no plausible adjustment to the multiplying factor could capture the thought that having to sacrifice her own life could represent for a person a catastrophe of near insuperable proportions.

This need not be the case, of course. My other values might mostly involve commitments to causes greater than myself, in which case my death might not seem a matter of such insuperable importance, even when it is considered from the perspective of the totality of my values.[50] Thus the suggestion is not that fairness never requires people to sacrifice their lives but rather than it gives them a general prerogative which, given the nature of most people's values systems, makes most such sacrifices optional rather than required. As Scheffler himself would say, we don't think morality requires a person to make a sacrifice for the overall good unless the prospective gain as measured from the impersonal point of view is by a sufficient degree greater than the prospective loss as measured from her own point of view. That much seems exactly right; but whereas Scheffler seems to identify a person's personal loss with that part of the impersonal loss that has to do with her, I think it should instead be measured from the vantage point that is defined by the totality of the values she possesses. This is what limits the demands of beneficence. From the impersonal point of view the sacrifice of one's life is a great loss but one that could always be outweighed, and by any degree you like, whereas from the point of view of one's entire value system it could be a major catastrophe that nothing could clearly outweigh. Fairness requires that this be acknowledged. It is not enough that people be allowed to give their own interests and desires some disproportionate weight when justifying their actions; they must also be allowed to measure their prospective gains and losses from the point of view of their entire value system. What this will mean for most people is that straightforward appeals to the overall good will never yield requirements that they sacrifice their own lives or even place them at grave risk, no matter how much good is at stake.[51] If such sacrifices are ever required of people, that must

[50] To mention only the most obvious of examples: if my greatest concern is in fact to contribute to the promotion of the overall good, then my prerogative will of course have no effect and I might be required to sacrifice. Notice, however, that this would not necessarily be to say that other people would be permitted to force my hand; although there would be no restriction against their doing so, it still might be ruled out on straightforwardly consequentialist grounds. In fact, there is sure to be a good consequentialist case for a *social policy* that forbids sacrificing any person, since endless difficulties are bound to arise if we regard sacrificing each other as something that might occasionally be permissible.

[51] I say this not because I believe that promoting the overall good has no value for most people but because I believe that people typically find greater value in preserving their own lives, in fact a value great enough to ensure that having to sacrifice their own lives would count for them as a loss that no straightforward appeal to the overall good could clearly outweigh.

be a reflection either of the fact that they place comparatively little value on preserving their own lives or of the fact that they have somehow incurred a special obligation.

Of course, if this is right, and if it is true that fair terms of cooperation will include a restriction against imposing on people harms that they are not required to bring upon themselves, a restriction the threshold of which is no less high than that of the prerogative itself, then it follows that most people could never permissibly be forced to sacrifice their lives for the sake of the overall good, no matter how much good was at stake. In Dostoevsky's case, for example, we might not be permitted to torture and kill the innocent child even though that would secure a life of great happiness for millions of other people, since that is a harm that the child might not be required to bring upon itself.[52] Is this a result we can live with, or should we rather take it as indicating that our account of prerogatives and restrictions has at some point gone badly astray?

No doubt some will be tempted to reply by insisting that we should be permitted to torture and kill Dostoevsky's child even if it would not be required to bring such harms upon itself, thereby calling into question my earlier claim that personal integrity and individual autonomy are interconnected ideals. Others will surely be tempted to reply by insisting that this child actually would be required to bring these harms upon itself, given the enormous amount of good at stake. It seems to me, however, that the arguments we have so far assembled are strong enough to overcome any such temptations we may feel to back down in the face of Dostoevsky's example, and that the conclusion they lead to is one we can in any event live with. It may turn out that reason would not forbid us to torture and kill a child in a case such as this; but *morality*, as I understand it, certainly might.

The truth is that I am much more worried by a rather different kind of objection. For I can well imagine someone objecting that, in trying to formulate a prerogative that might allow people to refuse to sacrifice their lives in cases like Dostoevsky's, I have not just limited the demands of impartial beneficence but in fact reduced them to almost nothing at all.[53] Suppose, for example, that my overwhelming concern is to live a life of

---

[52] I refer of course to the case that Ivan confronts Alyosha with in *The Brothers Karamazov*. He actually goes so far as to imagine that *everyone else* will be made happy if only the one child is made to suffer.

[53] Brink 1986 reads Scheffler 1982 as proposing a prerogative strong enough to prevent morality and self-interest from ever conflicting. This is clearly not Scheffler's intention; but the question here is whether it is a result that he can avoid.

total independence, a life in which I never receive help from other people and never give help either. Could I not then argue that, from the point of view of my total value system, helping other people would be disastrous, and hence that I should be permitted never to help?

That surely would be an indication that our account of prerogatives and restrictions has gone astray. It is simply not possible that an accurate characterization of morality's content will reveal the demands of impartial beneficence to be so easily escaped; nor is it a possibility that fair terms on which to promote the overall good would allow people so easily to avoid making any contributions. It is one thing to say that fairness allows people to decline to sacrifice their lives, quite another thing to say that it allows them to decline to make any sacrifices at all. We need, therefore, to show that our reformulated prerogative does not generate this embarrassing result, or else, failing that, to provide a formulation of the prerogative that will fare better here.

Now it might seem that our original difficulty has devolved into an outright dilemma. Either the measure of the agent's prospective loss is taken from the impersonal point of view, as Scheffler seems to be assuming, or it is taken from the different point of view defined by her own value system, as I have been urging instead. Scheffler's formulation seems to have the consequence that any person could be required to sacrifice her very life, which I have suggested seems unfair; my reformulation seems to have the consequence that some people could be permitted never to sacrifice at all, which does not seem any fairer. I suppose that some readers, put off by these difficulties, might conclude from this that we should be formulating the prerogative in terms entirely different from those Scheffler proposes, terms that in no way involve people's being allowed to give disproportionate weight to their own interests and desires.[54] But I would maintain, in response to this, that we should be extremely reluctant to abandon the broad approach to prerogatives that we have been pursuing, for that would also be to abandon the rationale for prerogatives that we uncovered earlier in this chapter. Perhaps we should take a moment to remind ourselves of what that rationale is. The idea, remember, was that fair terms on which to promote the overall good must take account of our nature as human beings, and in particular of the fact that we inevitably have values other than our concern for the overall good.[55] Our initial

---

[54] This is the tack taken in Murphy 1993.

[55] There is also the fact that we sometimes fail to comply with morality's requirements; but that is clearly not unrelated to the fact that we possess rival values, so perhaps we can allow the one fact to stand in for them both.

thought was that it would be unfair to require people fully to subordinate their rival values to the goal of promoting the overall good because that would be too demanding; though why it would be too demanding we at first sight found it difficult to say. But after some discussion we did determine what the answer to this question should look like; it would be too demanding because acting in ways that are true to all one's values is an important ideal of individual behaviour and so something that must be given some play. And how, exactly, are fair terms on which to promote the overall good to give some play to this ideal of personal integrity, if they in no circumstances allow people to give any sort of disproportionate weight to their own interests and desires?

This seems to me a compelling rationale that we should be loath to abandon. In consequence, it seems to me that we really must find some way to elude the dilemma that seems to confront anyone trying to formulate the prerogative in something like Scheffler's terms; and I see only two ways in which this might be managed. Either we must find a way to reconcile ourselves to the inescapable fact that Scheffler's formulation of the prerogative could leave any person having to sacrifice her life, or the lives of people dear to her, simply to help save the lives of some greater number of strangers, or we must find a way to defend my reformulation of the prerogative from the intolerable charge that it would reduce the demands of impartial beneficence to almost nothing, permitting some people never to sacrifice at all, simply because their overwhelming concern is to be totally independent of others. Not surprisingly, my own preference is to pursue the second of these two alternatives; that any person could be required to sacrifice her life or the lives of people dear to her is something I am willing to accept only as a last resort. So we come back to the question of how we can avoid this result. If we allow people to take the measure of their prospective losses from the point of view of their own value systems, no matter what their values are, we succeed in avoiding this result but reduce the demands of impartial beneficence to almost nothing.[56] Or so it seems; for it seems that a person could conceivably have as her dominant value a concern to live a life of total independence, and from a point of view dominated by that value having to help other people would seem to be an insuperable loss. But is this right? Is it possible that a person could have as one of her values a concern to live a life of *total* independence? Is it possible

---

[56] Not for all people in all circumstances, of course; but the worry is that it would be too much for this ever to happen.

that having to help other people could be for someone a loss that no other considerations could *ever* outweigh? We won't be in a position to answer these questions until we determine what it is for something to be a value; once we do that, however, I think we will find some very good reasons to answer these questions firmly in the negative.

Somebody could certainly believe that her dominant value was to live a life of total independence. In suggesting that further examination of the nature of values will reveal any such beliefs to be false, I am therefore suggesting that a person's values will turn out to be identical not so much with her actual beliefs or desires but with something that is more objective. Now this might seem a rather peculiar suggestion to make in the midst of a discussion of prerogatives, for it might be thought that the whole point of prerogatives is to allow people sometimes to give some disproportionate weight to the various personal concerns that they actu-ally have. After all, these are the concerns that people are naturally inclined to favour in their actions; why, then, should prerogatives refer to values that people might not even recognize as their own?[57] But it is important that we remember here what the rationale for the prerogative actually is. Fair terms of cooperation allow people sometimes to give some disproportionate weight to their own interests and desires not because their doing so is natural but because acting in ways that are true to all one's values is an integral part of an important ideal of individual behaviour. So it should come as no surprise that the interests and desires that get referred to in the final formulation of the prerogative will be the interests and desires that a person's actions must be true to in order for her to attain the ideal of personal integrity. If personal integrity requires that one be true to desires that have met certain objectifying conditions, those same conditions must be expected to appear in the final formula-tion of the prerogative.

My claim in subsequent chapters will be that values are indeed to be understood more objectively.[58] And as we shall see, this does make it possible to argue that nobody could really be committed to living a life of total independence, and hence that from nobody's point of view would having to make some sacrifices for the overall good necessarily be such a bad thing. As we shall also see, by making it possible to argue for a more generous conception of the commitments defining each person's

---

[57] On this point, compare Scheffler 1982: 9 and 62.

[58] The case for objective values will be made in the second half of Chap. 3; its impli-cations for these worries about morality's content will then be drawn in Chap. 4.

point of view, a more objective conception of value promises to alleviate not only these worries about morality's content but also worries about its authority. For it promises to help explain not only how morality can make real demands of people but also why those people of whom the demands are made have real reason to comply. But we should note already that the sailing here is likely to be far from smooth. For in a sense the whole premiss of this chapter has been that people who have commitments to things other than the overall good will be subject to an ideal of behaviour that in some respects differs from that of cooperating in the promotion of the overall good. If not for the fact that this rival ideal might call for people to organize these personal and impersonal values along rather different lines, there would be nothing preventing us from analysing the ideal of cooperating in the promotion of the overall good in more straightforwardly consequentialist terms. So even though a more objective conception of value may help with worries about morality's authority, it remains to be seen where the journey we have embarked on will ultimately lead us.[59]

We finish this chapter, therefore, with as many questions as answers. I have explained why fair terms on which to promote the good will include both prerogatives and restrictions. I have explained why the prerogatives will be limited to those of the 'no-harm' sort, and why the restrictions will cover only those cases 'too closely resembling' forced supererogation. I have also explained why there could never arise circumstances in which we would be permitted to impose on a person a harm that she was not required to bring upon herself; but when people are required to bring harms upon themselves is something about which we remain somewhat unclear. My claim has been that a satisfactory formulation of the prerogative will allow people to take the measure of their prospective losses from the point of view of their own value systems; but I need to say much more about those values before that claim can be made to stick.

---

[59] My claim in the Conclusion will be that it leads us to an account of morality's authority that can at least explain the feeling of inescapability that moral reasons have.

3

Initial Counter-Arguments Supporting Value Monism

To have a motive to perform an action is one thing; to have a reason to perform it is something rather different. Let us say that a person has a motive to perform an action in so far as, and only in so far as, her performing that action could be *explained* in light of the goals she *in fact* possesses, together with her *beliefs* about her circumstances. For example, if one of my goals is to avoid paying taxes, and if I believe that I can avoid paying the taxes I owe on part of my income by neglecting to declare it, then I have a motive that could explain my failure to declare my full income. One often finds a person's motives referred to as her reasons; but I would rather we reserve that term for something else. Let us say that a person has a reason to perform an action in so far as, and only in so far as, her performing that action could be *justified* from the perspective of the goals she *should* possess, together with the *truth* about her circumstances. So if my goal should be to pay whatever taxes I owe, or if I am wrong in thinking that I can avoid paying what I owe simply by failing to declare my full income, then my motive is not a reason that would justify my acting in this way.

Although questions about reasons must be distinguished from questions about motives, it nevertheless seems likely that they are related in important ways. In particular, many philosophers have been struck by the thought that there would be little point to claims about the goals that people should have unless they could adjust the goals that they do have through some process of deliberation. Many of these philosophers have then gone on to argue that people's current goals are fixed by their current desires and that their desires are not the sort of thing that people can adjust in any fundamental way through deliberation. A person might adjust her derived desires after some further deliberation, but not the underived or basic desires from which they stem.[1] Given this, it appears

---

[1] As I understand it, this is not necessarily to deny that changes in one's basic desires might be prompted by the acquisition of new beliefs. As we shall see, it is instead simply to deny that any new beliefs could bring about such changes through a process of practical deliberation.

to follow that we have no choice but to adopt an instrumentalist conception of practical reason, according to which people's reasons for action
are at bottom determined by facts concerning the optimal satisfaction of
their basic desires. For the implication appears to be that any more critical conception of practical reason would be without any real point, distinguishing itself only by its insistence that people's deliberations should
change desires that cannot possibly be changed by such means.[2]

As we saw in the Introduction, however, any such conclusion about
reason's nature would create grave difficulties for my characterization of
morality's content. For if people's reasons do depend in this way on their
desires, it becomes hard to see how any truly impersonal values could
exist. And yet, if all reasons are agent-relative, one would suppose that
morality should be characterized solely in terms of reasons of that kind.[3]
Can we really suppose that morality requires everyone to cooperate in
the promotion of the good, if no one need aim at its promotion? If no
way can be found to reject the line of thought I just briefly sketched, we
may do better to revert to contractualism. Notwithstanding the difficulties that contractualist theories encounter in their attempts to account for
impartial beneficence, we may have no viable alternative to them.

Now this line of thought might be challenged at several different
points. One possibility would be to reject the relevance of motives to
reasons, thereby allowing that it might be true that people should have
goals of some particular (say, beneficent) sort even if it were not always

---

[2] Arguments of this sort have been familiar at least since Hume—although I think
he drew a more radical conclusion from his argument, not contenting himself with an
instrumentalist conclusion about reasons for action, but concluding instead that there are
no reasons for action at all.

Notice that the instrumentalism to which I am suggesting this argument appears to
lead could be quite sophisticated. It need not maintain that deliberation simply seeks the
most efficient means to some one already-understood end. On the contrary, it would presumably allow that deliberation also seeks better understanding of what would constitute
achieving the various individual ends that one has, better understanding of the relative
importance that these different ends have, strategies by which several of these ends could
jointly be satisfied, and so forth. What instrumentalism would not allow, however, is that
there are some facts which do not in any way concern the optimal satisfaction of the basic
desires that a person has at a time but which nevertheless play a fundamental role in determining the reasons for action that she has then. (This notion of an instrumental reason
clearly resembles the notion of an internal reason familiar from Williams 1980; but by
virtue of its reference to basic desires, it may in fact be a somewhat narrower notion.)

[3] As I mentioned in the Introduction, I am not going to take time here to defend
these claims against 'externalist' claims to the contrary. For a sampling of the sorts of
arguments that might be offered on each side of this debate, see Brink 1989 and Smith
1994.

possible for them to acquire goals of that sort through a process of deliberation. Another possibility would be to reject the dependence of goals
on desires, thereby allowing that a person might be able to bring her
goals into line with the requirements of practical reason simply by forming true beliefs about the (say, beneficent) sorts of outcomes that are in
fact worth pursuing.[4] But I doubt that either of these challenges would
be very successful. It seems to me that a successful challenge to this line
of thought will not be one that confronts it head on, but will rather be
one that leaves each step of the argument in place while avoiding its
instrumentalist conclusion. I shall be arguing that this is possible but
much more difficult than most opponents of instrumentalism have hith-
erto realized, requiring us to embrace something like Donald Davidson's
view that the nature of desire is shaped by the demands of interpretation.

To what conception of practical reason would this view of desire lead?
In recent years, several philosophers have taken up Davidson's suggestion
that our conclusions about the desires people do have must be governed
by our views about the desires they should have and that, because of this,
people must be found actually to have more or less the desires that they in
point of fact should have. The obvious implication to be drawn from this
suggestion is that instrumentalists get things the wrong way round when
they maintain that people's reasons for action depend on the nature of their
desires, the truth of the matter being rather that people's desires depend on
the nature of certain values that exist somehow independently of them.[5]
But Davidson's suggestion might also be thought to yield a stronger result.
As we shall see, it might be thought that interpretation requires the
assumption not just that there are objective values but also that those values, and hence our reasons, must all be of the form that is nowadays often
described as agent-neutral. And since morality is on my view a normative
system that recognizes relative values in addition to the agent-neutral
ones, this might seem to imply that my characterization of morality's content has slipped one punch only to be decked by another.[6]

---

4   As we shall see, this is the line that many people nowadays take—influenced, in
most cases, by the famous treatment of these matters in Nagel 1970.

5   Inferences of roughly this sort (sometimes appealing to Wittgenstein rather than
Davidson) are drawn in Wiggins 1976, McDowell 1981, Lovibond 1983, and Hurley
1989. In fairness, it should be stressed that none of these writers explicitly goes on to
argue that all reasons must therefore be agent-neutral. However, it is also true that none
of them is very careful to point out that rejecting instrumentalism need *not* rule out
embracing agent-relative reasons.

6   Once again, it will have this implication only on the assumption that some form of
internalism about morality is true.

My principal contention in this chapter, however, will be that arguments of this sort read too much into the Davidsonian theory of desire. Davidson's theory can demonstrate that instrumentalism about practical reason must be rejected—in that respect, it is of almost inestimable importance to moral philosophy. But it cannot by itself put any other theory in instrumentalism's place. As we shall see, that requires theorizing of a more substantive sort. Nevertheless, Davidson's theory is useful here too, for it does help us to understand how substantive theorizing about practical reason might properly proceed. This again is help moral philosophy is very much in need of, and help it cannot easily acquire without embracing the Davidsonian programme. The lessons we learn here will be applied in the following chapter, where a dualistic conception of reason will be defended in some detail.

I. *Explanation and Justification*

Let us begin with the line of thought that is said to lead from some simple considerations about the explanation of action to an instrumentalist conclusion about the justification of action. What, more precisely, are these simple considerations? How, more precisely, does this argument run?

The considerations in question here have to do with the dependence of goals on desires. We might put them like this. First, it is said that the contents of the goals that a person has at any time are fixed by the contents of the desires that she has at that moment; bringing about an end E is a goal possessed by a person P if and only if P has a desire to perform actions that would contribute as causal or constitutive means to E. Second, it is said that the importance that a person assigns to her goals at any time is fixed by the strengths of the desires that she has at that moment; bringing about an end E is a goal important to a person P just in so far as P has a strong desire to perform actions that would contribute as causal or constitutive means to E. This account of goals is integral to a familiar theory of motivation. I shall refer to it as the Humean theory. This theory first states that the existence of a motive M for a person P to perform an action A always turns on two things—on P's having a *desire* to perform actions that would contribute as causal or constitutive means to some end E, and on P's having a *belief* that her action A would contribute as a causal or constitutive means to that end E. Then this theory states that the strength of this motive M that this person P has to perform this action A likewise turns on two things—on *how strongly* P desires to perform actions that would contribute as causal or constitutive means to that end E, and on *how well* P thinks her action A would contribute as a causal or a constitutive means to that end E.

These two claims about motives are then said to entail two corresponding claims about reasons. They might be encapsulated as follows. From the claim that the contents of people's motives depend crucially on the contents of their desires, it is inferred that the contents of people's reasons depend crucially on the contents of their desires; from the claim that the strengths of people's motives depend crucially on the strengths of their desires, it is inferred that the strengths of people's reasons depend crucially on the strengths of their desires. Evidently an important assumption is being made here. It is very similar to an assumption that Hume makes about morality. The Humean assumption, which is often referred to as the assumption that morality is *practical*, is that morality could not require a person to perform actions of a particular kind unless her recognition that an action was of that kind could move her to perform it, not just through the vagaries of chance, but through a process of practical deliberation.[7] The assumption here, which is often described as a sort of *internalism* about reasons for action, is that reason could not require a person to perform actions of a particular kind unless her recognition that an action was of that kind could move her to perform it, again through a process of practical deliberation, and not just the vagaries of chance.[8]

The validity of this assumption might of course be challenged; but that is not a possibility I shall entertain here. While the Humean thesis

---

[7] Although he doesn't refer to it in just this way, Hume defends this assumption in 1739: 455–70. It should be stressed that this is an assumption stronger than the internalism about morality I have occasionally been alluding to, for it makes morality's requirements dependent not just upon the existence of reasons but also upon the availability of motives. (It is effectively the result of combining internalism about morality with what I go on to call internalism about reason.)

[8] For a defence of this internalist thesis, see Nagel 1970, Williams 1980, and Korsgaard 1986. (None of these writers formulates the internalist thesis in precisely the way that I do; but I take it that the formulation I offer is one they all could accept.)

Notice that the internalist requirement is that it must be *possible* for a process of deliberation to have this result, not that it must always in fact have it—a point that Korsgaard rightly stresses in her paper.

It is also worth stressing that this internalist thesis about reasons for action has *nothing whatever* to do with internalism about psychological content, and so is not incompatible with externalist views about such matters. I explain what externalists might make of it later in this section.

about moral requirement has sometimes been rejected, this more basic thesis about rational requirement is almost universally accepted. I shall therefore assume that its validity can be established, the better to concentrate my attention on two other questions. How, exactly, is the Humean theory of motivation to be understood? What, exactly, are its implications for our theorizing about practical reason?

Obviously enough, the Humean theory of motivation is concerned with the role that facts about beliefs and desires play in the explanation of actions. What is less obvious is whether this theory is supposed to tell the whole story about their roles. If so, then it entails that a person's beliefs can move her to act only *in the service of* her desires; if not, then it allows that a person's beliefs might also move her to act *through the medium of* her desires. An example may help to make this distinction clearer. Thus suppose P believes that Q is suffering. Then, if it is true that a person's beliefs can move her to act only in the service of her desires, it must follow that P's belief that Q is suffering can move her to perform an action that she believes would help him only if she already has some desire to the satisfaction of which she believes her helping him would contribute, such as a general desire to alleviate suffering. However, if it is possible that a person's beliefs might also move her to act through the medium of her desires, it will follow that P's belief that Q is suffering might move her to perform an action that she believes would help him even if she currently lacks any desire to the satisfaction of which she believes her helping would contribute, for it might itself generate the requisite desire.[9]

Now I suggest that the Humean theory of motivation is properly to be understood as leaving room for this possibility. Whether or not Hume understood his theory in this way, there are at least two reasons that can be offered for our doing so. First, I think this is the only interpretation that gives the Humean theory some chance of being true, since it seems clear

[9] This distinction obviously owes a great deal to the distinction that Thomas Nagel draws between motivated and unmotivated desires in Nagel 1970, chap. 5. But Nagel's terminology here is rather unfortunate. For talk of motivation inevitably, and quite properly, brings to mind explanations by goals, and thus, I believe, explanations by desires. (I will be saying something in defence of this belief in just a moment.) This in turn creates the impression that Nagel's distinction must inevitably coincide with, or collapse into, the completely innocuous distinction between derived and underived desires, that is, very roughly, the distinction between desires that are and desires that are not generated by one's beliefs about how best to satisfy the other desires that one has. But clearly the position that Nagel is trying to stake out here cannot be so easily undercut. (This point is brought out very nicely in Wallace 1990, sect. 5.)

to me that a person's beliefs *can* bring about *fundamental* changes in the contents and the strengths of her desires (changes, that is, in the contents and the strengths of her basic or underived desires).[10] Second, I think this is the only interpretation that pays proper attention to what the term 'motive' means, for it seems clear to me that a person can be *moved* to perform an action by something that does not itself *motivate* her to perform that action (though not, I would argue, by something that does not cause her to become so motivated). It is easy to lose sight of the second of these two considerations. But a moment's reflection should suffice to bring it back into focus. After all, when we say that a person P has a motive M to perform an action A, we are not merely saying that P is in a state that could cause her to do A; we are also saying that that state is of a special sort, one that could rationalize her performance of A.[11] Looking back, that is why I insisted that a motive is a state partially constituted by the possession of a goal, and not just any state that is potentially explanatory of an action—the idea being that we rationalize the performance of an action by showing how it can be explained in a special way, in terms of the beliefs that the agent currently has about the steps that she might now take towards the goals that she currently embraces.

This suggests that theories of motivation are best understood as claims about what would constitute a person's being motivated to perform an action and not as claims about what might cause someone to be motivated to act that way. That is how I am recommending that we understand the Humean theory—as claiming only that people's motives are partially constituted by their desires.

---

[10]   If only because of the ineliminable holism of the mental. Of course this was not a consideration available to Hume. However, if he were to deny that beliefs can bring about fundamental changes in desires on a priori grounds (simply insisting that an 'original existence' couldn't be influenced by an 'idea'), that would seem to be at odds with his views about causality (in 1748, sect. 7), for it would seem to depend on some alleged insight into the causal powers that things possess rather than on our accumulated experience of their comings and goings. And yet, if he were to deny that beliefs can bring about fundamental changes in desires on empirical grounds (arguing instead that we can always get by without introducing that complication), that would seem to be at odds with his views about simplicity (in 1751, appendix 2), for it would seem to depend on the tacit assumption that the simplest explanations of our actions are the ones that make the simplest claims about basic desires. So even without considerations regarding the holism of the mental, Hume had some very good reasons to tread carefully here.

[11]   Granted, in *The Shorter Oxford English Dictionary*, the term 'motive' is defined as 'that which moves or induces a person to act in a certain way'. However, if 'moving' is understood as 'causing', this simply cannot be right. It is simply false to say that anything that causes a person to act in a certain way constitutes a motive for her to act in that way.

Of course, the Humean theory claims that motives are partially constituted by desires only because it holds that goals are wholly constituted by desires. This view about the nature of goals is one that I think
we have good reason to accept. For to say that a person P has as one of
her goals the bringing about of an end E is surely to imply that P is to
some extent *disposed* to perform actions that she believes would contribute as causal or constitutive means to E; but to say that P is to some
extent disposed to perform actions that she believes would contribute as
causal or constitutive means to E is surely to imply that P has a *desire* to
perform actions that would serve as means to that end.[12] Beliefs by
themselves could never constitute such dispositions, even if anti-Humeans
sometimes talk as though they could. For example, if anti-Humeans
thought that rationality required any person who believed that other people were suffering to be to some extent disposed to perform actions that
she believed would help them, and if they thought that our person P did
believe that certain other people were suffering, then, if they thought
that P was likely to meet rationality's requirements, they might be tempted to maintain that she was already disposed to help, even if they doubted that she had any desire that could account for the existence of that
disposition—as though it was actually her belief that was in this case
constituting the required disposition. However, if anti-Humeans doubted that rationality required any person who believed that other people
were suffering to be to some extent disposed to perform actions that she
believed would help them, or if they doubted that our person P was likely to meet rationality's requirements, then, even if they thought she did
believe that certain other people were suffering, they would not dream
of saying that she was therefore disposed to help, unless they thought
that she did have some desire that could account for the existence of that
disposition—indicating that even they don't really think beliefs can constitute the sort of dispositions goals involve.[13]

[12] This talk of people being 'to some extent' disposed to perform actions, and indeed
talk of people being 'disposed' to perform actions at all, obviously cries out for a more
rigorous formulation; but it should suffice for our purposes here. For some discussion
of the claim that propositional attitudes involve dispositions to act, see Levi and
Morgenbesser 1964; for some discussion of the idea that goals are constituted by desires,
see Smith 1987, sects. 5–7, and 1994, chap. 4.

[13] The point here is that P's belief that certain other people were suffering could not
constitute a disposition to perform actions that she believed would help them unless she
could not possibly have that belief without also having that disposition—something that
not even Hume's opponents are prepared to maintain.

What if P believed, not just that those other people were suffering, but also that reason
required her to help? Could not such a belief, a belief that was itself about practical reason,

This leads me to conclude that we have no choice but to accept the Humean theory of motivation. As long as it is construed as a theory about the constitution of motives, I do not see how it could plausibly be rejected. By the same token, however, construing the Humean theory in this limited way would seem to open up the possibility that it may have no bearing on the choice among competing theories of practical reason, for it allows that beliefs are still able to *generate* dispositions of the sort that goals involve, rejecting only the much narrower claim that beliefs can themselves *constitute* such dispositions. Returning to our example, therefore, it seems possible that rationality could require a person who believed that certain other people were suffering to be to some extent disposed to perform actions that she believed would help them, even if she did not then have any desire that would dispose her to act in those ways, since her belief could itself cause her to acquire just such a desire. What this suggests is that instrumentalists might confront a kind of dilemma, and that their appeals to the Humean theory of motivation might thereby be thwarted. Either they construe the Humean theory as making a claim even about the causes of motives, in which case it seems almost certainly false, since it seems clear that a person's beliefs can bring about fundamental changes in the contents and the strengths of her desires, or they construe the Humean theory as making a claim only about the constitution of motives, in which case it seems almost entirely innocuous, since it seems possible that a person's beliefs might bring about whatever changes in her motives practical reason deems to be necessary.

Such is the response standardly given in the literature to all those who would draw instrumentalist conclusions about reasons from Humean views about motives. It is perhaps most closely associated with the work of Thomas Nagel, and has more recently been refined in various ways by Christine Korsgaard.[14] I think it is a response that can be made to stand, but only if much more work is done to shore it up. For I think instrumentalists have at their disposal a counter-argument the real force of which has not been fully appreciated by their opponents.

We can begin to see this by reflecting on the assumption that we earlier described as a sort of internalism about reasons for action. The

---

constitute the sort of disposition that goals involve? I don't think so. It is difficult, I confess, to see how P could believe that reason required her to help without being at least somewhat disposed to comply; but, as we shall see, that is a fact that can be accounted for without having to call into question the Humean theory of motivation. See pp. 97–100.

[14] See Nagel 1970 and Korsgaard 1986.

claim, remember, was that reason could not require a person to perform actions of a particular kind unless her recognition that an action
was of that kind could move her to perform it, not just through the
vagaries of chance, but through a process of practical deliberation. So
far, however, all we have managed to establish is that a person who did
not have any desire motivating her to do what reason required might
be caused to acquire such a desire, and so to comply with reason's
demands, by some beliefs that she had acquired. We have shown that
beliefs could conceivably bring about the right outcomes, but not that
they could bring them about *in the right way*. Yet, as I tried hurriedly
to indicate in my earlier remarks, it is crucial to the internalist thesis
that people be able to transform the goals they do have into the goals
they should have through a process of deliberation. So, unless we are
prepared to abandon the internalist thesis altogether, it is obviously
incumbent upon us to look more closely at the process through which
beliefs might bring about fundamental changes in the contents and the
strengths of desires.

Now my guess is that many opponents of instrumentalism will object
to the spirit in which these remarks are made. They will readily agree,
no doubt, that not every case in which a belief gives rise to a desire is a
case of deliberation, and hence that they have more work to do before
their position is complete. A process of deliberation is presumably one
over which an agent can exercise a certain degree of control, and so one
for which she can be held in some measure responsible; that is why we
are drawn to the internalist thesis about reasons for action, so that
people can be held in some measure responsible for not acting on the
reasons they have.[15] There is no reason that I can see for opponents of
instrumentalism to deny this, nor to deny that it sets them some tasks
that they have yet to complete. What many will reject, however, is the
suggestion that they are unlikely to be able to complete these tasks in a
satisfactory way, that the notion of deliberation is for some reason the
special province of instrumentalism. Obviously the instrumentalist conception of deliberation is one that we all want to acknowledge, and one
where it is especially easy to understand why talk of control and responsibility might be warranted. But unless we are prepared simply to beg
the question in favour of instrumentalists and against their opponents,

---

[15] This is perhaps not the only consideration that draws us to the internalist thesis;
but it is surely the most important. See, for example, Pettit and Smith 1996. (Darwall
1983, chap. 5, and 1992 take a slightly different view of the matter.)

why should we suppose that this is the *only* sort of deliberation there is?[16]

But this is where opponents of instrumentalism tend to underestimate its strength. They tend to assume that instrumentalists have no more cards to play, when in fact they are still holding a card of some note. Perhaps we can best appreciate its importance by returning to our example.

Thus suppose that P believes that Q is suffering and that this belief has given rise in her to a desire to help him. We can all agree, I think, that if we want to maintain that this belief gave rise to that desire *through a process of deliberation*, we will also have to maintain that P judged there to be some reason why it should do so. Perhaps P also believed that Q was a friend, and judged that one should help one's friends when they are suffering; or perhaps P judged that one should help anybody who is suffering, whether or not one counts them among one's friends. It does not matter for our purposes what P's reasoning actually was. All we need suppose is that some such reasoning was at work. But now, it might be argued, if we are going to maintain that P's belief gave rise to her desire *in virtue of that reasoning*, we will also have to maintain that any suitably similar belief would have given rise to a correspondingly similar desire. Suppose that the operant judgement in this case was that a person should always help her friends when they are suffering; does it not follow that a belief that some other friends were suffering would have generated a desire to help them?[17]

It seems to me that this conclusion does follow and that opponents of instrumentalism are consequently in a tight spot. For if it is true that a belief that some other friends were suffering would have generated in P a desire to help them, it would seem to follow that P was to some extent *disposed* to perform actions that she believed would alleviate the suffering of her friends. But that would in turn entail that P must in some sense and to some degree have *wanted* to alleviate the suffering of her friends, unless a disposition to perform actions that one believes would contribute to some end need not involve a desire to bring about that end.[18]

---

[16]   This question is raised in Korsgaard 1986, sect. 6.

[17]   Of course this would at best follow ceteris paribus; but that does not undercut the point I am making, for obviously similar ceteris paribus clauses would have to be written in to any dispositional analyses of goals and desires.

[18]   Compare Williams 1980: 107, Smith 1987: 59, and Smith 1994: 122–5.

Perhaps Nagel would reject the dispositional analysis of desires upon which this argument rests. But then why does he grant that all actions involve desires of some sort? The point of the instrumentalists' counter-argument is precisely to show that their various

Where before there seemed to be a kind of dilemma keeping instrumentalists from their objective, there now threatens instead to be a kind of dilemma preventing their opponents from escaping. For it begins to seem that non-instrumentalists must either reject internalism about reasons for action, and its claim that a process of deliberation can always bring motives into line with reasons, which I have suggested one should be loath to do, or else work their way back in the argument and reject the Humean theory of motivation, and its claim that goals can be connected to desires through the notion of a disposition, which strikes me as being an equally hopeless way out.

I think this counter-argument is a very powerful one, indeed one that comes perilously close to settling the issue. Certainly it is not so easy to accept the Humean theory of motivation but blithely declare it to be innocuous; the dispositional analyses of goals and desires upon which that theory rests enables it to resist being treated too cavalierly. To see just how dire our predicament here has become, let us briefly consider several unsuccessful attempts to escape it.

I suspect that many opponents of instrumentalism will be tempted to respond to this counter-argument by trying to restrict its range of application. They will insist that it has force only so long as it is directed towards beliefs of a certain kind. Granted, they might say, if P's belief that Q is suffering really did give rise in her to a desire to help him through a process of deliberation, that must be because she judged there to be some reason why it should do so, such as that Q is a friend and that one should help one's friends when they are suffering. Moreover, they might say, if P's belief that Q is suffering really did give rise in her to a desire to help him in virtue of that reasoning, it must be true that a belief that other friends were suffering would have generated in her a desire to help them, indicating that P actually wanted to alleviate the suffering of her friends. But what are we to say about the origin of *this* desire? Here is where many opponents of instrumentalism will dig in their heels. They will insist that, for all we know, P's desire to alleviate the suffering of her friends could itself have been generated, through a process of deliberation, by her belief that one should help one's friends when they are suffering. And this could have happened, they will add, without P's having judged there to be some reason why this belief should have this

claims about desires hang together in ways that their opponents have failed to appreciate. The best reasons for endorsing the Humean theory of motivation are also reasons for denying that beliefs can bring about fundamental changes in desires through processes of deliberation.

effect, and so without the presence of any antecedent desire of the sort that instrumentalism invariably requires.[19]

The idea, therefore, is that the instrumentalists' counter-argument does not touch beliefs that are themselves about practical reason. The claim is that such beliefs can give rise to desires through a process of deliberation without signalling the presence of antecedent desires. Now, at first sight, this can seem quite compelling, for it is tempting to suppose that people's beliefs about practical reason must *always* be capable of influencing their practical deliberations. Whereas a process of deliberation could have led P from a belief that Q is suffering to a desire to help him only if she also believed that for some reason it should do so, it is tempting to suppose that deliberation could have led her from a belief that one should help one's friends when they are suffering to a desire to alleviate the suffering of her friends no matter what else she believed. Whether or not she was in fact led to form such a desire, it is tempting to suppose that this belief could have had that effect.[20] Tempting though this is, however, I think we misunderstand its significance if we take it to show that no antecedent desires need be involved here, for the following simple reason. Even if it is true of necessity, it remains the case that a process of deliberation could have led P from a belief that one should help one's friends when they are suffering to a desire to alleviate the suffering of her friends only because different beliefs about what one should do could have had a corresponding effect upon her desires—in short, only because she was already disposed to do what she believed reason required.

Thus it looks as if an antecedent desire would be at work even in cases like this. A process of deliberation could lead one from a belief about what one should do to a desire to do what one should only if one already had a desire to act as reason requires. So the instrumentalists still seem right in thinking that there can be no reasons without antecedent desires.

While conceding this point, some opponents of instrumentalism will insist that there is nonetheless the basis here for a decisive objection to the theory. And indeed there can seem something suspect about any acknowledgement by instrumentalists of a desire to act as reason

---

[19]   It is worth noting, for example, that when Nagel talks about beliefs 'motivating' desires, he invariably has in mind beliefs that are themselves about practical reason.

[20]   If P is depressed, for example, she may not succeed in forming this desire; but it is still tempting to suppose that there must be a real sense in which her belief about practical reason ensures that she could have done so.

requires. What does it matter whether instrumentalism is true, if at the same time it is true that people's foremost desire is of necessity to act as reason requires? If we need to know what people have reason to do *before* we can determine what instrumentalism requires of them, how much importance can the instrumentalist theory have? Certainly it will no longer suggest that all reasons must be agent-relative. Thus beliefs about practical reason may create a problem for instrumentalism after all. The problem is not that they constitute an exception to the instrumentalists' claim that there can be no reasons for action without antecedent desires but rather that they reveal the presence of a desire that threatens to render the instrumentalists' theory vacuous.[21] But notice that beliefs about practical reason create this problem only on the assumption that they really are capable of generating desires through a process of practical deliberation. So if the instrumentalists can convince us that beliefs about practical reason are in fact incapable of playing this role, that they are idle expressions of what one anyway desires and not effective cogs in the process of practical deliberation, then they will have rid themselves of this final problem—leaving us little choice but to conclude with them that people's reasons for action are exclusively agent-relative in nature.

How might the instrumentalists argue that beliefs about practical reason can only be idle expressions of what one anyway desires? As I see things, they need only take the argument that their opponents are now pressing against them and stand it on its head. Oversimplifying just a little, we might summarize that argument as follows: people obviously must have reason to act as reason requires; so, given the internalist thesis about reasons, it must be possible for their recognition that reason requires a certain action of them to move them to perform that action through a process of deliberation; but that, as we have seen, requires that they be disposed to perform any actions that they believe reason requires of them; so, given the dispositional analysis of desires, it follows that people must have a desire to act as reason requires.[22] In response, however, I think the instrumentalists can argue like this: there are no desires

---

[21] Perhaps the instrumentalists could neutralize this threat by arguing that a desire to act as reason requires is nothing more than a desire to act as instrumentalism requires; but any such argument would have to be supported by something other than the facts about the explanation and motivation of action that we are focusing on here.

[22] And since the reason must obviously be overriding, the desire must be strong enough to dominate—which is not to say that it always *will* dominate, for in any given case a person might act irrationally.

that people must of necessity have; so, in order to avoid concluding other-wise, some fault must be found with the argument that has just been advanced; but the only way to find fault with that argument is to attack its understanding of what beliefs about practical reason are; so, for want of any acceptable alternative, beliefs about what reason requires of one must be understood not as effective cogs in the deliberative process but as idle expressions of what one anyway desires. Deliberation occurs as these desires get filtered through one's beliefs about means. One's beliefs about reason merely reflect the resulting changes in one's desires. Now of course opponents of instrumentalism are likely to object that this extremely deflationary conception of practical deliberation is quite unacceptable, certainly much less acceptable than the idea that there are certain desires that people must of necessity have.[23] But it seems to me that the instrumentalists are well within their rights to chal-lenge the idea of a necessary desire, and that until more sense is made of it they must be judged the winner of this dispute.

If we are to accept the Humean theory of motivation yet avoid the instrumentalist conclusion, we must take a much more radical step than any we have contemplated so far. We need not necessarily reject the dis-positional analyses of goals and desires upon which the Humean theory of motivation rests; but we must radically rethink those analyses in light of the thought that explaining actions requires us to interpret them. This will provide us not only with a better understanding of why instrumen-talism is vacuous but also with the resources we need to put a better the-ory in its place.

Suppose philosophers like Davidson are right in maintaining that the nature of people's propositional attitudes is shaped by the demands of radical interpretation. What impact would this have on the instrumental-ists' argument? Davidson is of course himself one of the more celebrated proponents of the view that motives are constituted by belief/desire pairs, so perhaps we should not expect this view of propositional atti-tudes to overturn the Humean theory of motivation. If we are to interpret people we must make them out to be as rational as we can, and our first step must be to portray their actions as products of beliefs they have about means to ends they desire.[24] These desires will in some cases

---

[23] The charge that instrumentalists cannot make satisfactory sense even of instru-mental deliberation is very often made (e.g. in Smith 1988 and Korsgaard 1996)—though many who make it seem not to realize that it obliges them to acknowledge the existence of necessary desires.

[24] See Davidson 1963.

emerge spontaneously but will more often be the products of deliberations they have undergone. And these deliberations will in every case
involve their judging that they should act in certain ways. The question
then is whether interpretation requires that these judgements be rooted
in other desires that they have, or whether it allows that people's deliberations can bring about fundamental changes in the contents and the
strengths of their desires. Now, at first sight, it might look like interpretation *should* allow this, requiring only that their deliberations bring
about these changes in ways that are so far as possible rational. But that
would at the very least require that suitably similar beliefs normally
bring about correspondingly similar desires; and that would once again
seem to indicate that these changes are manifestations of underlying dispositions to act. Upon further reflection, therefore, it looks like instrumentalists might win here too—and indeed Davidson has suggested that
judgements about values are probably best interpreted as manifestations
of underlying desires.[25]

Thus it begins to look like the Davidsonian conception of propositional attitudes might leave each plank of the instrumentalists' argument
more or less intact. But notice how their argument has nonetheless been
defused. Instrumentalists would like to draw from their argument the
conclusion that people's reasons for action are in some important sense
dependent upon their desires, while all the time maintaining that their
desires are not in any important sense dependent upon their reasons. But
the Davidsonian conception suggests that people's desires actually *are*
dependent upon their reasons in an important sense, and so forces us radically to rethink the instrumentalists' claims about the ways in which
their reasons are dependent upon their desires. Thus it may well be true
that reason could not require a person to perform actions of a particular
kind unless her belief that an action was of that kind could move her to
perform it through a process of deliberation. And it may also be true that
her belief that an action was of that kind could not move her to perform
it through a process of deliberation unless she had an underlying desire
inclining her towards actions of that kind. Nonetheless, if the
Davidsonian conception of propositional attitudes is to be believed, our
conclusions about the underlying desires people do have will be governed by our judgements concerning the underlying desires they should

---

[25] In Davidson 1984b. (What exactly he means by this, however, is far from clear. I
explain how I think a Davidsonian should envision the relation between our desires and
such judgements in the next section.)

have. We must not suppose that our endeavour to make people out to be as rational as possible has no application at this point. But this means that we must have views about people's reasons that are in some sense independent of our views about their desires. Therefore, unless we are to suppose that those views are systematically in error, we are obliged to conclude that people's reasons cannot possibly depend upon their desires in the fundamental way instrumentalists think they do.[26]

This of course assumes that the Davidsonian conception of propositional attitudes is actually to be believed—an assumption the truth of which I have so far done nothing to establish. I shall say something in defence of the Davidsonian conception in the next section. But my main concern there will be to clarify its implications for theorizing about practical reason.

2. *Justification and Interpretation*

I said at the beginning of this chapter that there are some compelling considerations about the interpretation of action that might be thought to provide some support for the claim that all reasons are agent-neutral. What, more precisely, are those compelling considerations? How, more precisely, might this argument run?

The considerations in question here have to do with the dependence of interpretation on valuation. They might be put as follows. First, it is said that our warrant for attributing to a person P a desire D to bring about an end E typically depends on our judging that P's bringing about E would have some objective value—that is, some value that it would have independently of the existence of her desire D. Second, it is said that the strength that we are warranted in assigning to this desire P has to bring about E typically depends on the real importance that we judge P's bringing about E would have—that is, the importance that it would have independently of the strength of her desire D. This account of interpretation is integral to a familiar conception of desire, the one I have been calling the Davidsonian conception. Notice that the claim is not that, in consequence of our limitations as interpreters, *we* can do no better than to assume that people must have more or less the desires that we judge they should have. What the Davidsonian claims is rather that, due

---

[26] For a more thorough investigation of this line of thought, see the articles and books cited above in n. 5.

to the nature of interpretation itself, even an *ideal* interpreter would have no alternative but to allow her attributions of desires to be governed by her judgements about values.

And of course the Davidsonian also holds that this epistemological claim has important metaphysical implications. Thus we get the following inferences. Given that even an ideal interpreter would have no alternative but to allow her attributions of desires to be governed by her judgements about values, the Davidsonian concludes that this tells us something, not just about the properties that may justifiably be attributed to people's desires, but also about the properties that people's desires *really do have*. Given that an ideal interpreter's judgements about objective values must themselves be ideal, what the Davidsonian thinks we learn from this epistemological claim is that the contents and the strengths of people's desires must by and large correspond, not merely with the interpreter's own particular views about objective values, but with *the full truth* about such matters.[27] Obviously arguments are needed to substantiate these inferences, arguments linking the epistemology of interpretation to the metaphysics of desire and value. In particular, more needs to be said about the respects in which an ideal interpreter would have to be ideal; otherwise it remains unclear why such an interpreter must be in possession of the truth about objective value, and why indeed there must be truths about objective values for such an interpreter to be in possession of. However, in keeping with my decision to focus mainly on the implications of the Davidsonian conception of propositional attitudes, and not to get caught up in the many considerations that can be offered for and against it, I shall simply assume that the epistemology of interpretation does have implications for the metaphysics of desire and value.[28]

We have already concluded that the Davidsonian conception of propositional attitudes would undercut the instrumentalist theory of

[27] Most people are probably more familiar with the parallel inferences drawn for beliefs in Davidson 1977 and 1986a. But Davidson 1984b, 1985, and 1986b make it clear that similar arguments are meant to hold for desires.

[28] Discussion of the considerations that can be offered for and against Davidson's claims about beliefs are not far to find; but so far as I know the claims about desires have yet to receive the attention they so obviously deserve. As I have said, it is not my intention to try to provide a full defence of these claims in this book. I am more interested in the implications of these claims for the nature of value and the prospects for moral theory. Nevertheless, I think it should be emphasized that these two undertakings are not entirely independent of each other. If Davidson's theory indeed has implications favourable to moral philosophy, that may surely be admitted as evidence in its defence.

practical reason. Can we now conclude that exclusively agent-neutral conceptions of reason would stand to gain the most from this? That depends on how the Davidsonian conception of desire is finally to be understood, and in particular on what conception of objective value it finally commits us to.

As we have seen, the Davidsonian conception of desire commits us to the view that people's desires by and large conform to values that are in some important sense objective. The question is whether the Davidsonian conception commits us to the view that those values are at bottom agent-neutral. If so, then it entails that a person typically can have a desire to bring about an end only if her bringing about that end would actually have value *for everyone*; if not, then it allows that a person might typically have a desire to bring about an end even though her bringing about that end would have value *only for her*. An example might help to make this distinction clearer. Thus suppose we are wondering whether to ascribe to P a desire to learn to play Beethoven's piano sonatas. Then, if it is true that a person typically can have a desire to bring about an end only if her bringing about that end would actually have value for everyone, we should probably be thinking that P's learning to play those sonatas would be a good thing all around. However, if it is possible that a person might typically have a desire to bring about an end even though her bringing about that end would have value only for her, we can simply be thinking that P's learning to play those sonatas would be a good thing for her.[29]

Now I suggest that the Davidsonian conception of desire is properly to be understood as leaving room for this possibility. Two reasons for making this suggestion come immediately to mind, reasons which run roughly parallel to those that were tendered at a similar point in the previous section. First, I think it is this interpretation that gives the Davidsonian conception of desire the best chance of being true, since it seems at least possible that people typically do desire to bring about ends that have an intrinsic value only for them (so that only for them do those ends have a value that does not simply derive from the contribution that they would make to other outcomes that have value for them). Second, I think this is the only interpretation that pays proper attention to what the term 'objective' means, for it seems clear to me that a value can be objective in a perfectly good sense

---

[29] For both this distinction and this example, see Nagel 1980: 101–2. (As we shall see in Chap. 4, I think this distinction is actually more complicated than such simple examples might suggest. But they will do for the moment.)

even if it is agent-relative (that is, even if there is a sense in which it exists only for the agent herself, perhaps indeed only for that agent at that time and in those circumstances). The term 'objective' is admittedly one that gets used in many ways; but I think in this context its meaning should be sufficiently clear. So far as I can see, when we say that a person's bringing about an end that she desires would have a value that is objective, we are simply saying that its value does not depend on the fact *that she desires it*. So far as I can see, we are not denying that the value of that outcome might depend on other facts about that person, facts that might make it of value *only for her*.[30]

But even if it does make good sense to say that values could be agent-relative yet nonetheless objective, it may be that interpretation requires the assumption that values are objective in the stronger sense of being agent-neutral. I have indicated that I have grave doubts about this; but I have yet to say what those doubts are.

With this in mind, let us begin by asking why the interpretation of action should be thought to require the assumption that values are objective in any sense at all. The answer standardly given here is that this view of interpretation is one we have no choice but to accept.[31] We could always try, I suppose, to make do with the assumption that every person must have more or less the desires that we would have had if we had lived her life and now inhabited her circumstances. The trouble with this, however, is that we might have no idea what those desires would be if this person's history and circumstances were as different from our own as we must suppose they could have been. In order to protect ourselves against this possibility, we must abandon any thought of making do with a purely descriptive assumption and avail ourselves of a normative one. We must at least be prepared to assume that every person must have more or less the desires that we *should* have had if we had lived her life and now inhabited her circumstances. But of course this is to go so far as to assume that there are objective values that somehow determine what desires different people should have given their different histories and their different circumstances.

---

[30] A fact stressed in Nagel 1980: 102. (Notice that a value can be agent-relative in the sense under consideration here without also promising to make the agent fare better, without being self-interested in that narrow sense, though there may be some broader sense in which all agent-relative values will be tied to self-interest.)

[31] See, in the first instance, Davidson 1984*a*, Essays 9–12. These papers deal primarily with the attribution of beliefs, not desires. Desires are given greater attention in Davidson 1984*b*, 1985, and 1986*b*.

But why should interpretation be thought to require any assumption about the form people's desires must by and large take? Why can we not proceed instead in a piecemeal fashion, looking at each person's behaviour case by case and trying to build up an account of her desires? The reply standardly given to this objection is that we cannot form a hypothesis about the content and the strength of any one of a person's desires without at the same time forming connected hypotheses about the contents and the strengths of many other desires that she has, and that in the face of this holism of the mental we have no choice but to start with an assumption about the form people's desires must by and large take and then try to tailor it for each person in light of the behaviour she actually displays.[32] Now I must say that I find this entire line of thought quite convincing.[33] Thus I would agree that interpretation requires the assumption that values are somehow objective. At the same time, however, nothing that has been said so far would seem to indicate that these values must be at bottom *agent-neutral*. All we have said so far is that we must assume that every person must have more or less the desires that we should have had if we had lived her life and now inhabited her circumstances. That, as we have seen, is tantamount to assuming that there are objective values determining what desires people should have given their histories and their circumstances. But it seems to leave open the possibility that these objective values are agent-relative and hence that people who have had

[32] Against this, it might be objected that we do in fact have another option. For it might be thought that we could limit appeals to the 'principle of charity' to the problem of fixing beliefs, then fix desires on the simpler assumption that people's actions must by and large be rational in light of their beliefs. However, Davidson has shown quite convincingly that this alternative strategy will not work. Appealing to the 'principle of charity' will not enable us to fix beliefs with enough precision to make this strategy viable; a provisional assignment of desires is also necessary so that both assignments can subsequently be refined in light of the person's behaviour.

[33] The holist assumption underlying this line of argument has recently been attacked in Fodor and Lepore 1992. Although their criticisms are far too many to be addressed in any thorough way here, there is one point that I think is worth making, for it seems to bear on many of the objections they raise. When holists say that we cannot form hypotheses about any one of a person's attitudes without at the same time forming connected hypotheses about many other attitudes that she has, Fodor and Lepore repeatedly reply by asking for some perfectly general way of determining which these other attitudes would be, hoping to show that holists are in the unenviable position of maintaining that the nature of any one of a person's attitudes depends on the nature of *all* the others. But why should we suppose that holists are obliged to go along with this request? Surely we might know which of a person's attitudes are relevant in any given case, simply in virtue of our understanding of the concepts involved, and not in virtue of some more general rule that can be applied across the board.

different histories and now inhabit different circumstances would be right to desire different things.

If the Davidsonian conception of desire is going to provide any special support for exclusively agent-neutral conceptions of reason, some way must be found to rule this possibility out. I do not myself think it can be ruled out; but it must be admitted that we have not yet considered all the arguments that are relevant to this question.

Thus suppose we were trying to interpret a person whose history and circumstances were very much different from our own. And suppose we did try to begin by assuming that this person must have more or less the desires that any person should have after having lived such a life and upon now inhabiting such circumstances. The possibility we must consider, once again, is that we might have no idea what those desires would be, given how different her history and circumstances were. How could we even identify the differences in her history and circumstances that should have generated differences in her desires, if we could not begin by assuming some familiarity with the desires she should have? The conclusion to draw from this, I think, is that interpretation must guard against this possibility by starting with an assumption that is less schematic in nature. It must start by assuming that there is some one set of basic or underived desires that everyone should have, and that differences in people's desires should emerge only as differences in their histories unfold.[34] Such an

---

[34] Compare this with the more familiar idea that some beliefs are so basic or central that we would be hard put to imagine any turn of events that would call for us to interpret someone as lacking them.

By this point, some readers may be finding a certain objection hard to suppress. Why, they might ask, must the assumptions necessary for interpretation be normative ones? No doubt it would not be enough simply to assume that every person must have more or less the desires that we would have had if we had lived her life and now inhabited her circumstances. It would not be enough to assume that the same or similar desires would result from the same or similar causes because these causes could be ones with which we have little or no experience. This suggests that interpretation requires an assumption of some less schematic sort; but why exactly could that less schematic assumption not still be causal? Instead of insisting that interpretation must start out with the assumption that there is some one set of desires that everyone should have, why not allow that it might start out with the assumption that there is some one set of desires that everyone *will* have? This is in effect to ask why interpretation must be governed by views about objective value and not simply by theories of human nature. Perhaps the quickest way to respond is to point again to the case of belief. If we feel that some beliefs are so basic or central that we would be hard pressed to imagine any turn of events that would call for us to interpret someone as lacking them, that is surely not simply a reflection of some theory that we hold about human nature but flows instead from some view that we take about certain truths that are independent of those beliefs. As far as I can see, there is no reason whatever to treat desires any differently.

assumption would enable us to formulate views about how people's different histories and circumstances should lead to differences in their
desires. It would therefore enable us to give some content to our claims
about the desires that our interpretees must more or less have. Of course,
even if it is true that such an assumption would be *sufficient* to get interpretation going, it does not follow that it would also be *necessary*. But I
doubt that any weaker assumption would still be strong enough to do the
job. The conclusion to which this line of thought leads me, therefore, is
that in some important sense people should have desires that are at bottom the same. And that might seem to establish that values must at bottom be agent-neutral in character.

Now I believe that this line of thought does establish that basic values
must be objective not just in the minimal sense of being desire-
independent but also in the stronger sense of applying to everyone.[35] But
I think this would still leave open the possibility that those basic values
might be exclusively agent-relative. In conceding that people should have
desires that are at bottom the same, we would be conceding that basic
values must all be universal, but this is not to say that those values must
be agent-neutral, since a value could be universal and yet nonetheless be
agent-relative. Perhaps it is true that every person should desire her own
well-being, and perhaps also the well-being of her friends and family, in
which case the values of self, friends, and family would be universal, but
that does not mean that those values would be agent-neutral. For it does
not mean that every person should desire the well-being even of family
members and friends who are not hers. It does not even mean that every
person should desire that other people have family and friends and be
able to help them.[36] Another way of putting the point here would be to
say that there is an ambiguity in the claim that people's desires should be
at bottom the same, for their desires might be at bottom *of the same type*
without being at bottom directed *towards the same outcomes*. They might
each have a desire for (for example) their own well-being, without there
being any person whose well-being is desired by them all. Unless interpretation can be demonstrated to require the assumption that people's
desires should be at bottom the same in the second sense as well as in the
first, we will have no grounds for concluding that the Davidsonian conception of desire favours exclusively agent-neutral conceptions of reason.

---

[35] Derivative values, of course, are different; they will apply to people only in virtue
of their histories and their circumstances.

[36] For some reservations, see Korsgaard 1993.

We will have to concede that anti-instrumentalism could take several forms, according to one of which reasons are exclusively agent-relative in character.

I can think of only one route that we might take here. It involves arguing that the attribution of desires runs in every respect parallel to the attribution of beliefs, then arguing that the attribution of beliefs requires something parallel to the assumption of agent-neutral values. This road is a precarious one that we must negotiate with care.

Parallels between the attribution of desires and the attribution of beliefs are not far to find. Just as we would not get very far trying to interpret people only on the assumption that they must have more or less the desires that we would have had if we had lived their lives and now inhabited their circumstances, because we might have no idea what those desires would be, so too we would not get very far trying to interpret people only on the assumption that they must have more or less the beliefs that we would have had if we had lived their lives and now inhabited their circumstances, because we might have no idea what those beliefs would be. Here again we have no choice but to invoke an assumption that is normative in character. And just as it did not seem sufficient to assume that people must have more or less the desires that we *should* have had if we had lived their lives and now inhabited their circumstances, because we also might have no idea what one should desire in that case, so too we would need something stronger than the simple assumption that people must have more or less the beliefs that we should have had if we had lived their lives and now inhabited their circumstances, for we might have no idea what one should believe in that case either.[37]

But now consider the assumption that we do seem to make in the case of beliefs. We do not simply assume that people should have beliefs that are at bottom of the same type (whatever that might mean); what we assume is that people should have beliefs that are at bottom directed towards the same *outcomes* (and to the same degree). We assume that there is one world composed of various different objects behaving in their various different ways, and that people should have beliefs that are true to the nature of those objects and events. Interpretation proceeds only on the assumption that every person must have more or less those beliefs. So why do we not likewise assume that there is one world (if we

---

[37] See the works cited in n. 31 above, in particular Davidson 1985. See also Lewis 1974.

may call it that) composed of the truth about value, the truth about what outcomes it would be good (or bad) to have happen and how good (or bad) it would be? Why do we not assume that it is this one world that determines what desires people should have, and that interpretation proceeds only on the assumption that every person must have more or less those desires?[38]

This is a powerful argument that deserves our respect. If we are to avoid its troubling conclusion, we must explain why the attribution of desires requires something different from the attribution of beliefs. We have conceded that they begin by requiring very similar things. If they finish by requiring very different things, one would suppose that we should be able to uncover a convincing explanation of that fact.

I think such an explanation can be found in the following difference between beliefs and desires. It seems that we could allow ourselves to suppose that we and other people might very often assign radically different *utilities* to the same token outcomes, because that supposition need not undercut the assumption that it is to the same token outcomes that those radically different utilities were actually being assigned, since we might still be able to identify those outcomes in terms of our shared beliefs. But surely we could not allow ourselves to suppose that we and other people might very often assign radically different *probabilities* to the same token outcomes, because that supposition certainly would undercut the assumption that it is to the same token outcomes that those radically different probabilities were actually being assigned, since we might no longer have sufficient shared beliefs in terms of which to identify those outcomes.[39] Yet interpretation requires the assumption that utilities and probabilities are being assigned to the same token outcomes. In the case of beliefs, therefore, a commitment to agent-neutrality cannot be avoided; interpretation does not allow that there is any interesting sense in which 'the world' could be different for different people. In the case of desires, however, a commitment to agent-neutrality has to be earned; interpretation by itself leaves open the possibility that 'the good' is to be found in different places by different people.[40]

---

[38]   Compare Williams 1985, chap. 8.

[39]   This point is used to devastating effect against external-world scepticism in Davidson 1991.

[40]   Although I think this has always been his view of the matter too, it must be admitted that Davidson has not always made this very clear. Perhaps most misleading was his claim (in 1970: 222) that, in our need to make sense of a person's behaviour, 'we will try

The only way this possibility might be ruled out is through substantive theorizing about practical reason. Adopting the Davidsonian conception of desire does enable us to avoid instrumentalist theories of practical reason; it also enables us to conclude that some values must be not just objective but universal. But it does not enable us to say what these universal values in fact are; it does not even enable us to say how we might conduct the search for them. It does tell us that our judgements about values must be by and large correct. But it is one thing to be inoculated against radical forms of scepticism about practical reason, and quite another thing to be given a reliable *method* by which to investigate its nature. It is one thing to be able to answer most questions that arise about objective value, but quite another thing to be able to settle the hard cases that separate competing theories. Theories that recognize only agent-relative values are able to account for *most* of the judgements that we feel inclined to make about objective values; that is why they continue to draw adherents. So the fact that our judgements about objective values must be by and large correct does not entail that we can rule out such theories; a limited form of scepticism still threatens us.

How then are we to decide among competing theories of practical reason? Although I have just argued that appealing to the Davidsonian conception of desire cannot enable us to avoid engaging in substantive theorizing about practical reason, I do want to insist that there are several important lessons we can learn from the Davidsonian conception about the form such theorizing should take. I shall close this chapter by briefly explaining what these lessons are.

Let us begin by turning our attention back to the internalist thesis about reasons for action. If this thesis about reasons is correct, reason cannot require us to perform actions of some particular kind unless our recognition that an action was of that kind could move us to perform it

for a theory that finds him . . . a believer of truths and a lover of *the good*' (emphasis added).

I suppose it might be wondered why the holism of the mental I was endorsing earlier does not undermine the distinction I'm espousing here. After all, if desires depend for their existence on beliefs in the ways that holism suggests, how could a commitment to agent-neutrality be unavoidable in the one case but problematic in the other? But all holism commits us to is the claim that a person couldn't have certain particular desires if she didn't have certain minimal beliefs. A person could not have a desire for things to be some specific way, for example, if she believed that no such things existed or that such things could not possibly be that way. But evidently a person could believe that such things existed and that they could be that way without desiring them to be that way. Given this, I don't see why the agent-neutrality present in the one case must carry over to the other, and so don't see why holism presents any threat to the distinction I'm drawing here.

through a process of deliberation. As we saw in the preceding section, what this apparently means is that the desires we have must of necessity be such that we could through a process of deliberation come to the truth about our reasons for action. There we were offered two radically different ways in which this claim might ultimately be understood. According to the instrumentalists, our desires are necessarily such that deliberation could lead us to the truth about our reasons because reason simply directs us to optimize the satisfaction of whatever desires we happen to have. According to their opponents, our desires are necessarily such that deliberation could lead us to the truth about our reasons because our foremost desire is always to do whatever it is that reason happens to require.[41] The instrumentalists' account seemed at the time quite troubling, for it appeared to require that we accept a markedly deflationary picture of what practical deliberation consists in, one according to which beliefs about means do all the work and beliefs about reasons are in a way just epiphenomenal.[42] But the opponents' alternative seemed if anything even worse, for it appealed to the idea of a necessary desire without giving us any clear sense of what that could be, and so without giving us any clear answer to the charge that there could be no such things.

Now I believe that the Davidsonian conception of desire gives us the resources to answer this objection. For if it is in general true that one's desires must by and large reflect the truth about objective value, then it does not seem so very surprising that one's foremost desire should of necessity be to act as the balance of those values requires. This assertion can now be seen to be a natural extension of a perfectly general view about what desires are, and not just an ad hoc device baldly designed to avoid the instrumentalist conclusion to which the internalist thesis about reasons otherwise seems to lead.[43] The Davidsonian conception of desire also gives this assertion a deeper significance than it had before. If all we know is that people's foremost desire is of necessity to act as reason requires, then, while there is indeed a sense in

[41] This, recall, was the position that opponents of instrumentalism seemed driven to, given that they could not avoid either the internalist thesis about reasons or the dispositional analysis of desires.

[42] Recall that the instrumentalists were forced to adopt this markedly deflationary picture in order to avoid conceding that people's foremost desire is necessarily a desire to act as reason requires.

[43] The parallel claim in the case of beliefs would be that a person's deepest belief must of necessity be that there are objective truths to which her views should correspond. (This very Davidsonian claim, that one cannot have beliefs without also having the concept of objectivity, is one I find extremely compelling; but obviously this is not the place to defend it.)

which instrumentalism must be considered vacuous, since we first need to know what reason requires of people before we can tell what instrumentalism would have them do, there is another sense in which the theory might still hit the mark, for it might still prove true that what reason requires of people is that they optimize the satisfaction of whatever other desires they have. Moreover, we are left without any indication of how to rule out this possibility. By contrast, once we know that the truth about objective value must be reflected more generally in people's desires, then we know that the instrumentalist theory is in a deeper sense false, and that in order to determine what reason requires of any given person at any given time we need to know, not what would optimize the satisfaction of her desires as they actually are, but what would optimize the satisfaction of her desires as they would be if they more accurately reflected the truth about objective value. In addition, we now have some indication of how to set about identifying those truths.

We have some indication of how to set about identifying these truths because we know they are reflected in the desires we already have. Of course, we can also be pretty sure that their reflection in any given person's desires will be neither fully accurate nor fully complete. So a limited form of scepticism will threaten us until we uncover a reliable method by which to follow the clues our desires provide. A completely satisfactory statement of this method has yet to be produced; but some of its broader features would seem to be reasonably clear.

At a general level, it seems reasonable to suppose that the method we seek will look very much like the method of 'reflective equilibrium' that John Rawls has famously advocated for our theorizing about distributive justice (and perhaps also about moral issues more generally).[44] Now to speak here of a *method* is undoubtedly a bit optimistic. To date, all the Rawlsians have really told us is that we are to begin by stockpiling 'considered judgements' about distributive justice, both about the verdicts we think it would render in various concrete cases and about the relations we think it bears to other areas of inquiry, then try to articulate a set of principles that will mesh smoothly with all these judgements, before finally, upon discovering (as we are quite certain to) that no set of principles can mesh smoothly with all our considered judgements, making adjustments both to our judgements and to those principles until a happy state of equilibrium is reached.[45] The trouble with this, however, is that it leaves all

[44] See Rawls 1971.
[45] For a helpful account both of the many attractions of Rawls's method and of the problems that it still faces, see Daniels 1979.

the really hard questions unanswered, for any set of principles can be brought into reflective equilibrium with our considered judgements about distributive justice, no matter what they are, so long as we are prepared to make the requisite adjustments along the way; a complete statement of the method would therefore have to explain how we are to distinguish adjustments that consolidate our considered judgements about distributive justice from adjustments that distort them, presumably by explaining how we are to distinguish those of our considered judgements that are more central from those that are less so. But this task, while undeniably difficult, doesn't strike me as being insurmountable. On the contrary, it strikes me as being remarkably of a piece with a task that the Davidsonian conception of desire must anyway confront, so that we can try to find people wrong about 'peripheral' matters before ascribing to them 'central' mistakes.

Having said all this, I must confess that (for want of time and ingenuity) I am not here going to offer any general criteria by which to distinguish the more central of our considered judgements about objective values from the less so. But there is one *negative* point that I should like to make. Just as Moore once argued that a perfectly 'substantive' judgement, such as his judgement that he had lived all his life at or very near the surface of the earth, could be central to his considered views about the world, and so among the last things he should jettison in search of theoretical understanding, so too I would suggest that a judgement can be central to our considered views about objective values, and so among the last things we should be willing to abandon in our search for reflective equilibrium, without there having to be any sense in which it is 'merely formal' in nature.[46] I believe this to be a point worth stressing because, among those philosophers who have been concerned to reject instrumentalism, there has long been a strong temptation, no doubt encouraged by consistency models of rational requirement, to assume that a desire to act 'reasonably' must have a stronger claim to the title of rational requirement than most other desires, and certainly a much stronger claim than any desire having anything at all to do with the promotion of the overall good, for the simple reason that it seems more 'purely formal' in nature, whereas any reference to the overall good seems clearly to introduce a 'substantive' element. Thus many philosophers assume that opposition to instrumentalism must lead to contractualism. But I find contractualism no less problematic as a theory of reason than it was as a theory of morality,

---

[46] I refer here, of course, to Moore 1925.

so I think it important that we not start out with any preconceived notions about what might be most central to our considered judgements about objective values.

Having established that instrumentalism is false, we are now at last in a position to consider what might be true. We have also gleaned at least some indication of the method by which we should proceed. Taking our lead from Rawls's work, we must somehow identify the most central of our considered judgements about objective value, then determine what support they offer the claim that reason is at bottom dualistic in nature.

4

Self-Governance and Value Dualism

IN the preceding chapter, we concluded that people's desires must by and large correspond to certain values that exist independently of them, and that their foremost desire must of necessity be to act as these objective values dictate. We also concluded that the best way to identify these objective values is probably to follow some analogue of Rawls's method of reflective equilibrium, which method requires that we be able to distinguish between those of our considered judgements about objective values that are more central and those that are less so. Now at this point some people will maintain that an unprejudiced assessment of our considered judgements about objective values clearly reveals at least a very strong presumption in favour of the conclusion that they are dualistic in nature. As they see things, once it has been established that neither the explanation nor the interpretation of action settles the question in favour of value monism, the burden of proof lies squarely on the shoulders of anyone who would deny that both agent-relative and agent-neutral values do in fact exist.

I too find a strong presumption in favour of agent-relative values. I do not mean by this to deny that problems could arise and that we might conceivably find ourselves having to decide against their existence in the end; in fact, as we shall see in the Conclusion, anyone concerned to defend a plausible thesis about morality's authority is bound to feel some real pressure in that direction. But I do think such pressure meets stiff resistance from considered judgement. It can be no easy matter to overturn our sense that some outcomes have a value for the agent that they do not have for people more generally. Who wants to deny that the death of a friend or the failure of a project is especially unfortunate for the person whose friend or project it was? To be sure, many consequentialists will argue that such judgements must ultimately be re-evaluated. They will insist that certain outcomes appear to have a special importance for certain people only because they are best placed to promote them, only because it happens that those people will contribute most to the overall good if they develop an especially strong concern for those things.[1] But the urgency with which this claim typically gets made is itself quite suggestive. It indicates that even most consequentialists find a strong presumption in favour of agent-relative values that they feel obliged somehow to explain away. But then of course the question for us to ask is why it should be explained away and not accepted on its own terms.[2]

Some find the presumption in favour of agent-neutral values equally imposing. And at first sight it can seem overwhelmingly likely that many such values exist, for having once given up the instrumentalists' insistence that reasons be anchored in desires, it does become hard to deny that many outcomes are of value to everyone, for example that everyone has at least some reason to alleviate a stranger's pain.[3] But is this enough to suggest that such values are agent-neutral? They appear to satisfy the condition on agent-neutrality specified in the preceding chapter, for they appear to be outcomes the realization of which has value for everyone; but the question is whether meeting this condition would be sufficient for agent-neutrality, or whether truly agent-neutral values would have to meet some more exacting standard. I think a little reflection will reveal that there is a further difficulty here. If the problem were simply that some contractualists are going to try to explain the appearance of neutrality in terms of merely relative ends, then we could again reply that those very efforts betray their acknowledgement of a presumption that might better be accepted on its own terms.[4] But this is not the only problem afflicting the case for agent-neutral values. For even if everyone has some reason to alleviate a stranger's pain, and that reason is not derivative upon other reasons that they have, this still might not signal the existence of an agent-neutral value, not anyway in the sense required by my cooperative conception of morality.

To see how difficulties might arise here, consider how Bernard

---

 [1] As I have mentioned, some consequentialists, such as Brink 1986, take a different line, allowing that relative values really do exist but insisting that morality is completely indifferent to them. But my own feeling is that this more conciliatory approach fatally undermines their position, for I don't see how morality can avoid addressing itself to all the values there are.

 [2] In light of our findings from Chap. 1, we might also wonder whether the appearance of agent-relativity actually can be explained away as easily as these consequentialists are suggesting.

 [3] Compare Nagel 1986: 160 ff.

 [4] And again, in light of our findings in Chap. 1, we might question whether the appearance of neutrality can be explained away as easily as these contractualists are maintaining.

Williams responds when his assaults on the universalistic pretensions of moral theory meet constructions like mine.[5] He exhibits surprising agreement with their Davidsonian elements, even conceding that people's desires might actually start out answering to values that are both universal in their application and neutral in their content.[6] But he maintains that both the intrinsic content and the relative importance of these values would inevitably come to vary from person to person with differences in their histories and their circumstances. He thinks people in different classes or different cultures, undergoing different experiences and doing different things, would rightly understand and rank these values in different ways. He insists that this fate would befall even those values (if any) that are essential to morality, and concludes on this basis that the universalistic pretensions of moral theory would remain unrealized. If both the intrinsic content and the relative importance of such values would inevitably vary among classes or cultures, how could any one theory of morality possibly have application to every person?

Now some may wonder whether truly objective values could be so mutable. As we shall see, however, there is in fact no very good reason to deny that assessments of value are in one sense always relative to people's histories and circumstances; the question is rather whether there might be another sense in which the values of things remain for every person at all times the same. The universal pretensions of moral theory require this deeper sort of dualism.[7] Neutrality of content is not enough; what must be shown is that there is a perspective from which the intrinsic content and relative importance of values is not susceptible of variation, and this despite the fact that there is another perspective from which the intrinsic content and relative importance of values change with history and circumstance. In any event, this is the sort of neutrality that my moral theory requires. Some proponents of contractualism might include a concern for the overall good in the profile of the agents whose negotiations will determine morality's content, then try to explain why everyone should agree to the same set of rules even though

---

[5] See Williams 1995: 140 ff.

[6] For our purposes here, it is not necessary to determine how far Williams would actually take his agreement with Davidson; it would not matter if he were granting the elements of Davidson's theory merely for the sake of the argument.

[7] To be more precise, the universalistic pretensions of moral theory require this deeper sort of dualism if I am right in thinking that internalism about morality is true and that contractualists cannot provide a fully satisfactory account of morality's content.

the relative importance of their concerns may vary.[8] But we have seen how such approaches would jeopardize our stipulations about morality's content. Fully vindicating all three of our stipulations about morality's content required us to postulate the existence of two comprehensive perspectives on questions of value, so we need to show that there is a perspective from which the relative importance of outcomes is for everyone always the same.

And obviously this neutral perspective must be shown to be reason-generating. Its mere existence is not enough; what is required is not just that there be a perspective from which the relative importance of different outcomes is for everyone always the same, but also that this perspective have throughout the course of their lives a significant role to play in the determination of each person's reasons for action. We need to show that reasons really are determined from two perspectives. As I indicated in the Introduction, I shall attempt to do this by arguing that a truly self-governed person is precisely one who divides her allegiance between competing value systems, not one who simply follows the particular system of values that is continually being reshaped by the slings and arrows of her own outrageous fortune. Or rather, I shall argue that this is a plausible view of self-governance. My goal in this chapter is not to prove that self-governance is a matter of dividing one's allegiance between neutral and relative values but to show that such a view can be made plausible enough to lend some very important support to my cooperative conception of morality. It will be helpful in what follows to think of the issue like this: if even self-governance can plausibly be characterized as a matter of dividing one's allegiance between agent-neutral and agent-relative values, then the fact that my cooperative conception of morality depends on the assumption of value dualism can hardly be a strong count against it.

1. *The Mutability of Objective Value*

Let us begin with the suggestion that the intrinsic content and relative importance of objective and even universal values will vary from person

---

[8] Nagel himself sometimes talks as if he understands contractualism in this way, even though he is without question the foremost proponent of value dualism. But I take it that he really means us to be imagining negotiators who share a much less mutable commitment to the overall good.

to person with differences in their histories and circumstances. Before seeking to determine what the implications of this suggestion might be, we need to decide what the chances are that it is true.

One source of worry here is not far to find. For if developments in people's lives can cause both the intrinsic content and the relative importance of values to change for them, it might seem that the values to which their desires originally answered could cease to have any application to them at all. And this, it might be argued, would return us once again to the predicament of the radical interpreter; for if we were first to encounter a person only after such changes had had a chance to take effect, we would no longer know how to frame an assumption about the form her desires must by and large take.[9] Instead of tailoring some such assumption in light of her behaviour, our interpretation would have to be constructed from the ground up; yet that is something that we have concluded to be impossible, given our guiding assumption about the holistic nature of the propositional attitudes.

The worry here does not concern desire-change per se. Our imagined objectors could certainly grant that people whose lives have developed in very different ways might rightly desire very different things; but the claim would be that these differences can emerge only among desires that are not basic but in some sense derived. Thus people in different classes or different cultures, after undergoing different experiences and performing different actions, might rightly come to regard very different things as possible means to becoming liked or respected, and might rightly come to assess the relative effectiveness of these means very differently as well. But the claim would be that such variations in intrinsic content and relative importance must somehow be confined to people's derived desires, so that their basic desires can always be seen as answering to a single set of values that has application to everyone.

If this proved unconvincing, our imagined objectors might try to take the line of thought a step or two farther, much as some moral theorists tried to do in response to Williams's famous attacks on the usefulness of impersonal theory as a guide to practical deliberation. For example, instead of relying solely on the very simple distinction between basic and derived desires, they might appeal to the rather more complicated

---

[9] Even if they would always retain at least some application to people, the possibility that the relative importance of these values could now be very different might seem problematic enough. For how could we assign a provisional allocation of desires to people if we did not know to which permutation of these values they were more or less to correspond?

distinction between different orders of desire. That is to say, they might allow that people's *first*-order desires can diverge as differences in their histories unfold, insisting only that the higher-order attitudes that people take towards their first-order desires must continue to reflect the values to which they originally answered—roughly speaking, that everyone should always want themselves to have whatever first-order desires would in their circumstances lead them to satisfy that set of values as fully as possible.

On occasion, in fact, it might even be argued that people could better satisfy those values by *denying* their applicability, and thus by forming higher-order desires to have whatever first-order desires would in their circumstances lead them to satisfy some *rival* set of values.[10] This suggests an even deeper sense in which different people might rightly desire different things; indeed, it suggests that in some circumstances people might rightly share no desires at all. Even so, however, the claim will still be that these variations affect only people's desires and not their values; the values to which desires answer must remain for everyone always the same, even if they can sometimes call for people's desires to differ very widely. It is the immutability of these basic values that our imagined objectors will insist on—again, because the assumption of their immutability seems necessary if interpretation is to be possible.

But I believe closer inspection will reveal this appearance to be illusory. Radical interpretation *would* require the assumption of the immutability of values *if* its success depended on its guaranteeing that people could be interpreted even by someone who knew nothing of the particular ways in which their individual lives had developed. In any event, a good case for that conclusion could be made. Certainly it is hard to see how we could admit the possibility of any very significant value change and still determine how to select among the widely varying interpretations that could then be offered of people we did not know. But must we really guarantee that interpretation is possible in such cases? While the approach I am taking evidently does presuppose that people's propositional attitudes must meet some sort of 'publicity' condition, it seems enough to guarantee that people could be interpreted by anyone with sufficient knowledge of their

---

[10] For some discussion of the idea that certain values might be 'self-effacing' in this way, see Kavka 1978 and Parfit 1984. I myself wonder whether it is possible that a person's desires could best reflect one set of values by aiming at another. For our purposes here, however, the point to note is simply that Williams's opponents might invoke this possibility in their defence.

histories and circumstances.[11] And securing that guarantee seems perfect-ly compatible with tolerating some value change. For if one knows enough about a person's life, about the particular things she has experi-enced and done, there seems no obvious reason why one could not chart the ways in which the values of things have changed for her.

Some may feel that this leaves me open to a devastating objection. For they may feel that an interpreter who had in her possession sufficient knowledge of a person's history and circumstances wouldn't need to start with any assumptions about the form that her beliefs and desires must by and large take. Couldn't such an interpreter solve for her beliefs and desires more directly? But in that case Davidson's theory of inter-pretation would not give agent-neutral values any protection against the instrumentalist attack, and so the defence of value dualism that I am try-ing to mount here would come crashing down around us. In fact, how-ever, there's no danger at all of this happening. Even if our interpreter were in possession of all actual and even counterfactual information regarding a person's history and circumstances, the holism of belief and desire would still mean that indefinitely many different interpretations could be offered of her behaviour. So there's no getting away from the need for some guiding assumptions.[12] What is true is that the nature of

[11] Ludwig 1992 goes even farther, arguing that the theory of radical interpretation need only guarantee that people could be interpreted by anyone with sufficient know-ledge, not necessarily of their histories and circumstances as they have unfolded in the actual world, but rather of their histories and circumstances as they would have unfolded in some suitable—but perhaps non-actual—world. (For example, in a world that actually contains external objects!) Others would go less far, insisting that the theory of radical interpretation must surely guarantee that people can be interpreted by anyone whose knowledge of their (actual) histories and circumstances, though not necessarily complete or even close to complete, is of roughly the kind and amount that people typically have of each other. Obviously this is not the place to rebut these different possible readings of the 'publicity' condition. The point to stress here is simply that there are plausible readings of that condition that would by no means rule out Williams's speculations about the likely mutability of objective value.

[12] As we saw in Chap. 3, n. 34, some will argue that the need for expressly *norma-tive* assumptions could be avoided if radical interpretation were allowed to make use of the straightforwardly *empirical* generalizations that might be culled from the long record of prior attempts at such interpretation. After all, as Fodor and Lepore 1994 and Fogelin 1997 both assert, there is no good reason to suppose that people must be interpretable even by someone who knows nothing of how other interpretations have fared. As I men-tioned in Chap. 3, however, I find it difficult to see why the generalizations that might be formulated on the basis of such information should be thought to be uncontaminatedly empirical in nature. So while I grant that radical interpreters could make use of them, I do not see how this changes the fact that their interpretations would be guided by substantive assumptions about the nature of objective value. (For more on this, see Davidson's 1994 response to Fodor and Lepore.)

these assumptions will depend on the interpretative predicament that we are imagining; and my claim is that the interpreters we should be considering would not need to assume that values are immutable.

No doubt they would have to make other assumptions about value change. Knowledge of a person's life would not enable us to chart the ways in which the value of things have changed for her unless we could assume that such changes were governed by certain principles that are universal in application. Otherwise we would still have no way of selecting among rival interpretations.[13] And of course it would once again not be enough simply to assume that people's values must change in more or less the ways that ours would have changed if we had lived their lives and now inhabited their circumstances. Some assumptions much less schematic than this would have to be made. But if we *do* assume that value changes are governed by appropriately substantive principles, and also that everyone starts out owing allegiance to the same set of values, there remains no good reason to deny that real change is possible. And once we grant its possibility, why should we deny its actuality? Once the purely theoretical objection is recognized to be groundless, why not simply acknowledge what has always seemed so obvious—that differences in people's lives can give rise to differences even in the fundamental values that things have for them?

Thus imagine two women, the first of whom has devoted great time and energy to the pursuit of her career, at considerable cost to her enjoyment of family and friends, the second of whom has devoted comparable time and energy to the enjoyment of such relations, at considerable cost to the successful pursuit of her career. The suggestion then is simply that these differences in their lives may have led different things to become fundamentally important for them. They need not have, of course; much would depend on how these women acquired their different histories and on what they make of the fact that they did.[14] But still, they might have done; it seems absurd to insist that any differences here must somehow be confined to the derived values that things have for them. It is of course true that these differences in their lives now leave them with different opportunities to satisfy more fundamental values. But in part for that very reason it seems likely that these two women will now be right to take very different views

---

[13] Compare Williams 1985: 199, and 1995: 142 ff., on the importance of uncovering psychological and sociological principles that govern value change.

[14] For more on this, and in particular on the possibility that people can have reason to rebel against their pasts, see p. 148 below.

even of these fundamental values, either because they should now rank these values against each other in different ways or because they should now have a different understanding of what these values involve. Perhaps the careerist should care less about certain conceptions of family, while the housewife should care less about certain conceptions of achievement. As I have acknowledged, we cannot very well concede this possibility without at the same time insisting that such changes must be governed by principles that are universal. That said, however, it seems fair to insist that the burden lies on Williams's opponents to explain why people's fundamental values could not change in this way.

In response to this, it might be objected that a parallel line of argument would suggest that differences in people's lives might lead different facts to hold true for them, and that the palpable absurdity of this conclusion should lead us to wonder whether fundamental values could really be as mutable as I have been maintaining. But while there are indeed many parallels between facts and values, there is also an important asymmetry that blocks any such *reductio*. The difference is that we can formulate the principles governing changes in people's values in terms of facts about the ways in which their lives have actually developed, saying for example that people tend over time to find more value in activities to which they have willingly been devoting a greater amount of time and energy. But in what terms could we hope to formulate parallel principles governing changes in the facts that ultimately hold true for people? It seems perfectly clear that any such principles would again have to be formulated in terms of facts about the ways in which their lives have actually unfolded, and that because of this these and all other facts would have to be safe from the forces of change that the principles were meant to be revealing. Since these are supposed to be principles to guide anyone's interpretation of anyone else, they need to be formulated in terms of facts that hold true for everyone. And since any fact could in principle be implicated in the story explaining how one person's life has developed in ways that distinguish it from all the others, there seems no credible way to avoid allowing that every fact must after all be safe from the forces of change that the principles were intended to reveal. So the idea that the facts might differ for different people is a non-starter; there is simply no possibility of formulating principles to govern variation of that sort.[15]

---

[15] The point here is of course intimately related to the one that I made in Chap. 3 when considering why attributions of belief could not exhibit the kind of agent-relativity that attributions of desire might.

Of course, just as one would like to know a lot more about the nature of the values to which everyone's desires must be assumed originally to have answered, so too one would like to know a lot more about the nature of the principles that must be assumed to govern subsequent changes in those values. We know that they would have to be substantive in nature, but nothing at all about the content that they actually have. The one example that I have ventured indicates just how complicated a subject this could be; for while it does seem true that people often find more value in activities to which they have been devoting more time and energy, one does not have to look very far before uncovering many apparent exceptions to this rule. My remarks so far have evidently been very abstract and exploratory, giving only the barest indication of how Williams's argument might go. For our purposes here, however, I think this is all that is required; for my strategy here will not be to contest the validity of Williams's argument. I propose to grant him his claim that any values to which people's desires prove to be answerable will also turn out to be highly mutable in nature. What I want to contest is the idea that the truth of this claim would reveal the universalistic pretensions of moral theory to be unrealizable or somehow fraudulent. It goes without saying, I trust, that I do not intend to do this by championing some formalistic view of morality that drains it of all distinctive content. My plan is not to argue that moral theory can survive Williams's onslaught because it allows people to do whatever their highly divergent values require that they do. It is rather to argue that people with highly divergent values still have reason to endorse a single and substantive moral theory of the sort I have defended.[16]

Keeping these goals in mind, therefore, let us now consider whether there is not after all some way in which we can allow Williams to have his argument while at the same time refusing to accept his conclusion. Does the mutability of objective value show the universal pretensions of moral theory to be unrealizable?

2. *Initial Considerations Favouring Value Dualism*

The claim I wish to defend is that Williams's argument establishes the mutability only of agent-relative values, leaving untouched the possibility

---

[16] It should be said, however, that some difficult questions will remain about whether this theory could be substantive in precisely the way that, or to the full extent that, Williams says no theory could be.

that there are also agent-neutral values that remain for everyone always the same. Our next step, therefore, must be to get clearer about the critical distinction between agent-relative and agent-neutral values.

So far, we have been distinguishing between these two sorts of values by pointing to the indexicality of their contents.[17] Conceding that neutral values are not distinguished by either their objectivity or their universality, we have focused on the fact that they direct everyone towards the same outcomes. Thus a value has been counted as agent-relative if, and *only* if, its content includes some ineliminable token reflexive, as is the case, for example, with the value to be found in advancing one's *own* interests or promoting one's *own* friendships. By contrast, any value to be found in advancing interests or promoting friendships quite generally has, to this point, been counted as agent-neutral. The contents of these values do not include ineliminable token reflexives; they point everyone to whom they apply towards the same particular outcomes. Instead of giving me special reason to attend to *my* interests and friendships and you special reason to attend to *yours*, any such values would give us all reasons to do what we can to advance interests and promote friendships quite *generally*.

Drawn in this way, the distinction between agent-relative and agent-neutral values poses no problem at all for Williams's argument. He can happily allow that there might be agent-neutral values in *this* sense, insisting only that the intrinsic content and relative importance of these values can change.[18] For example, he could concede that friendship-in-general is one of the values to which people's desires originally must answer, but insist that its intrinsic content and relative importance will vary from person to person as differences in their lives unfold. Certainly there is nothing in his argument to suggest that originally applicable values will prove mutable *only* if their contents include ineliminable token reflexives. Thus Williams might very well grant that there are agent-neutral values in this sense and that morality weighs them against agent-relative ones. His claim will simply be that, since the intrinsic content and relative importance of these values will vary from person to person, there is no hope of arguing that the right way of striking this balance is for everyone always the same.

---

[17] Following e.g. Parfit 1984: 143, and Nagel 1986: 152–3. Nagel states the position very succinctly when he says that the contents of agent-relative values, but not of agent-neutral ones, contain 'essential references' to the agent.

[18] As we shall soon see, however, if he does admit that values can be agent-neutral in this sense, he may find it difficult to fend off another kind of agent-neutrality, one that does create difficulties for him.

If it is to pose a problem for Williams's argument, therefore, the distinction between agent-relative and agent-neutral values needs to be drawn differently. But now there is, I believe, good independent reason to conclude that we are not yet drawing the distinction correctly; for surely values that are fully agent-neutral should be for *every* person in *all* respects the same, pointing everyone towards one univocal set of outcomes that are ranked against each other in one univocal way.[19] This is the sort of agent-neutrality that my cooperative conception of morality presupposes, a sort that ensures the principle of impartial beneficence the same importance for everyone. Given this understanding of agent-neutrality, however, Williams could not so easily grant that agent-neutral values exist and that morality weighs them against agent-relative ones; it looks like he might instead have to find some way of arguing that there are no values that are agent-neutral in this much more demanding sense.

Now it might be suggested that Williams has already provided that argument; for was his claim not precisely that all values will prove to be mutable? That is to say, was the conclusion of his argument not precisely that any values that prove to be among the ones to which people's desires must answer will also prove to be such that their intrinsic content and relative importance vary from person to person with differences in their histories and circumstances? That was no doubt his intention; but the point I think we need to stress here is that any such argument will run aground on a crucial ambiguity. For as we are now drawing the distinction between agent-relativity and agent-neutrality, it is possible for an unindexed content to pick out values of both types; so the fact that something has a value that varies from person to person does not prove that it lacks a value that remains for everyone the same.[20]

The point here is not simply that the same *outcome* can sometimes be described in two ways, and that under these different descriptions it will sometimes be found to have values of different kinds—as happens, for example, when the flourishing of a friendship is more specifically the

<hr/>

[19] If truth be told, I don't believe that philosophers like Parfit and Nagel really mean to deny this. Certainly it accords very well with many of the substantive claims they make about neutral values. But I do believe that in defining agent-neutrality they very often lose sight of it, and that in Nagel's case this occasionally generates problems in his formulation of contractualism. (Recall n. 8 above.)

[20] Another way to put the point here would be to say that it is *systems* of values that are agent-neutral or agent-relative and that an unindexed content (such as friendship-in-general) can for each person serve to pick out values that figure in *two* systems—one in which its import remains for everyone the same, another in which its import differs from person to person.

flourishing of my friendship, and so has an additional importance for me that it lacks for other people.[21] What I am further suggesting is that the same *description* can sometimes be considered from two perspectives, and that from these two perspectives it will sometimes be found to reveal values of different kinds—an agent-relative value that varies from person to person with differences in their histories and their circumstances, and an agent-neutral value that remains for everyone always exactly the same.[22] For example, considering the different ways in which their lives have unfolded, different people might now be quite right to rank the general flourishing of friendships and the general promulgation of knowledge very differently. Some people, having devoted themselves to the nurturing of friendships, might find the greater value there, while others, having worshipped instead at the temple of learning, might rightly decide in its favour. Considering the matter from a more neutral perspective, however, it might seem that these two ends should still be ranked in whatever way they had been ranked before differences of this kind emerged. After all, even if differences in our biographies can affect the relative importance things have for us, why should we suppose they affect the relative importance things have in and of themselves?

Such talk of the importance things have 'in and of themselves' is sometimes dismissed out of hand on the ground that things can have value only for people or perhaps sentient creatures more generally. What are we to believe—that outcomes can be good or bad, or better or worse, from the point of view of the universe, or from no point of view at all?[23] But the neutral perspective I am imagining here is not well described as a view from nowhere; if we must indulge in such metaphors, it would be better described as the view from everywhere. For what I have in mind is a perspective that is equally the perspective of everyone and from which the relative importance of different outcomes is always in every

[21] The goal of Nagel 1970 was precisely to deny that an outcome could have an importance for one person that it lacked for others. In the terminology he employed at the time, it could not have any 'subjective' value without having a correlative 'objective' value too. It is only as he came to reject this view that Nagel decided that this talk of 'objective' and 'subjective' values was potentially misleading. Now he talks instead of relative and neutral values and allows that an outcome's neutral value need not match its relative value. Unfortunately, however, he tends to state his new position using essentially the same distinction he had used in stating his old position. My point here has so far simply been that this makes it difficult to appreciate the full ramifications of his value dualism.

[22] Of course, this could at best be true only of unindexed contents; indexed contents could not succeed in picking out anything but relative values.

[23] The first of these two images is of course drawn from Sidgwick 1907; the related image of 'the view from nowhere' comes from Nagel 1986.

respect the same. It of course remains to be seen whether this fully neutral perspective on value really does exist; but I think we can safely assume that the idea of such a perspective is perfectly coherent. It is after all no different from an idea that most people are happy to accept, for most people are happy to accept that the facts must be the same for everyone.[24] Indeed, in the case of facts, the idea of a fully neutral perspective has no serious competitor, for the idea that the facts might be different for different people does not make any sense. When it comes to values, however, the idea of differences among people does make good sense—so much so that one may wonder what need there is for the idea of neutrality.

Having himself provisionally granted that every person's desires are originally answerable to a single set of values, it is difficult to see how Williams could reject the very idea of this more neutral perspective.[25] He might conceivably try to argue that unindexed contents cannot after all pick out objective values, thereby denying that values can be agent-neutral even in the limited sense we considered earlier.[26] But it is not easy to see how a compelling argument to this effect could be formulated. Why should something's having value for a person depend on its bearing some special relation to her? Any such requirement would seem simply to be a vestige of instrumentalism, the view that nothing can be of value for a person unless she stands in some relation of desire to it, together with the assumption that people's desires never take the promotion of general ends as their object, at least not until the person in question has actively embraced some such end as her project (in which

---

[24] Obviously enough, some people find the idea of neutral reasons for belief every bit as problematic as the idea of neutral reasons for action. Surely, they will say, reasons for belief can exist only for particular people in consequence of their own particular histories and circumstances. As must by now be clear, however, this deeply relativistic position is one for which I have little understanding and even less sympathy. As I keep insisting, it seems to me that the theory of radical interpretation leaves no room for relativistic conceptions of truth. Relativists talk as if truth and agreement are just illusions generated by the happy fact that people's individual attitudes are in many respects compatible, whereas the theory of radical interpretation reveals that we cannot begin to talk of individual attitudes without first assuming truth and agreement.

[25] Also relevant here is the fact that Williams does believe that the idea of a fully neutral perspective makes sense in non-evaluative contexts (witness Williams 1978). This makes it that much harder to see why he should then want to deny that it makes any sense in the context of value.

[26] I mention this as a possibility; but in fact I see no indication that this line of thought has ever held any real appeal for Williams. So far as I can see, his worries about agent-neutral values have always been directed not at their indexless contents but at their immutable importance.

case the value in question would by our definition still count as agent-relative, since its application and in particular its importance would not be the same for every person). If only for the sake of the argument, however, Williams is now tempering his earlier allegiance to such views and allowing that people's desires might themselves be answerable to values that are objective. So he would have to argue that some more objective relation is necessary for the existence of value; yet it is difficult to see what this more objective relation could possibly be.

Think again of the example that I mentioned at the beginning of this chapter. How can we deny that everyone has at least some reason to do what they can to alleviate the pains of even the most distant strangers?[27] Why should we suppose that a person acquires a reason to be concerned about strangers only when certain developments in her life somehow make their well-being important for her? No doubt we should not expect very young children to recognize that they have such reasons for action, just as we would not expect their beliefs to conform as closely to certain kinds of truths as an older person's would. But just as we would say those truths are all the while still true for them, so too we should say the well-being of strangers still generates reasons for them. By itself, of course, this does not establish the existence of agent-neutral values. For everyone could have a reason to alleviate a stranger's pain even though the relative importance of that reason was not for everyone exactly the same.[28] But I think the case for agent-neutral values begins to look much more promising when we consider examples such as these in the light of Davidson's theory of interpretation. For Davidson's theory tells us that everyone starts out owing allegiance to the very same set of values. And our example of the stranger seems strongly to suggest that at least some of those values are free of token reflexives. Taken together, therefore, there seems to be a case for saying that a fully neutral perspective on value may play a role in determining everyone's original reasons for action.

In view of the concessions that he has provisionally made, therefore, it would seem that Williams has no real choice but to grant that unindexed contents can pick out objective values whose initial importance is for everyone the same. He has no real choice, in other words, but to

---

[27] Once again, compare Nagel 1986, chap. 8, pp. 160 ff.
[28] Nagel is led to overlook the relevance of this possibility, and so to underestimate the difficulty of establishing value dualism, by his overly narrow account of what value dualism is.

grant that there may well be a fully neutral perspective on value that has an initial application to every person. This is not to deny that more relative perspectives on value may also have application to people from the beginning, if only because each person may also start out owing some special concern to her own self and immediate family.[29] It is just to allow that some subset of the values initially governing people's desires may prove to exhibit precisely the sort of univocality that is characteristic of full neutrality. Where Williams might still try to dig in his heels, however, is at the idea that this neutral perspective on value will continue to have relevance for people even after differences in their histories and circumstances begin to emerge. After all, we have already conceded his claim that the intrinsic content and relative importance of values will inevitably vary from person to person as differences in their lives unfold. So why can he not insist that this initial perspective on value will apply to people only in their youth, and that as time passes their desires will become assessable only from the relative perspectives defined by their individual biographies? And yet, if people's desires are never simultaneously assessable from the neutral and the relative perspectives, how can morality be a matter of weighing these different perspectives against each other?[30]

I believe this is the question upon which the prospects for value dualism—and so also for moral theory—depend. Too often discussions of these matters get bogged down in questions about the sort of objectivity that is at issue. And indeed, if truth be told, proponents of value dualism often bring this upon themselves by analysing objectivity in ways that make the notion of competing value systems somewhat problematic. Thus—to mention only its most celebrated proponent—Thomas Nagel analyses objectivity in terms of a kind of absolute intelligibility that leads some people to deny that agent-relative values could be objective in the way agent-neutral values are.[31] Even Nagel, at times, talks of

---

[29] Another possibility, however, is that these relative values emerge *only* as people's histories and circumstances cause their own selves and immediate families to acquire a special salience for them.

[30] Once again, this assumes that internalism about morality is true.

[31] The danger here is that absolute *intelligibility* is very easily conflated with neutral *applicability*, with the result that relative values come to seem intelligible only from subjective points of view. The source of the difficulty here is again to be found in Nagel 1970—this time in the idea that we cannot fully understand a value without becoming answerable to it. For some criticism of this aspect of Nagel's earlier work, see Sturgeon 1974; for some worries about the tenability of Nagel's subsequent value dualism, see Korsgaard 1993 and Dancy 1993.

agent-relative values as if they were really nothing more than the varying appearances agent-neutral values present to people who are variably
circumstanced.[32] I would like to think that, by discussing value dualism
in the context of radical interpretation, we have seen how agent-relative
and agent-neutral values could be objective in exactly the same sense
and to exactly the same degree. For if objective values exist whenever
there are substantive constraints on the ascription of desires, then value
will be dualistic so long as these constraints stem from two different systems. And we are getting close to establishing that they do, for even if
different people's desires come to be answerable to different sets of constraints, they apparently start out by answering to some constraints that
are the same for everyone. What remains, however, is to determine
whether these different sets of constraints ever hold court together, or
whether the neutral one withdraws as soon as the relative ones emerge.

   This is not an issue that can be resolved simply by appealing to the
requirements of radical interpretation. As we have seen, interpretation
does require that there be a single set of values to which everyone's
desires are originally answerable. But it does not require that the contents of any of these values be free of token reflexives; nor does it
require that any such unindexed values retain their authority over people
even after the particular developments in their lives have led them to
develop divergent perspectives on these things. These issues, if they can
be resolved at all, must be resolved by arguments of a different sort.
What we need to ask ourselves, I think, is how the requirements of radical interpretation are themselves most credibly to be interpreted. How
credible is it to suppose that there are no unindexed values to which
desires originally must answer? Assuming there are some, how credible
is it to suppose that their intrinsic content and relative importance mark
nothing more than a starting point from which different people then go
their separate ways?

   I have already indicated why I think it would not be very credible to
dismiss unindexed values altogether. A person need not stand in any special relation to something in order for it to have some real value for her.

---

[32]   See e.g. 1986: 168. Korsgaard 1993 rightly traces the difficulty here to something
she describes as the 'strong objectivist' account of the distinction between relative and
neutral values. She thinks the distinction must ultimately be abandoned because the only
alternative account of it is equally objectionable in that it privileges relative values and
makes neutral ones mere 'constructions'. But what I am trying to demonstrate here is that
we can safely chart a course between these unacceptable extremes by adopting a
Davidsonian account of what values are.

As I have continually insisted, a stranger's pain is something that gives everyone some reason to act.[33] Moreover, until differences in their histories and circumstances lead them to develop different perspectives on things, the general alleviation of pain must be assumed to have the same value for everyone. The question we need to consider, therefore, is how it can have the same value for everyone. The fact that radical interpretation demands it does not by itself give us any clear indication of how it can be true. After all, why should the general alleviation of pain start out having the same value for every person? Is this most credibly understood as a consequence of some fact about our shared human nature? Or is it better understood as a consequence of some fact about our shared normative world?

The obvious answer to this question, in my view, is that the general alleviation of pain starts out with a value that is for everyone in every respect the same because there is a single normative world in which we all go on to live our individual lives. The fact that the general alleviation of pain eventually comes to be valued in different ways *within* those different lives does not mean that those lives are not *themselves* unfolding within a common world. Values that lack token reflexives cannot credibly be construed as nothing more than a starting point from which people then go their separate ways, for there is no good reason why people should share such a starting point unless their lives are unfolding within a single normative world. But if their lives are unfolding within a single normative world then surely it does make sense to suppose that they must somehow split their allegiance between its dictates and their own evolving priorities. Rather than taking their own evolving priorities to be replacing or eclipsing the common set of values that originally had application to them all, they should see them as defining their particular positions within a world that does not itself ever change and yet remains always their own.[34]

The situation would be very different, I take it, if our earlier arguments had come out rather differently, and we had after all found some good reason for thinking that the values to which desires are originally answerable do *not* include any that are free of token reflexives. In that case, it could with some credibility be argued that people share a single

---

33 I have also been assuming that this reason is for everyone a basic one, one not dependent upon the existence of some chance that their efforts will be rewarded.

34 This talk of 'a common normative world' may once again seem to raise the spectre of 'the view from nowhere'; but I mean by it nothing more than a space of reasons that at all times has application to everyone.

starting point only because they share a basic nature that over the course of time develops in different ways. And if the reason people share a single starting point were only that they share a basic nature that then develops in different ways, it might plausibly be argued that there is no reason for the starting point to retain any authority once those developments have actually occurred. But the presence of values that lack token reflexives makes this a very difficult row to hoe. Why should facts about our shared nature imply that the *general* alleviation of pain has universal value? If it is only what we have in common as individual human beings that leads certain values to start out by applying to us all, shouldn't those values themselves be confined to contents that in one way or another refer back to us as the individuals that we are?

I suppose Williams might reply by insisting that this is just bluff—and rather unconvincing bluff at that. Why, exactly, could claims about our basic nature not underwrite the assignment of objective value to unindexed contents?[35] After all, if facts about our basic nature could make the flourishing of our communities valuable for us, why could they not do the same for the flourishing of our nations or our species? Yet once things reach that point, what's to keep them from going all the way to unindexed contents? Why not allow that they could make the flourishing of our (= the) world valuable for us too? But then, by our own admission, we would also have to allow that the intrinsic content and relative importance of this value would vary from person to person as differences in their lives unfolded. And since its original content and importance would owe nothing to the existence of a common normative world, its subsequent relevance to people would depend entirely on the particular ways in which their individual lives developed. For some, this original interest in the overall good might develop into a commitment of central importance; for others, it might recede into the background as they become more heavily invested in different things. This really would create serious difficulties for any conception of morality that makes the overall good centrally important, and so, as we have seen, any conception of morality that might satisfactorily accommodate our initial stipulations about the subject. For how can a moral theory give central importance to something whose value varies widely among people and still aspire to have something substantive to say about how every person should properly be acting?

---

[35] Strictly speaking, of course, the value is found not in the content but in the outcomes that fall under it; in order to keep matters simple, however, I shall not always hold myself to standards as strict as this.

I do not see any logical barrier preventing someone from trying to run an argument along these lines; but I do believe that this way of looking at the matter is at least initially less credible. It is no coincidence that broadly Aristotelian accounts of morality, which ground pronouncements about objective value in claims about our shared nature, typically recognize as values only things that are designated by indexed contents—things like the development and exercise of one's *own* capacity for reason, or the creation, promotion, and enjoyment of one's *own* family and friendships, or the discovery and occupation of one's *own* place in broader society. If they allow unindexed contents to have any objective value, it is typically only a relative value holding for a particular person, in consequence of certain facts about the way her life has developed—usually the fact that over some extended period of time she has been actively pursuing the general promotion of such contents in a way that has led her to develop a real commitment to their promotion. For once you start assigning objective values to unindexed contents, and insisting that their initial importance is for everyone exactly the same, it just does look like you are postulating a common normative world—a space of reasons that initially have application to everyone precisely because they *always* have application to everyone, because their application to people is in no way dependent on the particular features of their individual biographies. Even if there are other possible interpretations of the matter, this seems on the face of it the obvious way to go—unless and until problems emerge that force us down a different path.

But perhaps it will be said that value dualism is itself the problem that forces us down a different path. For how are we to make sense of the idea that people should split their allegiance between different value systems? If objective value was ultimately to be found only in unindexed contents, and if the value found there was always perfectly immutable in nature, talk of a common normative world might then prove unproblematic. But of course we are supposing that the objective value found even in unindexed contents will be mutable in nature, and in any case that objective value is also to be found in contents that are indexed to the agent. So we can maintain that some values have their source in a common normative world only if we are prepared to pay a price, the price of explaining how people can serve two masters. And that price could conceivably prove to be so high that we would do better to revert to the rival account, which explains the initial commonality among our values entirely in terms of the fact that we share one basic nature. That would require us to abandon the idea that a conception of morality giving central place to the overall good, as my conception does, could still make substantive demands having application to every person. But if it really is so difficult to make good sense of the idea that people's allegiance should be divided, perhaps this just is the price we have to pay in order to retain our commitment to agent-relative values. So even if we could get Williams to agree that there is a presumption in favour of the conclusion that agent-neutral values exist, he might still insist that he's holding the winning hand.

What we therefore need to do is explain how a person could divide her allegiance between two comprehensive value systems. Can we make sense of this in a way that will reinforce the initial presumption in favour of value dualism? Now it might be said that we have already done so; for have we not shown how cooperating in the promotion of the good requires one to balance agent-neutral against agent-relative considerations? As I mentioned in the Introduction, however, what we really need to provide is a dualistic conception of *reason*; and we have as yet no good grounds for thinking that our account of morality can play that role too. Morality may require that weight be given to agent-neutral considerations; but why should we suppose that this is a demand that reason can embrace as its own and not merely an external imposition? We need to ensure that reason can embrace these considerations as its own before we can count them as values. What I therefore think we should consider is how agent-neutral considerations might figure in an account of self-governance. For even if they do not always present themselves this way, it seems fair to say that different theories of reason's nature can always be depicted as differing accounts of what self-governance requires. This characterization may seem somewhat unfair to those theorists who hold objective values to be exclusively agent-neutral in nature; but in fact they are effectively saying that self-governance requires everyone to bend their will to the same truths.[36] If value dualism can be made plausible in this arena too, then I think we can feel reasonably confident that the initial presumption in its favour will not be cancelled out after further reflection.

The task that next confronts us, therefore, is to determine what self-governance would require if value dualism were indeed true (and true in the sense I have described, in the sense of two comprehensive value

---

[36] Think, for example, of Plato; although he holds that the same 'forms' apply to everyone, he clearly believes that complying with these forms is ideally a result of self-governance.

systems). Would its requirements be plausible enough to reinforce the initial presumption in favour of value dualism?

3. *Self-Governance and Objective Commitment*

What self-governance appears to require of people is that they act in ways that *fully and accurately* reflect *their own* values and commitments. So the question we must answer is how they can do this if values of the agent-neutral and agent-relative sorts both exist.

Many contemporary accounts of self-governance take as their point of departure Harry Frankfurt's analysis of free will; so perhaps we should do the same ourselves. Frankfurt's original suggestion, very roughly, was that willing freely requires people, when considering what to do, not to take the contents and strengths of their desires as given but to ask themselves how they would like their desires to be.[37] What sorts of things would they like themselves to desire? What would they like the relative strengths of those desires to be? By asking themselves these questions, people uncover second-order desires, desires seemingly more deserving of their allegiance, in as much as they emerge from a process of self-assessment and not simply from an assessment of the outcomes available to them. Of course, they might find that their second-order desires are conflicting; they might find themselves torn between incompatible visions of the people they would be. In that case, Frankfurt insisted, they are to repeat the process, to continue their self-appraisal, not taking the contents and strengths of their second-order desires as given but asking themselves how they would like those desires to be. Eventually, Frankfurt maintained, their higher-order desires will start speaking in unison, and the demands of willing freely will become perfectly clear. As he originally put it, a 'decision' will be made, one further reflection would only reaffirm, after which people willing freely would proceed to form all and only the first-order desires they had 'decided' they would like to have.[38]

But this initial formulation of the analysis met with a good deal of

[37] See Frankfurt 1971. Frankfurt himself carefully distinguishes between higher-order desires and higher-order volitions, between answers to questions about how one would like one's lower-order desires to be and answers to questions about which of them one would like to be one's will. However, the interesting questions this raises are not ones that need detain us here.

[38] See Frankfurt 1971: 22.

criticism, much of which was directed towards its reliance on higher-order decisions.[39] One worry here, of course, was that people's higher-order desires would always be multiple and conflicting, no matter how many stages of higher-order reflection they worked through, since desires are by nature conflicting, most options having some appeal. This is not something that can be changed by decision. The only matter for decision is what to make of these conflicts. However, once this is conceded, Frankfurt's analysis of free will no longer carries so much conviction, for it no longer singles out any desires to be one's will, but simply calls for a decision, one that could take any form. And even if higher-order desires were not always multiple and conflicting, Frankfurt's analysis of free will would threaten people with an endless regress of desires. For the basic idea, again, was that people willing freely do not take their desires as given but instead ensure that they are validated through a process of reflection, specifically reflection about how they would like their desires to be. But wouldn't the results of this process also require validation, raising the question how these people would like their reflections to go?[40] The upshot, it would seem, is that reflection of this kind could never fully validate a desire and hence that Frankfurt's criterion of willing freely could never be met, unless again he allowed such regresses to be stopped by arbitrary choices.

Some readers, perhaps, might regard this as a result to be welcomed, a long-overdue acknowledgement that willing freely requires nothing more than a capacity to bring one's first-order desires into line with one's choices however made. But not Frankfurt; he conceded that there must be more to say about the decision into line with which one's first-order desires are to be brought, and hence that his analysis of free will must be reformulated. He is now inclined to present his view in

[39] See, in particular, Watson 1975. (In Watson's case, however, the 'regress' worry I go on to describe here is by no means the only worry that he raises about Frankfurt's analysis. It is really just symptomatic of a deeper worry about Frankfurt's failure to emphasize the importance of acting not just on one's desires but on one's *values*. I turn to such worries next.)

[40] The familiar point here is that these higher-order desires would after all still be nothing but desires. So if one shouldn't take one's desires as given, but should instead ensure that they can be validated, then it would seem that one should also check to ensure that one's higher-order desires are validated. The fact that they emerge through a process of higher-order reflection does not by itself seem to validate them—certainly not so long as those reflections consist simply in asking oneself how one would like one's desires to be. Cf. Watson 1975: 107–9, and 1987: 147–51, and Christman 1987: 283–7, and 1988: 112–14.

the following terms.[41] Suppose that a person's higher-order desires really do conflict at every possible level. No matter how many stages of higher-order reflection she works through, she finds them still at odds. It might nevertheless be the case, Frankfurt remarks, that a certain pattern will emerge. Although her desires continue to conflict, it may be that one side comes out stronger at every level. This might not happen straightaway, of course, but it seems inevitable after some point. She might continue to ask herself how she would like her desires to be, but eventually her desires will become stable under any further such reflection. Suppose, therefore, that a person has worked through several stages of higher-order reflection, and that a pattern of this sort seems clearly to be emerging; one higher-order desire seems likely to continue winning at every level.[42] Given that her deliberations must eventually come to an end, that she must eventually decide what she would have her first-order desires be, would a decision to give victory to this higher-order desire necessarily be arbitrary?

Surely it wouldn't be; such a decision might be in other ways problematic, but if it is the problem will not be that it is arbitrary, but rather that it is for some reason not itself freely rendered. Thus Frankfurt would seem to have provided a satisfactory response to 'regress' objections; since it is possible for desires to become stable under higher-order reflection, it is possible that higher-order reflection could validate lower-order desires.[43] Now whether or not this will prove to be a fully satisfactory analysis of free will is not a question I wish to take up here. The question I want to pursue here has rather to do with self-governance: does self-governance require anything more of people than that their actions conform to such

---

[41] See Frankfurt 1987: esp. 169. It is perhaps not entirely clear that Frankfurt means this as a reformulation of his earlier position, rather than simply as a clarification of the position that he had in mind all along. But that is not something that it is important for us to get clear about here; what matters here is that we be clear about how the underlying position is best expressed.

[42] If we say, as I will, that higher-order desires take the form of desires to have whatever desires will lead one to A, where A is some valued activity, then the 'same' desire will re-emerge at higher levels just when the value of that activity is reaffirmed.

[43] Notice that the adoption of this formulation of the position obliges us to reject any suggestion to the effect that every higher-order desire must actually receive validation through a process of yet higher-order reflection. What becomes essential is rather that every desire *would* receive such validation *if* one were to press on through ever higher orders of reflection. This of course raises the interesting possibility that actually working through even the first few stages of higher-order reflection might on some occasions be unnecessary for and perhaps even positively detrimental to freely willed action. Sometimes one might maximize one's chances of acting on desires that would stably be endorsed by higher-order reflections simply by acting on habit.

higher-order reflections? Pretty clearly it does, if only because it also makes some demands on the relevance of these choices; a person is not governing herself if her choices are made to no effect.[44] But the more pressing worries for our purposes here stem from the thought that self-governance may make further demands on the contents of people's choices. After all, self-governance requires people's choices to reflect not their desires or inclinations but their values or commitments; moreover, self-governance requires people's choices to reflect those values and commitments not just accurately but also fully. Yet it does not seem very plausible to suppose that the full story about a person's values and commitments will always be encapsulated in the one higher-order desire that happens to triumph in her higher-order reflections.

We are following Davidson in assuming that people's desires do not create their values but should instead be reflecting them; so the obvious suggestion to be considered at this point is that self-governance requires people to bring their wills into line not necessarily with the higher-order desires that they *do* have but rather with the higher-order desires that they *should* have. As we have seen, even if all objective values are also universal, the relative importance of certain values may vary from person to person with differences in their histories and their circumstances. Thus different people should often take different views about the first-order desires they would like to have, which suggests that a self-governed person is one who adopts and enacts the view appropriate for her. It is not enough simply to conform one's will to whatever higher-order desires one happens to have; one must also succeed in forming higher-order desires that capture the truth about one's own value system. If one does not, one might still be commendable in many ways, for it is often no small feat to conform one's will to the higher-order desires that one has adopted, and there might after all be much to say for one's higher-order reflections even if their results are flawed. But so long as we are following Davidson in distinguishing between people's views about their values and the truth of the matter, it is hard to see how self-governance could simply be a matter of conforming one's will to the values one accepts.[45]

---

[44] Here I draw on a point that I made in Chap. 2, that individual autonomy and personal integrity are both facets of self-governance.

[45] One could of course just stipulate that self-governance is simply a matter of conforming one's will to the values one accepts, and so insist that some other term be introduced to capture the idea of being true to the values one really has. I think there is ample precedent, going back through Rousseau to Plato, for rejecting this narrower notion of self-governance; but what matters here is not the term but the conception of reason that it is being used to convey.

If all objective values were also agent-relative, the implications of this account of self-governance would be reasonably clear. Even if these agent-relative values were also universal, their different lives would make different rankings of these values applicable to different people, so the trick would be to determine which ranking was applicable to each person, and what action would best meet its demands.[46] The resulting conception of reason would be similar to decision-theoretic conceptions, differing only in so far as it replaced their references to subjective attitudes with its references to objective (but still relative) values. In particular, it would still be a maximizing conception, for it would call for each person to perform an action that would satisfy as fully as possible the particular ordering of values that applied to her. However, our interest here lies with value dualism, so something more must be said about what it would take for a person's actions to be true to all of the values that apply to her. If we assume that agent-neutral values exist alongside agent-relative ones, how are we to understand the requirement that people's actions should fully reflect the values that generate reasons for them? It might seem strange to suggest that *self*-governance requires people to ensure that their actions reflect agent-*neutral* values; but that is only because one naturally emphasizes the importance of being true to whatever distinguishes one's own values from other people's, not because it is not equally important to be true to those aspects of one's values that are necessarily shared by everyone.[47]

Now it might be suggested that people can acknowledge the existence of agent-neutral values by acknowledging that the overall good has universal value and so must have some importance within any ranking of values that could truly have application to them. The claim would then be that people's higher-order desires should always take the form

---

[46] Perhaps it is worth stressing the fact that I do believe each person will be committed to some particular ranking. In this respect, the view I am developing here differs from the one described as 'cognitive underdetermination' in Wiggins 1976. We both draw on Davidson in order to defend the claim that there are universal values. And we both allow that the relative importance of these values can differ for different people. But whereas Wiggins denies that there is any truth of the matter concerning how these values should be ranked for any given person at any given time, I believe that there is. (This is not to deny that there will inevitably be some indeterminacy in our ascriptions of desires to people; it is simply to deny that any such indeterminacy will also afflict people's values themselves.)

[47] In 1986: 140, Nagel makes a similar point by insisting that the 'objective' (he presumably means the 'neutral') self is a real part of each one of us. Perhaps this puts the matter more dramatically than necessary, but the underlying idea is sound. If agent-neutral values exist and are reason-generating, self-governed people cannot ignore them.

of desires to have whatever first-order desires would lead them to strike a suitable balance between promoting the overall good and promoting their more personal values. The appeal of this suggestion, of course, is that it seems to acknowledge the existence of agent-neutral values without abandoning the familiar maximizing conception of reason; it simply insists that the overall good is always to appear in the particular ordering of values that determines what a person has reason to do.[48] The problem with this suggestion, however, is that it ends up treating this end as an agent-relative value instead of as an agent-neutral one; for it nowhere denies that the relative importance of the overall good might vary from person to person with differences in their histories and their circumstances. As we know from the previous section, so long as we treat this end as just another value to be placed alongside agent-relative ones, varying in importance from person to person, we effectively treat it as an agent-relative value itself. We may succeed in capturing the important thought that the overall good will have some importance within each and every person's agent-relative system of values, but we fail to capture the further thought that it also has some quite neutral value.[49]

We have already seen how important it is when theorizing about morality to recognize not just the neutral value that exists in (say) people helping their own friends but also the special value that such activity typically has for the agents themselves.[50] What I am urging here is that any conception of reason that treats the overall good as just one value alongside others may succeed in capturing the relative value that the overall good has but fails utterly to capture its neutral value. Now what I want to suggest is that the solutions to these two problems will be in an important sense mirror images of each other too, for both will turn on the idea that people should not countenance too much damage to the overall good when pursuing their own more personal concerns. But how they frame this idea will depend in each case on the way in which reason and morality balance agent-neutral and agent-relative values, and in reason's case the fact that self-governance requires people fully and accurately to reflect their own values and commitments favours a quite straightforward solution. As we have seen, from morality's perspective,

---

[48] It might actually be wondered whether even *intra*-systemic judgements weighing only agent-relative values would be maximizing in any very strict or robust sense. (If this is all Wiggins means when he speaks of cognitive underdetermination, then we are more in agreement than I suggested in n. 46 above.)

[49] Or, better, that it stands proxy for a *system* of such values.

[50] See Chap. 2 above—and also, for example, Williams 1973 and Scheffler 1982.

the emphasis on cooperation will recommend a *prerogative* permitting people to pursue the satisfaction of their own more personal concerns subject to the condition that they not countenance too much damage to the overall good. But self-governance, and so therefore reason, would seem to favour a more straightforward *requirement* that people actually maximize the satisfaction of their own more personal concerns so far as that is possible without countenancing too much damage to the overall good.

Morality and reason respond in different ways to the fact of value dualism because they are concerned with different things. Morality's concern is with fair terms on which to promote the overall good, so it takes the fact of value dualism to indicate that limits must be placed on the demands that can be made of people in the name of impartial beneficence. But should a person decide to forsake her more personal concerns and sacrifice everything for the overall good, morality is not likely to have anything to say in criticism of her choice. Morality requires people to moderate their pursuit of their relative values with a concern for agent-neutral value, but leaves them free to pursue agent-neutral value without giving their relative values any thought at all. So long as their pursuit of agent-neutral value does not lead them to violate other people's prerogatives, morality will find nothing to fault and much to commend in the decision to sacrifice oneself for others.[51] But reason is certainly going to find something to fault in any such decision, for its concern lies with self-governance and so with fully and accurately reflecting one's values and commitments. A person who ignores her relative values and focuses exclusively on the overall good is clearly not meeting this condition. Personal integrity requires that she pay allegiance in her actions both to the relative values that she happens to have and to whatever neutral values there should happen to be.[52] It does not give her the option of forsaking either side for the other.

A further important difference between morality and reason lies in the fact that only the former makes room for restrictions. As I argued in Chapter 2, morality's concern with fairness requires that, both in our

---

[51] Morality might fault such a decision if it led one to violate one's special obligations to certain particular people (family, friends, and the like). As I mentioned at the beginning, however, these are not possibilities that I can take time to enter into in this book.

[52] I say this because, as I have said before, I believe that integrity requires one to be true to *all* the values that one has. A rather different account of what integrity requires will be considered below.

pursuit of the overall good, and in our exercise of our individual prerogatives, we not impose upon other people harms that they would not be required to bring upon themselves. Without some such restrictions against any actions too closely resembling forced supererogation, it is difficult to see how we can be cooperating with each other in the promotion of the overall good. But reason, with its focus on self-governance, does not seem to have any scruples about such conduct; for the notion of integrity refers one back to one's own values and commitments and not other people's. Of course, if harming others has neutral disvalue, self-governance will always have something to say against it, since it is not only her agent-relative values that a person should be acknowledging as her own. And if harming others has in addition some relative disvalue for people, then it scarcely needs to be said that the complaints self-governance brings against it will be that much stronger. But they won't amount to a restriction against harming others, as we saw earlier when discussing Nagel's version of contractualism. No matter how much agent-relative disvalue is to be found in harming others, there could be circumstances where the value to be gained thereby is even greater, in which case self-governance would seem to call for one to do the dastardly deed.[53]

To be sure, this view of things has met with resistance from more than one quarter throughout the history of philosophy; many philosophers have tried to show that self-governance in fact requires adherence to much the same restrictions as morality does. Speaking very generally, many of these arguments are attempts to make something of the obvious fact that a self-governed person cannot simply take her circumstances as given but must do what she can to shape them according to her own lights. A self-governed person is not someone who simply performs actions that will reflect her values and commitments as fully and accurately as the circumstances allow; she is someone who also tries to make the circumstances ones in which her values and commitments can be reflected as fully and accurately as possible. Of particular concern to a self-governed person will be the written laws and unwritten conventions that to a large extent shape the possibilities for action; she will want to ensure that they are such as to maximize the possibility of actions giving

---

[53] In fact, in retrospect, one wonders whether Nagel doesn't find it so difficult to accommodate prerogatives and restrictions, despite his value dualism, because he never clearly distinguishes morality's ideal of cooperation from reason's ideal of self-governance.

full and accurate expression to her values and commitments. And this, it might be argued, requires that she participate in negotiations of the sort that contractualists have long been exploring, negotiations in which the participants are trying to uncover and live by rules from which each one of them would profit.[54] And if these rules include restrictions, it might further be argued that self-governance requires her to acknowledge and honour them; for why should anyone be allowed to participate in these negotiations if she cannot be trusted to abide by their results?

But does the possibility of exercising influence over one's circumstances necessarily require that one participate in such negotiations with other people? And does the possibility of participating in such negotiations necessarily require that one can be trusted to abide by their results? Why could it not sometimes be possible to maintain a façade of trustworthiness while at every opportunity cheating on the side? Could it not sometimes also be possible to imprint one's values and commitments on one's circumstances without securing other people's blessing? No doubt arguments can be offered showing that the chances of succeeding at either of these endeavours is for most people in most cases very small. And no doubt it can also be argued that the penalties likely to be incurred if these endeavours go wrong are in most cases very large.[55] It might further be argued that negotiating with one's fellows and abiding by the results is something that in fact has considerable value for most people. And to the extent that this is true the distance between the demands of self-governance and the demands of morality will naturally be correspondingly diminished.[56] As we shall see in the Conclusion, arguments of these sorts may be of some help with questions about morality's *authority*; but they are never going to rule out the very possibility that people could sometimes have overriding reason to shirk morality's requirements. So even with questions about morality's authority, we must be careful not to overestimate the help such arguments might provide us;

---

[54] The contractualists I have in mind here are naturally the ones I earlier described as Hobbesian or Lockean. Contractualists of a Rawlsian or Scanlonian sort are more likely to press the objection that I consider next.

[55] Gauthier 1986 takes arguments of these sorts about as far as they can go, but still falls short; he does succeed in greatly reducing the gap between Hobbesian reason and Hobbesian morality, but never closes it.

[56] A lot, of course, will depend on why such activity is thought to have value for most people. Little will be gained if its value for people depends on their being taught to care for it, for it will not infrequently happen that people's elders could expect to gain more by training them differently. The gap here will be significantly diminished only if everyone has an objective interest in cooperating with others.

and we certainly shouldn't expect them to establish that the *content* of self-governance's demands is invariably the same as morality's.

If one really wants to show that self-governance makes room for the prerogatives and restrictions that we have been attributing to morality, one must somehow do without the idea that it is a matter of fully and accurately reflecting one's own values and commitments. Indeed, one must somehow go so far as to deny that self-governance is a matter of *reflecting* anything at all; for reflection, whether it be of objective values or subjective desires, seems much too straightforward a matter to yield such complex structures.[57] But in what terms is one to think of self-governance if not as a matter of fully and accurately reflecting one's own values and commitments? Where groups are concerned reflection can be replaced with cooperation; but what can one do with one's own values but reflect them as faithfully as possible?

Perhaps it will be objected that I am overlooking the fact that self-governed agents cannot be bound by anything outside their will, not even by those aspects of their values and commitments that are dependent upon developments peculiar to their own histories and circumstances. For of course the idiosyncratic features of people's histories and circumstances are never to be explained solely in terms of their choices, and even if they were those choices would themselves have to be assessed in terms that did not recreate the original difficulty.[58] Mustn't the self-governed person decide for herself how she is going to proceed, regardless of the history she has lived and the circumstances she now inhabits? And couldn't it turn out that the right decision for her to make will reveal that self-governance does make room for both prerogatives and restrictions?

But how are we to give content to talk of the 'right' decision for a person to make without at some level returning to the idea that certain values are objectively hers? And why should we find it so upsetting to be told that the values that are objectively hers are in some part determined by processes that are not fully under her control? It seems to me that people who press objections of this sort are almost without exception fleeing from false pictures of what values are. Kantians in particular are very often guilty of construing desires as nothing more than brute

---

[57] This is of course the lesson we were to have learned in the first half of this book.

[58] The objection here might be put by saying that personal integrity cannot after all require one to be true to the values that one has. Alternatively, it might be put by saying that the sorts of things we have been describing as values cannot be values in the end.

impulses and values as nothing more than external impositions.[59] If one paints the possibilities in these colours, then of course self-governance will seem to require that one not submit to such things; a purely formal, if possibly empty, decision procedure such as Kant is sometimes said to provide may then seem one's only avenue of escape. But if one analyses desires and values along Davidsonian lines, as I have been suggesting one should do, the threat they pose to self-governance becomes very much more difficult to discern. Davidsonian desires and values are dependent upon each other in ways that prevent people's desires from systematically leading them astray while allowing their values to reflect their own particular histories and circumstances. Moreover, as I mentioned in Section 1, the idea is not, for example, that every woman who has been putting her efforts more into her family than into her career will now be right to find more value for herself in the former than in the latter. By allowing that much depends on why people have been acting as they have, the Davidsonian account can portray values in a way that makes them look not like external impositions but like personalized indicators of the direction that the next stage in one's life should ideally take.

Still, it might be objected, even if a person's relative values would be sensitive to the idiosyncratic features of her own biography, her biography is not itself entirely her own doing, so how can a self-governed person not take some distance from it? And, it might be added, what better way is there to do this than to limit or constrain pursuit of the relative values that one actually has by rules that one would have found agreeable even if one's values had been decidedly different? I mention this because reflections along these lines sometimes seem to hold out the promise that self-governance ultimately could be linked to prerogatives and restrictions, in as much as truly self-governed people could be shown to owe all their possible selves the same respect that truly co-operative people owe each other.[60] But even if it were true that a self-governed person should take into account what her other possible selves would say, the fact that she cannot interact with them as she does with other people would surely make prerogatives and restrictions quite unnecessary. And in any event it simply does not follow from the fact that we are never fully responsible for being who we are that self-governance requires us somehow to make allowances for all the very different people we might have been. Having already acknowledged that

59 For one example of this tendency, see Korsgaard 1996.
60 Korsgaard 1989 seems to be headed in this direction.

the agent-neutral system of values would not continue to possess authority over people if it represented only a common starting point, surely we're not now going to allow that agent-relative systems of value can claim authority over people just because they might possibly have been theirs.

Before moving on to other things, let me acknowledge once again that there very often is a substantive point of some importance behind these worries about the proper characterization of self-governance. I don't see why the fact that our individual biographies are not entirely our own doing should be thought to disqualify them as partial determinants of what our reasons for action are. But at the same time I do agree that it would be a mistake to suppose that people are literally trapped by their histories, as the housewife of our example would be if the mere fact of her housewifing somehow settled what her relative values must now be. Obviously a plausible account of self-governance must allow that people sometimes have very good reasons to rebel against the lives they have led. My claim is simply that the reasons why they should do so will have to be found within the details of those lives themselves.

It seems to me, therefore, that we can and should stick with our general definition of self-governance as a matter of fully and accurately reflecting one's own values and commitments. The question, as I see things, is not whether this definition of self-governance is correct but whether it reveals value dualism to have implications that considered judgement is unable to accept. Now my claim in this section has been that the existence of both relative and neutral values would imply that a self-governed person is a person who satisfies her own relative values so far as that is possible without countenancing too much damage to the overall good. So the question we must now consider is whether this emerging account of self-governance will prove to be sufficiently palatable to considered judgement, or whether it will prove to offend against considered judgement in a way that will oblige us to forsake the thesis of value dualism.

Probably the worry that comes first to mind here is that the truth of value dualism, and in particular the existence of neutral values, would make self-governance too demanding. So let us begin by considering whether our account of self-governance really is vulnerable on this score.

4. *Self-Governance and Impartial Beneficence*

How demanding value dualism would make self-governance evidently depends on what it takes not to countenance too much damage to the overall good. And as we saw back in Chapter 2, that in turn depends on how the different quantities being compared here are to be measured.

Let us therefore imagine, as we did before, a case where the only way I have to save N total strangers from a certain death is to offer up my own life in sacrifice. Clearly, from the point of view defined by agent-neutral values, the loss of my life would be just the loss of one life—a terrible outcome, no doubt, but (we might plausibly suppose) N times less bad than the loss of N lives.[61] From the point of view defined by my relative values, however, the loss of my life might be a loss of quite staggering proportions—and so, in all likelihood, an outcome worse (perhaps very much worse) even than the loss of N lives. These are the two quantities to be compared; the relevant question is not how N compares to some multiplying factor but how the one assessment of the situation compares to the other. Does the loss of N lives represent from the impersonal point of view a catastrophe greater than the catastrophe that the loss of my life represents from my own point of view? Does the former surpass the latter by more than the specified factor? Only if it does would the refusal to sacrifice my life countenance too much damage to the overall good and so be something that self-governance and reason forbid me to do. But whether it does will depend on a variety of different things—not just on the number of lives at stake and the size of the multiplying factor but also on the importance that my own life and the overall good have for me. Whether refusing to sacrifice my life would countenance too much damage to the overall good therefore depends on a comparison of the prospective gains or losses as they are measured from two different perspectives.

This of course still leaves us with many difficult questions about how I am to measure the prospective gains or losses from my own point of view, and about how I am then to compare these prospective gains or losses to the prospective gains or losses as measured from the impersonal point of view. But at least it shows us how self-governance could require me to give some independent weight to considerations about the overall good without making demands on me that are implausibly onerous. Perhaps there are scenarios wherein self-governance would require me to sacrifice my own life for the sake of the lives of mere strangers. It

---

[61] Strictly speaking, of course, this will be true only if we focus exclusively on the 'intrinsic' value of people's lives—and even then it might well be challenged. However, as this simplification in no way affects the point I am trying to make, I shall proceed as if the impersonal value of every life is the same.

is possible, after all, that the loss of my life could represent from my own point of view a catastrophe significantly smaller than the catastrophe that the loss of N lives would represent from the impersonal point of view. What seems implausible, however, is that the sheer number of lives at stake could by itself entail that self-governance requires me to sacrifice my life no matter what its preservation would represent from my own point of view. That is why it is important not to take the suggestion here to be that we should be comparing N and some multiplying factor. That would be the relevant comparison only if the loss of my life somehow represented from my own point of view nothing more than it represents from the impersonal point of view. But surely most people's relative values are such that the loss of their lives would have a quite special significance when considered from their own point of view, so much so that for many people it is difficult to imagine circumstances where self-governance would require them to sacrifice their lives for mere strangers.

At a similar point in our discussion of morality's content, we wondered whether this way of limiting the demands of impartial beneficence might not free some people from the requirement to make any sacrifices at all for the overall good. If a person's dominant value was to live a life of total independence, might not even the smallest sacrifice represent an unacceptably large loss when measured from her own point of view? It seems that it very well might, and hence that morality might not be able to require even the smallest sacrifice of this person. As we noted in Chapter 2, that conclusion is simply not credible, and so threatens to stand as a *reductio ad absurdum* of our treatment of morality. Now the same line of thought would seem to indicate that reason might actually forbid some people from making any sacrifices at all for the overall good. This conclusion is perhaps not quite as incredible as the parallel conclusion regarding morality's content, but I think we should still view it with some considerable trepidation. For can we really suppose that agent-neutral values might exist and yet that reason would prohibit certain people from making any sacrifices for the overall good? I think this is hard to accept, and hence that we should again be worried that our arguments here might be leading us astray. If morality and reason require people to give agent-neutral values their due, that can only be because doing so is compatible with giving one's agent-relative values their due as well. So the demands of beneficence clearly must have real limits; but surely not limits that would go so far as to leave some people morally free and indeed rationally required to pay no heed to agent-neutral values at all.

Towards the end of Chapter 2, however, we noted that worries of this sort would seem much less pressing if values were understood to be something objective rather than something subjective. If a person's values are simply identified with the higher-order desires that she does or will have, small sacrifices for others might indeed represent unacceptably large losses for her, since her dominant desire might well be to live a life of total independence. But if a person's values are identified with the higher-order desires that she should have, it may be possible to rule out scenarios of this unwelcome sort, for a life of total independence may be one that no person should want to live. Now of course we have already decided in favour of the view that values are objective; so the question for us is whether anyone could be objectively committed to a life of total independence. I think it is hard to see how this could be regarded as a real possibility, notwithstanding the fact that the lives to which people are objectively committed can differ in many important respects. Certainly it is difficult to see how, if agent-neutral values exist, providing help can fail to have at least some agent-relative value for every person and hence at least some place in any life to which a person can be objectively committed. Nor is it easier, looking at the matter the other way round, to believe that there is not always at least something to be said for receiving help, even if fending for oneself always has at least something to be said for it too. Given our objective view of value, therefore, I think we can safely conclude that having to make minimal sacrifices for other people is from nobody's perspective necessarily such a bad thing.[62]

Thus we need not fear that our efforts to limit the demands of beneficence may have reduced them to nothing at all. We can allow that the measure of people's prospective gains or losses is to be taken from their own point of view and still conclude that every person will sometimes have to make sacrifices for others if she is not to be countenancing too much damage to the overall good. Much of course will depend on the degree by which impersonal gains must surpass personal losses before incurring those losses becomes required. But the point remains that morality and reason will not exempt anyone from the requirement to make sacrifices because everyone will sometimes confront circumstances where the prospective gain as measured from the impersonal

---

62 However, whether or not it will always be a good enough thing to anchor a credible thesis about morality's authority is another question—the question to which I shall turn in the Conclusion.

point of view surpasses the prospective loss as measured from their own point of view by more than the specified factor.

Of course, if what we are envisioning is really to be a form of value dualism, then we cannot allow any variation whatever in the degree by which impersonal gains must surpass personal losses before incurring those losses becomes required. The same multiplying factor must be applicable to every person, regardless of their history or circumstances; otherwise we are simply envisioning a form of value monism in which the promotion of the overall good has a universal, but relative, value. So a fair question to ask at this point is whether it really is credible to suppose that self-governance requires everyone to understand the requirement not to countenance too much damage to the overall good in the same way. On the contrary, doesn't the fact that we find it so difficult to agree on a universal interpretation of the multiplying factor indicate that the relative importance to be assigned to the overall good must vary from person to person?

It seems to me, however, that agreement here is actually not so hard to reach, not in any event so long as we take a realistic view of the degree of precision that can be attained in this area. For example, even if friends and family have acquired a special importance within an individual's life, she would surely be giving neutral considerations short shrift if she left a stranger to die just to keep a date with a friend. Obviously this agreement would become harder and harder to maintain if we were to work through a series of cases where the prospective gain in neutral value became progressively smaller while the prospective loss in relative value became progressively larger. But I see no reason why this should be taken to indicate that there is no universally applicable multiplying factor to be uncovered here rather than that the factor that is to be uncovered here admits of no very precise formulation. Matters might be different, of course, if we were wrong to find an initial presumption in favour of value dualism; all else being equal, perhaps we should favour an account of value that makes more precise comparisons among values possible. But we have already seen that matters are not equal; the fact that everyone starts out owing allegiance to one set of values, many of which are neutral in content, speaks strongly in favour of the truth of value dualism. So far as I can see, therefore, the question is simply whether the greater imprecision that value dualism brings in its train is troubling enough to outweigh the initial presumption that we have already found to exist in its favour.[63]

---

[63] We should also be careful here not to exaggerate the amount of precision that is attainable on monistic views.

And once again my feeling is that it is not; it seems to me that the level of imprecision we are threatened with is not as great as all that, well within the boundaries of what considered judgement deems possible.

I believe it is also worth considering where we would be left if we did embrace the view that all values are agent-relative in nature. How then could we explain the agreement we do seem to find about the importance of not countenancing too much damage to the overall good? Value monists could of course argue that a concern for the overall good must figure in every person's list of relative values. But they would have to admit that people with very different histories and circumstances might be right to rank this value in very different ways. So how could they avoid admitting that self-governed people might sometimes be right to let a stranger die rather than leave a friend waiting? I suppose they might try to argue that the relative value of promoting the overall good varies only within a certain range. They might hope in this way to allow that some people may rightly value promoting the good of their friends over promoting the overall good, while at the same time denying that the difference could ever be great enough to justify sparing a friend's feelings rather than a stranger's life. But it seems to me that the only good reason for thinking that relative values might have such boundaries is that neutral values really do exist. That is, if there is a neutral perspective from which the overall good is more important than the well-being of one's family and friends, then, perhaps, there may be certain limits on the extent to which the idiosyncratic features of one's own history and circumstances can reorder their ranking.[64] But if all we share is a starting point, not an enduring world, the idea of such boundaries becomes harder to accept.

Of course, value monists might choose to bite this bullet, acknowledging that relative values have no such boundaries and hence that self-governance could conceivably require someone to let a stranger die rather than miss a date with a friend. And I think it must be admitted that our considered judgements about reason do not speak against such proposals as clearly or forcefully as our considered judgements about morality speak against related attacks on the principle of impartial beneficence. But I think they still do say something against them, and in any event the general case we have constructed for value dualism seems to me more than strong enough to overcome any resistance we might

[64] This is a thought that I shall be trying to take advantage of in the concluding discussion of morality's authority.

encounter over such examples. Indeed, it seems to me that we have reached the point where we can confidently proclaim our analyses of reason and morality to be individually above reproach. The only question that remains is whether they are jointly compelling too.

We have already noted that reason and morality may not always agree about when a person is countenancing too much damage to the overall good; there may be cases where morality would judge that enough is at stake to require a particular sacrifice but reason would take a different view. And we have also noted that morality might permit people to make certain sacrifices that reason would expressly forbid them to make. But the most glaring discrepancies between reason and morality seem likely to occur in cases where much might be gained by forcing a supererogatory sacrifice; for we have to this point uncovered no grounds for thinking that reason will follow morality in prohibiting actions that too closely resemble forced supererogation. The final question we need to consider, therefore, is whether value dualism is compatible with a credible view of morality's authority.

Does the assumption of value dualism, by opening a gulf between self-governance and cooperation, put reason and morality more starkly or frequently at odds than considered judgement can allow? Or can our cooperative conception of morality's content be made compatible with a credible view about its authority?

Conclusion

Implications for the Question of Morality's Authority

IN a justly celebrated paper, T. M. Scanlon maintains that 'a satisfactory moral philosophy will not leave concern with morality as a simple special preference, like a fetish or a special taste, which some people just happen to have. It must make it understandable why moral reasons are ones that people can take seriously, and why they strike those who are moved by them as reasons of a special stringency and inescapability'.[1] Hoping to meet this condition, he proceeds to argue that 'an action is wrong if its performance in the circumstances would be disallowed by any system of rules for the general regulation of behaviour which no one could reasonably reject as a basis for informed, unforced general agreement'. Apparently the assumption is that we can account for the special authority of moral reasons simply by uncovering a better account of their content. As Scanlon puts his point, his version of contractualism provides an especially good account of morality's authority because 'the desire to be able to justify one's actions (and institutions) on grounds that one takes to be acceptable [as a basis for informed, unforced general agreement] is quite strong in most people. People are willing to go to considerable lengths, involving quite heavy sacrifices, to avoid admitting the unjustifiability of their actions and institutions'.

Now I agree that Scanlon's contractualism is better able to account for the special authority of moral reasons than 'philosophical utilitarianism' is.[2] It does seem plausible to suppose that the desire to be able to justify their actions to others will for most people be stronger than the desire to promote the overall good. But I doubt that the strength of even this desire could account for the special authority we believe

---

[1] Scanlon 1982: 106. The other two passages that I quote are from pp. 110 and 117.

[2] 'Philosophical utilitarianism' is the term that Scanlon uses to describe the view that morality is at bottom concerned solely with the promotion of overall happiness. Such a view may or may not lead to the further conclusion that some version of the utilitarian formula provides the correct 'normative theory' of morality.

moral reasons to have. So far as I can see, there is in fact no very plausible way to account for the special authority of moral reasons from within an instrumentalist conception of what reasons are. Pointing to facts about the special strength of certain desires can no doubt help to explain why people *often* have some considerable reason to comply with morality's demands; but I think it is hard to deny that we have something more in mind when we describe moral reasons as inescapable. What we seem to have in mind in saying this is some claim to the effect that people *always* have quite considerable reason to comply with morality's demands; and this seems to attribute a greater inevitability to morality's authority than facts about the nature of people's desires can account for.[3]

Some will conclude from this that we should be trying to ally Scanlon's version of contractualism with a different conception of reason.[4] As I argued in Chapter 1, however, we have some very good grounds to reject his version of contractualism even when it is assessed simply on its implications for morality's content. Scanlon is certainly right to reject the consequentialists' claim that morality is about nothing more than the promotion of the overall good. That claim, as we saw in Chapter 1, makes it impossible to account for the fact that prerogatives and restrictions are no less central to morality than the principle of impartial beneficence. But, by the same token, Scanlon surely takes opposition to consequentialism too far by neglecting to guarantee the principle of impartial beneficence some place within his system. Morality cannot be represented as a set of principles that no one could reasonably reject as a basis for agreement with others. Arguably, people who share an interest in reaching an agreement could disagree about so many other things that every proposal could reasonably be rejected by someone among them. And clearly the principle of impartial beneficence

---

[3] Unless, of course, some desires are necessary; but that, as I argued in Chapter 3, is not something instrumentalists are entitled to claim. The most they might be entitled to claim is that some desires are 'naturally' very strong; but that, I think, cannot secure for morality the sort of inescapability that most people want for it.

[4] For an interesting discussion along these lines, see Freeman 1991. His idea, very roughly, is that the desire to be able to justify oneself to others will have an overriding authority *for every person who has it* not because of the strength it will necessarily have relative to their other desires but because of the form it will enable their practical deliberations to take. But this claim, while interesting, seems problematic in two respects. For one thing, it is never made sufficiently clear why the regulative role Freeman assigns to this desire could not equally be played by other desires that the person has at the time; and since no attempt is made to argue that people *should* want to be able to justify themselves to others, the promised result is in any case significantly weaker than we are seeking.

could reasonably be rejected by those of them who are indifferent to the overall good.

If there were no alternative to the instrumentalist conception of practical reason, we might decide that Scanlon's version of contractualism, despite its various shortcomings, offers us the best available compromise between a solution to the problem of morality's content and an explanation of the authority of its reasons. By avoiding any reliance on a desire to promote the overall good, it makes it possible to argue that morality's authority is often considerable. And yet, by focusing attention on the desire to be able to justify one's actions to others, rather than on the more familiar desire to advance one's own interests, Scanlon's version of contractualism avoids taking opposition to consequentialism to quite the extremes reached by its Hobbesian and Lockean predecessors. But we have concluded that instrumentalism about practical reason must be replaced with a conception that recognizes the existence of objective values. Moreover, we have concluded that some of these values are agent-neutral, and hence that every person will always have at least some reason to comply with the principle of impartial beneficence, no matter what the state of her desires. This suggests that it might after all be possible to uncover better accounts of these two matters by granting beneficence a more central place within morality than Scanlon's version of contractualism allows.[5]

As I have said before, it is Thomas Nagel whose views on these matters come closest to the ones developed here.[6] He too recognizes that agent-neutral values exist, and hence that the problem of morality's content and the problem of its authority are both in large part problems of striking the right balance between these values and agent-relative ones. More importantly for the purposes of our discussion, he recognizes that the problem of morality's content and the problem of its authority can in this sense have the same general form without for that reason being exactly the same problem. This is because reason and morality balance the competing claims of agent-neutral and agent-relative value from different perspectives, or anyway from perspectives the equivalence of which has to be established through substantive argument and not through simple definition. Reason, as he understands it, looks at things from the agent's point of view; it recognizes that agent-neutral values exist but insists that the relative importance of the reasons they generate

---

[5] Indeed, if we take the view that morality must be characterized in terms of every sort of value that does in fact exist, as I have suggested we should, then it will seem not just advisable but essential that we find room for beneficence within our account.

[6] See Nagel 1986, esp. chap. 10.

must be determined from the vantage point of the agent.[7] Morality, on the other hand, looks at things from the impersonal point of view; it recognizes that agent-relative values exist but insists that the relative importance of the reasons they generate be determined from a vantage point that encompasses everyone. Because this impersonal assessment is supposed to result in principles by which to assess the actions that individual agents perform, Nagel believes that morality will go to some considerable lengths to accommodate itself to reason's way of balancing these values. He speculates that it may even go so far as to ensure that its verdicts will never conflict with reason's.[8]

My view clearly shares some important features with Nagel's; but the points of disagreement are very important too. As I argued in Chapter 1, we need to supply the moral perspective with sufficient content to explain how it can be true that morality includes all three of impartial beneficence, prerogatives, and restrictions. It is not enough simply to say that morality is a matter of striking a reasonable balance between an appreciation of impersonal value and one's own more personal concerns, not even when we add that this balance is to be struck from the impersonal point of view. Though this helps us to understand why one's personal concerns must be given the sort of independent weight that would set real limits on the principle of impartial beneficence, the emphasis on balancing would seem to support a principle of moderated beneficence rather than prerogatives and restrictions.[9] As I argued in Chapter 2, what we need to add to Nagel's picture is the idea that morality is a matter of cooperating to promote the good. It is the notion of cooperation that gives the moral perspective the content that it needs to generate a rationale for prerogatives and restrictions.

I believe Nagel's account of reason is likewise undercharacterized.[10] It is not enough simply to say that reason is a matter of striking a different balance between an appreciation of impersonal value and one's own

---

[7] This is of course not meant to deny that reason is in some important sense universal.

[8] As he says on p. 199: 'I am inclined strongly to hope, and less strongly to believe, that the correct morality will always have the preponderance of reasons on its side, even though it needn't coincide with the good life.' Or again, on p. 200: 'I am strongly disposed to the view that morality must at least be rational in this weak [not overridable] sense—not *ir*rational—though I should be more satisfied with a theory that showed it to be rational in the strong [overriding] sense.'

[9] See above, pp. 45 ff., and Kagan 1984.

[10] In fact, in the crucial pages (200 ff.) of Nagel 1986, there is really no characterization of reason offered at all.

more personal concerns, a balance that this time will seem reasonable when considered from one's own point of view. For that gives us no sense whatever of the way in which reason's method of striking the balance is different, and no sense either of the chances that its verdicts might nevertheless coincide with morality's. Is it enough to acknowledge that impartial beneficence has a place alongside our agent-relative values, or does reason require that we also grant it some different sort of authority over the determination of our will? I would like to think that we have avoided this shortcoming of Nagel's picture by showing how practical reason can be characterized as a kind of self-governance. We have seen that impartial beneficence has a role to play in the determination of objective commitments, but that it also influences what people can reasonably do in the pursuit of their commitments.

What I want now to argue is that these differences oblige us to temper Nagel's optimistic speculations about morality's authority. We have already uncovered some serious grounds for concern here; for we noted, in Chapter 4, that cooperation may not always allow people to countenance as much damage to the overall good as self-governance would require them to countenance. And even if they were always to agree about how much people are required to sacrifice for the overall good, discrepancies would emerge in as much as self-governance would forbid people to make various supererogatory sacrifices that cooperation would happily permit. But the threat to morality's authority is probably most clearly visible in cases where self-governance would require one person to impose upon another person a harm that cooperation would permit the second person to decline to take upon herself. Imagine a situation something like the one that Dostoevsky described; suppose N perfectly innocent people will meet a certain death unless one equally innocent bystander agrees to take their place or we take it upon ourselves to force her hand. Now even if N is not great enough for self-governance to require the innocent bystander to sacrifice her life, it seems clear that it might still be great enough for self-governance to require us to force her hand.[11] But since N might in addition be too small for cooperation to require the innocent bystander to sacrifice her life, it seems clear that it might also not be great enough for cooperation to allow us to force her hand. The fact that cooperation requires us to abide by restrictions would seem to make some conflict with self-governance inevitable.

---

[11] If this seems less than perfectly clear, imagine that the N people, though all perfect strangers to the bystander, are good friends of ours.

Now of course some readers may object that results of this sort really testify, not to the limits on morality's authority, but to the inadequacy of our analyses. It is hard to see how anybody could object to the general idea that reason and morality are to be understood in terms of self-governance and cooperation.[12] But some will take issue with our analysis of cooperation; they will try to argue that cooperation does not require prerogatives to be accompanied by correlative restrictions, or perhaps simply that it does not require strong prerogatives to be accompanied by equally strong restrictions. Others will take issue with our analysis of self-governance; they will try to argue that self-governance in fact requires agent-neutral and agent-relative values to be weighed against each other within something like an amalgam of impartial benefi-cence, prerogatives, and restrictions. Others will confess uncertainty about where to direct their fire, but will nonetheless maintain that our analyses of self-governance and cooperation must somehow have gone wrong because they take it as given that the correct analyses must show moral reasons to be inescapable. It is ultimately this last group that con-cerns me the most; for their worries cannot be laid to rest by meeting some specific objection that they have raised, since what lies behind their worries is not any specific objection but rather a more general dogma. They are convinced that moral reasons are inescapable and that what this means is either that such reasons are always overriding or that they are never overridden themselves. So their worries can be laid to rest only by providing some independent grounds for thinking that moral reasons are *not* inescapable in either of these two senses.

Evidently it will be easier for these people to agree that moral reasons are not inescapable in their favoured sense if they have a serviceable alternative to fall back on. Let us therefore consider whether there is not a different but still perfectly good sense in which moral reasons might be inescapable even though they are on some occasions overridden. Now the possibility that I think comes to mind here is that moral reasons might on some occasions be overridden and yet be inescapable in the sense that their authority is always at least quite considerable. Perhaps the inescapability of moral reasons lies neither in the fact that they are always triumphant nor in the fact that they are never vanquished but in the fact that they are always quite serious contenders. For surely it would

[12] Pettit and Smith 1993 may seem to deny that reason is a matter of self-governance; but I take it that what they really mean to be rejecting is the idea that reason might be as relativistic as some accounts of self-governance would lead one to suppose.

not be inappropriate to describe moral reasons as inescapable if indeed they were guaranteed always to be there, and always to be difficult to overcome, no matter what one's history and circumstances. Even when other considerations did overcome them, one would not really have escaped them, for in such cases one should at least regret the fact that circumstances had conspired to pit even stronger reasons against them. Obviously this notion of inescapability is weaker than the others; but the point is that its very weakness obliges us to consider whether the others are not much too extreme.[13] Why insist that moral reasons are overriding or even non-overridable, when it is possible to defend their claim to inescapability simply by showing that their authority is always quite considerable?

Some might object that this question is moot on the ground that we are not in a position even to establish that moral reasons are inescapable in this weaker sense. After all, they might say, having admitted that reason and morality can be at odds, how can we deny that the distance between their verdicts might sometimes be very great? Suppose, for example, that I find myself in one of those fantastic philosophical scenarios where I am going to be forced to sacrifice my life unless I can somehow get you to sacrifice your life instead. Since the prospective gain from the impersonal point of view is not likely to be greater than the prospective loss from your own point of view, morality is not likely to require this sacrifice of you.[14] It follows, then, that morality is likely to forbid me to force you to sacrifice your life even though that is the only way I have in the circumstances to save myself from a similar fate. But precisely because there is so little to choose between our two deaths when they are compared to each other from the impersonal point of view, reason may well require that I force you to sacrifice. The point, in other words, is that cases can almost certainly arise where honouring another person's prerogative not to sacrifice her life would effectively require me to sacrifice my own. Are we really to suppose that even in such cases moral reasons have an authority that will always be at least considerable and so *never* lapse into comparative insignificance?

I believe this challenge seems as powerful as it does only because we have not had a chance to consider the full range of things that have

---

[13] Just how much weaker it is will evidently depend on what exactly it takes for reasons to be 'quite' considerable.

[14] Even if my life generates more neutral value than yours, your prospective personal loss probably outweighs the prospective impersonal gain.

agent-relative value. In particular, we have not had a chance to consider the possibility that cooperating with others in the promotion of neutral value may *itself* have some value of this sort.[15] This is not the place to try to show that it does; but the point is that, if it does, the inescapability of moral reasons might suddenly become something that we can reasonably hope to establish. For suppose we could show not just that cooperating to promote neutral value has agent-relative value but also that this value is universal, and moreover that its relative value is for every person quite considerable. Much as they may differ with differences in people's histories and circumstances, suppose each person's (objective) ranking of the agent-relative values would give quite a prominent place to cooperating in the promotion of neutral value.[16] It would evidently follow from this that I would have considerable reason not to save my own life by forcing you to sacrifice yours, since by forcing you to sacrifice I would be failing to cooperate. Even considered from my own point of view, the choice between being forced to sacrifice my own life and forcing you to sacrifice yours would not be easy to make. Perhaps reason's verdict would still differ from morality's; but it would not do so in a way that would create any difficulties for the claim that moral reasons are inescapable.

As we saw a moment ago, Nagel's idea is that moral reasons might ultimately prove to be inescapable because morality will do what it can to accommodate itself to reason. As we also saw, however, there is no way that this process can be taken far enough to span the gap that seems to exist between reason and morality.[17] What I am in effect suggesting

[15] The suggestion here is not that the existence of agent-relative reasons to co-operate serves to explain why morality includes restrictions that sometimes prohibit people from sacrificing others. The idea is rather that morality (being a cooperative undertaking) does include such restrictions and complying with them may turn out to have a special agent-relative value.

[16] Having argued that the relative importance of agent-relative values can vary from person to person, it might now be wondered how any agent-relative value could be guaranteed a special prominence. Isn't it bound to be possible that some people's histories and circumstances could be such that cooperating in the promotion of neutral value would have little relative value for them? I think this is far from clear; it seems to me just as likely that the principles regulating change in the relative importance of values will ensure that certain of them always remain very important. That would of course need to be argued; but it suffices for our purposes here simply to note that there is no a priori reason to suppose that an argument of this sort could not possibly succeed.

[17] This is of course not to deny that securing a credible account of morality's authority will depend very heavily on our ability to defend an attractive account of its content. If cooperating in the promotion of the overall good were to make crazy demands of us, the claim that it has a special agent-relative value would evidently be harder to defend.

here is that the gap between reason and morality can be spanned only if reason is also in some measure prepared to accommodate itself to the demands that morality makes. It cannot very well alter its requirement that people fully and accurately reflect their own values and commitments; but what it can do is alter its view about what those values and commitments will actually be.[18] Even this, as we have seen, will not be enough to ensure that moral reasons are inescapable in the strong sense favoured by Nagel—the sense of always being overriding or anyway never being overridden themselves. As we saw in Chapter 4, agent-relative values are defined partly by the fact that their importance can vary from person to person. So no one value is going to be dominant for every person. But this is perfectly compatible with the claim that cooperating in the promotion of neutral value may be found to have a relative value that is always at least considerable. And that may be sufficient to ensure that people will have considerable reason to comply with the demands of cooperation even when that puts their other values at grave risk.

To be sure, these remarks are somewhat speculative; I am certainly not pretending to have shown that cooperating in the promotion of neutral value really does have this special status. But I believe that this could be shown; moreover, I believe that we can see a sign of this in our earlier readiness to endorse Scanlon's claim about desires. Why does it seem so plausible to suppose that the desire to be able to justify one's actions to other people will in most people be very strong? I think the answer is that we believe possession of this ability to have a special value and expect this fact to be reflected in most people's desires.[19] If time permitted, we might try to corroborate this belief by considering how the ability to justify one's actions to other people is connected to other central values. For example, we might try to show that possession of this ability is something without which it would be almost impossible for anyone to enjoy the benefits of self-esteem.[20] But even without such corroboration I think we are justified in feeling that a belief as strong as

---

[18] As Nagel 1986 and Scheffler 1992a both point out, certain kinds of personal and political transformations can also help to close the gap between reason and morality. But such transformations can account only for what Scheffler describes as the *potential congruence* of reason and morality; they do not explain why moral reasons are *necessarily inescapable*.

[19] If we take seriously the Davidsonian conception of propositional attitudes, this expectation will be grounded in a claim of necessity; for people's beliefs and desires will necessarily be such as by and large to reflect the truth about objective values.

[20] As Freeman 1991 intimates, we might also try to show how it is connected to the values of liberal community.

our belief in the value of cooperating is unlikely to prove mistaken. So I think we are also justified in feeling that the chances are pretty good that moral reasons will prove to be inescapable in the weaker of our various senses.

Of course, some readers will still insist that we should be holding out for an argument that will show moral reasons to be inescapable in the stronger senses as well. In their view, that result is not negotiable and so some fault must be found in any analyses of self-governance and co-operation that threaten to put it at risk. Either prerogatives and restrictions must have a place in our account of self-governance, or all trace of such principles must be removed from our account of cooperation. It does not matter how strongly our intuitions about self-governance and cooperation rebel; the most important thing is to achieve the ultimate harmonization of reason and morality. However, I see no reason why our intuitions about the relations between reason and morality should take priority over our intuitions about what reason and morality are.[21] On the contrary, it seems to me that we should be treating these intuitions equally and looking for a view that explains as many of them as possible. I think we will best be able to do this if we abandon Nagel's strong reading of the inescapability thesis and replace it with the weaker reading I have proposed. The resulting view is surely going to be less revisionary than one that links self-governance to prerogatives and restrictions or one that decouples prerogatives and restrictions from cooperation.

Nagel clearly does not have any desire to decouple prerogatives and restrictions from cooperation; so his hope must somehow be to link self-governance to prerogatives and restrictions. That is of course a hope that many philosophers have had before him; but it is also a hope that no one of them has successfully realized. The difficulty here is not hard to understand, for what seems to be required is some argument to the effect that people can be fully and accurately reflecting their own values and commitments even while declining to pursue them as efficiently as they could.[22] That seems on the face of it an impossible case to make; yet any suggestion to the effect that self-governance is not after all a matter of fully and accurately reflecting one's own values and commitments would surely be revisionary in the extreme. What leads Nagel to underestimate

---

[21] Neither, obviously, do I see any reason why the former should take a back seat to the latter. A theory that was too sceptical of morality's authority would certainly have a very important count against it.

[22] See above, Chap. 4, Sect. 3.

the difficulties here, of course, is his tendency to suppose that we can provide an adequate account of morality's content simply by characterizing it as a matter of striking a reasonable balance between agent-neutral and agent-relative values. Since reason is also seeking to strike such a balance, this characterization can make it very tempting to assume that there must be some pretty good chance that its way of achieving this result will never conflict with morality's way of doing the same. But we must not overlook the fact that morality includes both prerogatives and restrictions, neither of which requires that people maximize the satisfaction of their values or commitments. So long as morality's conception of a reasonable balance includes both prerogatives and restrictions, there is no way its verdicts can be kept from sometimes conflicting with reason's.

Upon reflection, therefore, it seems likely that prerogatives and restrictions must be rejected before Nagel's optimistic speculations about morality's authority can have any chance of being correct. This is evidently not a price that Nagel himself would be prepared to pay; but perhaps others would not be so reticent. They might agree to abandon prerogatives and restrictions, perhaps opting for the view that morality contains only a principle of moderated beneficence.[23] Just as we earlier said that self-governance requires people to maximize the satisfaction of their relative values so far as that is possible without countenancing too much damage to the overall good, so they might now argue that morality requires people to maximize the satisfaction of neutral values so far as that is possible without countenancing too much damage to their own more personal concerns. They might argue, in other words, that reason and morality could prove to be in perfect harmony because they could prove to be two sides of one coin. If they were always to agree about how much individuals must sacrifice for the overall good, then their verdicts would never conflict.[24] They would be in perfect harmony, notwithstanding the fact that they would have reached this point from opposite ends of the spectrum.

But is it really possible that morality might include nothing but a

---

[23] As we saw in Chap. 1, this is arguably the conclusion to which Nagel's talk of balancing neutral and relative values must itself lead.

[24] Of course, in as much as reason is analysed in terms of self-governance, whereas morality is analysed in terms of cooperation, it might be difficult to show that they *do* agree about how much individuals must sacrifice for the overall good. However, it would now at least be true that the verdicts of reason and morality *could* always be in perfect agreement, since there would be no deep structural dissimilarities preventing them from treating each case in a similar sort of way.

principle of moderated beneficence? I do not see how we can admit this as a possibility unless we are prepared to sever the link between morality and cooperation. We could not even formulate the principle of moderated beneficence if we did not grant the existence of both agent-neutral and agent-relative values; but given the existence of both agent-neutral and agent-relative values, it is impossible to believe that cooperation involves nothing more than moderated beneficence. On the one hand, it seems absurd to suppose that we might charge a person with failing to cooperate simply on the ground that she is countenancing too much damage to *her own* more personal concerns; cooperation does not rule out supererogatory sacrifices in the way that moderated beneficence does. On the other hand, it seems absurd to deny that we might charge a person with failing to cooperate simply on the ground that she is imposing too much damage on *someone else's* personal concerns; cooperation does rule out forced supererogation in a way that moderated beneficence does not. Moderated beneficence does not require one to make any serious concession to the fact that other people have relative concerns as well as neutral ones; it depends on the assumption that everyone has values of the relative sort, but then directs everyone to pay special attention only to their own.[25] I think we have seen enough by now to recognize that cooperation requires something very different; so moderated beneficence can be counted as the full story about morality only if morality is not to be analysed in terms of cooperation.

But can we really allow that morality is not to be analysed in terms of cooperation? Surely this would be to draw a conclusion far more revisionary than any conclusion that I have drawn about the inescapability of moral reasons. To my mind, it would be to draw a conclusion no less revisionary than the conclusion that reason is not to be analysed in terms of self-governance or the conclusion that self-governance is not after all a matter of fully and accurately reflecting one's own values and commitments. It seems to me, therefore, that anybody who is intent upon rejecting prerogatives and restrictions would be well advised to take a different tack; instead of trying to sever the link between morality and cooperation, they should be trying to sever the link between cooperation and prerogatives and restrictions. As we

---

[25] This is not to deny that it might find some special neutral value in the fact that people are free to satisfy their more personal concerns; but that of course is not the same as guaranteeing people the prerogative to give their more personal concerns some disproportionate weight in their practical deliberations.

have seen, however, there is no plausible way to do this as long as value is assumed to be dualistic in nature; if people owe allegiance to relative as well as neutral values, then any plausible account of cooperation must make room for both prerogatives and restrictions. Because of this, it looks as though anybody who hopes to harmonize reason and morality by rejecting prerogatives and restrictions must argue that agent-relative values do not exist and hence that self-governance and cooperation both require people always to do everything they can to promote the overall good. If it could be shown that there are no values other than agent-neutral values, then perhaps it could also be shown that self-governance and cooperation both demand that people always act as unfettered beneficence requires them to.[26]

My feeling, not surprisingly, is that denying the existence of agent-relative values is far more revisionary than accepting my weaker thesis about the inescapability of moral reasons. But of course I say this partly because it seems to me so clear that morality does include both prerogatives and restrictions. Those who do not share my enthusiasm for prerogatives and restrictions may assess the relative credibility of these two alternatives very differently. As we saw in Chapter 3, abstruse considerations about the nature of value and the demands of interpretation in no way rule out the possibility that at least some values are agent-relative. To rule out agent-relative values, one would somehow have to demonstrate that we can actually provide a better account of our considered judgements if we assume that all values are agent-neutral. My worry, however, is that opponents of prerogatives and restrictions might now insist that an exclusively agent-neutral conception of value really does provide the better account. In their opinion, as we know, the fact that it cannot accommodate prerogatives and restrictions is no very important mark against it. On the contrary, they might say, it is a price well worth paying in order to bring reason and morality into harmony.

It is undoubtedly tempting to suppose, with Nagel, that morality and reason can be brought into harmony only if morality can 'lower' its requirements to a point that reason can accept. This is a thought that has moved many people to embrace contractualism; by construing morality as a matter of cooperating for mutual advantage, rather than as a matter

---

[26] Of course, what unfettered beneficence requires is itself a good question, as we saw back in Chap. 1. But at least reason and morality would be agreeing, even if it remained unclear what they agreed on.

of promoting the overall good, they have hoped to make its requirements more palatable to reason.[27] What our discussion seems to reveal, however, is that morality's requirements will never be perfectly harmonized with reason's unless they are 'strengthened' by the removal of prerogatives and restrictions.[28] One cannot bring morality into line with reason by reducing its demands, for one can reduce its demands only by strengthening its prerogatives, yet cooperation requires that prerogatives be accompanied by correlative restrictions, and such restrictions inevitably place morality in some conflict with reason. As paradoxical as it may seem, therefore, it looks as though impartial beneficence must be given free rein within morality before its verdicts can ever be harmonized with reason's. If one wants reason and morality always to be in perfect harmony, one must argue that all values are agent-neutral in nature, for only then will morality direct people to maximize value in the way that is characteristic of reason.

As I have indicated, however, it seems to me that this cure is much worse than the disease by which we are in fact afflicted. To be sure, I say this in part because I believe more firmly in the real existence of prerogatives and restrictions than I do in the perfect harmonization of reason and morality. As a result, I find it easier to accept a slightly weaker thesis about morality's authority than to accept that prerogatives and restrictions are not after all real determinants of its content. But it is important to see that my reluctance to abandon agent-relative values is not to be explained solely by my enthusiasm for prerogatives and restrictions. If that were the whole story, there would be nothing to stop somebody else from abandoning agent-relative values out of an enthusiasm for morality's authority. Consequentialists may not be able to accommodate prerogatives and restrictions as real determinants of morality's content, but they can certainly find room within their theories for things that resemble prerogatives and restrictions.[29] So if I can argue that we should settle for a weaker thesis about morality's authority, they can counter by arguing that we should settle for a weaker thesis about its content. We will quickly find ourselves at an impasse here unless we can

---

[27] A similar thought is clearly motivating Scanlon's rather different sort of contractualism.

[28] The imagery here is potentially misleading, for rejecting restrictions might equally be regarded as 'weakening' morality's requirements. What really matters here is not the strength or weakness of morality's requirements so much as their structure.

[29] This is especially true, as we have seen, for those who adopt 'indirect' versions of consequentialism.

provide further grounds for settling this dispute in the way that I favour.[30]

I would like to think we can provide these further grounds by considering where the rejection of agent-relative values would leave the notion of reason. Surely the rejection of agent-relative values is troubling not just because it would leave morality in the hands of unfettered beneficence but also because it would do the same for reason. It would put reason in the position of requiring people to give their own more personal concerns only as much weight as was deemed optimal from the standpoint of impartial beneficence. This is a result that is going to strike many people as unacceptable; even many consequentialists find that it is more than they can swallow. In fact, many consequentialists try to avoid this result by allowing that agent-relative values exist but denying them any relevance to questions about morality's content.[31] But of course this tired stratagem, born of an almost palpable desperation, leaves them vulnerable to the charge that their account of morality's content makes its authority quite impossible to understand.[32] So far as I can see, they do better to be bolder, by trying to justify their account of morality's content precisely on the ground that it alone can secure morality's authority.[33] But I think that most people are going to concede that this gamble, although exhilarating, runs aground on the undeniable fact that agent-relative values do exist.

Of course, there will be some consequentialists who are so unwavering in their hostility towards agent-relative values that nothing I could say would have any chance of convincing them. As we saw in Chapter 4, something similar is true of contractualists; we cannot prove to them that agent-neutral values exist, since they might not share the considered judgements about objective value upon which any such proof would have to be based. But these are not difficulties that we should allow to dispirit us; for any inquiry must start with some shared sense of the problems that are in need of solution. I have been assuming that one important problem confronting moral theory is to accommodate all three

---

[30] We could try, of course, to argue that our account of morality's authority is *less* revisionary than their account of its content, but the point is that that would inevitably turn out to be a very difficult case to make.

[31] Brink 1986 is again useful here.

[32] As I have repeatedly insisted, it also offends against a kind of internalism about morality, according to which any and all values are relevant to the assessment of moral judgements.

[33] Kagan 1989 seems quite sympathetic to this approach.

of impartial beneficence, prerogatives, and restrictions, and that this problem is at bottom bound up with the problem of understanding how objective value could be dualistic in nature. If I have shown how these two problems can be solved, and solved in a way that makes morality's authority intelligible, then I have done all that can reasonably be asked. Consequentialism and contractualism owe much of their appeal to the fact that each is perceived as the only alternative to the other. If I have simply shown that a middle way is possible, I will have done much to relegate them to the margins.

REFERENCES

BARRY, BRIAN (1989), *Theories of Justice* (Berkeley and Los Angeles: California University Press).

BRINK, DAVID (1986), 'Utilitarian Morality and the Personal Point of View', *Journal of Philosophy*, 83: 417–38.

—— (1989), *Moral Realism and the Foundations of Ethics* (Cambridge: Cambridge University Press).

—— (1992), 'Mill's Deliberative Utilitarianism', *Philosophy and Public Affairs*, 21: 67–103.

BROOK, RICHARD (1991), 'Agency and Morality', *Journal of Philosophy*, 88: 190–212.

CHRISTMAN, JOHN (1987), 'Autonomy: A Defense of the Split-Level Self', *Southern Journal of Philosophy*, 25: 281–93.

—— (1988), 'Constructing the Inner Citadel: Recent Work on the Concept of Autonomy', *Ethics*, 99: 109–24.

DANCY, JONATHAN (1993), *Moral Reasons* (Oxford: Blackwell).

DANIELS, NORMAN (1978), *Reading Rawls* (Oxford: Blackwell).

—— (1979), 'Wide Reflective Equilibrium and Theory Acceptance in Ethics', *Journal of Philosophy*, 76: 256–82.

DARWALL, STEPHEN (1983), *Impartial Reason* (Ithaca, NY: Cornell University Press).

—— (1992), 'Internalism and Agency', *Philosophical Perspectives*, 6: 155–74.

DAVIDSON, DONALD (1963), 'Actions, Reasons and Causes', repr. in Davidson 1980.

—— (1970), 'Mental Events', repr. in Davidson 1980.

—— (1977), 'The Method of Truth in Metaphysics', repr. in Davidson 1984*a*.

—— (1980), *Essays on Actions and Events* (Oxford: Clarendon).

—— (1984*a*), *Inquiries into Truth and Interpretation* (Oxford: Clarendon).

—— (1984*b*), 'Expressing Evaluations', *The Lindley Lecture* (Lawrence, Kan.: University of Kansas Press).

—— (1985), 'A New Basis for Decision Theory', *Theory and Decision*, 18: 87–98.

—— (1986*a*), 'A Coherence Theory of Truth and Knowledge', in E. Lepore (ed.), *Truth and Interpretation: Perspectives on the Philosophy of Donald Davidson* (Oxford: Blackwell).

—— (1986*b*), 'Judging Interpersonal Interests', in J. Elster and A. Hylland (eds.), *Foundations of Social Choice Theory* (Cambridge: Cambridge University Press).

References

DAVIDSON, DONALD (1991), 'Epistemology Externalized', *Dialectica*, 45: 191–202.
—— (1994), 'Radical Interpretation Interpreted', *Philosophical Perspectives*, 8: 121–8.
FODOR, JERRY, and LEPORE, ERNEST (1992), *Holism: A Shopper's Guide* (Oxford: Blackwell).
—— (1994), 'Is Radical Interpretation Possible?' *Philosophical Perspectives*, 8: 101–19.
FOGELIN, ROBERT (1997), 'Quine's Limited Naturalism', *Journal of Philosophy*, 94: 543–63.
FOOT, PHILIPPA (1985), 'Utilitarianism and the Virtues', *Mind*, 94: 196–209.
FRANKFURT, HARRY (1971), 'Freedom of the Will and the Concept of a Person', repr. in Frankfurt 1988.
—— (1987), 'Identification and Wholeheartedness', repr. in Frankfurt 1988.
—— (1988), *The Importance of What We Care About* (Cambridge: Cambridge University Press).
FREEMAN, SAMUEL (1991), 'Contractualism, Moral Motivation, and Practical Reason', *Journal of Philosophy*, 88: 281–303.
FREY, R. G. (1984), 'Act-Utilitarianism, Consequentialism, and Moral Rights', in R. G. Frey (ed.), *Utility and Rights* (Minneapolis: University of Minnesota Press).
GAUTHIER, DAVID (1986), *Morals by Agreement* (Oxford: Clarendon).
GIBBARD, ALLAN (1991), 'Constructing Justice', *Philosophy and Public Affairs*, 20: 264–79.
HARE, R. M. (1981), *Moral Thinking* (Oxford: Clarendon).
HOBBES, THOMAS (1651), *Leviathan*.
HUME, DAVID (1739), *A Treatise of Human Nature*, ed. L. A. Selby-Bigge (Oxford: Clarendon Press, 1978).
—— (1748), *An Enquiry Concerning Human Understanding*, ed. L. A. Selby-Bigge (Oxford: Clarendon Press, 1975).
—— (1751), *An Enquiry Concerning the Principles of Morals*, ed. L. A. Selby-Bigge (Oxford: Clarendon Press, 1975).
HURLEY, S. L. (1989), *Natural Reasons* (Oxford: Oxford University Press).
JACKSON, FRANK (1991), 'Decision-theoretic Consequentialism and the Nearest and Dearest Objection', *Ethics*, 101: 461–82.
KAGAN, SHELLY (1984), 'Does Consequentialism Demand Too Much?' *Philosophy and Public Affairs*, 13: 239–54.
—— (1989), *The Limits of Morality* (Oxford: Clarendon).
—— (1992), 'The Structure of Normative Ethics', *Philosophical Perspectives*, 6: 223–42.
—— (1994), 'Defending Options', *Ethics*, 104: 333–51.
KAMM, FRANCES MYRNA (1989), 'Harming Some to Save Others', *Philosophical Studies*, 57: 227–60.
KANT, IMMANUEL (1785), *Groundwork for the Metaphysics of Morals*.

KAVKA, GREGORY (1978), 'Some Paradoxes of Deterrence', *Journal of Philosophy*, 75: 285–302.

KHOLBERG, LAWRENCE (1981), *The Philosophy of Moral Development* (San Francisco: Harper & Row).

KORSGAARD, CHRISTINE (1986), 'Skepticism about Practical Reason', *Journal of Philosophy*, 83: 5–25.

—— (1989), 'Personal Identity and the Unity of Agency', *Philosophy and Public Affairs*, 18: 101–32.

—— (1993), 'The Reasons We Can Share', *Social Philosophy and Policy*, 10: 24–51.

—— (1996), *The Sources of Normativity* (Cambridge: Cambridge University Press).

LEVI, ISAAC, and MORGENBESSER, SYDNEY (1964), 'Belief and Disposition', repr. in Raimo Tuomela (ed.), *Dispositions* (Dordrecht: Reidel, 1977).

LEWIS, DAVID (1974), 'Radical Interpretation', repr. in his *Philosophical Papers*, vol. i (New York: Oxford University Press, 1983).

LIPPERT-RASMUSSEN, KASPER (1996), 'Moral Status and the Impermissibility of Minimizing Violations', *Philosophy and Public Affairs*, 25: 333–51.

LOVIBOND, SABINA (1983), *Realism and Imagination in Ethics* (Oxford: Blackwell).

LUDWIG, KIRK (1992), 'Skepticism and Interpretation', *Philosophy and Phenomenological Research*, 52: 317–39.

LYONS, DAVID (1994), *Rights, Welfare, and Mill's Moral Theory* (New York: Oxford University Press).

MCDOWELL, JOHN (1981), 'Non-Cognitivism and Rule-Following', in S. Holtzman and C. Leich (eds.), *Wittgenstein: To Follow a Rule* (London: Routledge & Kegan Paul).

MILL, JOHN STUART (1859), *On Liberty*.

—— (1861), *Utilitarianism*.

MOORE, G. E. (1925), 'A Defence of Common Sense', repr. in Moore 1959.

—— (1959), *Philosophical Papers* (New York: Collier).

MURPHY, LIAM (1993), 'The Demands of Beneficence', *Philosophy and Public Affairs*, 22: 267–92.

MYERS, ROBERT H. (1994), 'Prerogatives and Restrictions from the Cooperative Point of View', *Ethics*, 105: 128–52.

—— (1995), 'On the Explanation, the Justification and the Interpretation of Action', *Nous*, 29: 212–31.

—— (1999), 'The Inescapability of Moral Reasons', *Philosophy and Phenomenological Research*, 59: 281–307.

NAGEL, THOMAS (1970), *The Possibility of Altruism* (Princeton: Princeton University Press).

—— (1980), 'The Limits of Objectivity', in S. McMurrin (ed.), *The Tanner Lectures on Human Values*, vol. i (Salt Lake City: University of Utah Press).

NAGEL, THOMAS (1986), *The View from Nowhere* (New York: Oxford University Press).

—— (1991), *Equality and Partiality* (Oxford: Clarendon).

PARFIT, DEREK (1984), *Reasons and Persons* (Oxford: Oxford University Press).

PETTIT, PHILIP (1987), 'Rights, Constraints and Trumps', *Analysis*, 47: 8–14.

—— and SMITH, MICHAEL (1993), 'Practical Unreason', *Mind*, 102: 53–79.

—— (1996), 'Freedom in Belief and Desire', *Journal of Philosophy*, 93: 429–49.

RAILTON, PETER (1984), 'Alienation, Consequentialism, and the Demands of Morality', *Philosophy and Public Affairs*, 13: 134–71.

RAWLS, JOHN (1971), *A Theory of Justice* (Cambridge, Mass.: Belknap Press).

ROUSSEAU, JEAN-JACQUES (1762), *Émile*.

SCANLON, T. M. (1982), 'Contractualism and Utilitarianism', in A. Sen and B. Williams (eds.), *Utilitarianism and Beyond* (Cambridge: Cambridge University Press).

SCHEFFLER, SAMUEL (1979), 'Moral Scepticism and Ideals of the Person', *Monist*, 62: 288–303.

—— (1982), *The Rejection of Consequentialism* (Oxford: Clarendon); rev. edn., 1994.

—— (1988a), *Consequentialism and Its Critics* (Oxford: Oxford University Press).

—— (1988b), 'Agent-centered Restrictions, Rationality, and the Virtues', in Scheffler 1988a; repr. in the rev. edn. of Scheffler 1982.

—— (1992a), *Human Morality* (Oxford: Oxford University Press).

—— (1992b), 'Prerogatives without Restrictions', *Philosophical Perspectives*, 6: 377–97; rev. and repr. in the rev. edn. of Scheffler 1982. (References are to the rev. edn.)

—— (1995a), 'Individual Responsibility in a Global Age', *Social Philosophy and Policy*, 12: 219–36.

—— (1995b), 'Families, Nations and Strangers', *The Lindley Lecture* (Lawrence, Kan.: University of Kansas Press).

SIDGWICK, HENRY (1907), *The Methods of Ethics* (7th edn.).

SOSA, DAVID (1993), 'Consequences of Consequentialism', *Mind*, 102: 101–22.

SMITH, MICHAEL (1987), 'The Humean Theory of Motivation', *Mind*, 96: 36–61.

—— (1988), 'Reason and Desire', *Proceedings of the Aristotelian Society*, *1987-88*, 243–56.

—— (1994), *The Moral Problem* (Oxford: Blackwell).

—— (1995), 'Internal Reasons', *Philosophy and Phenomenological Research*, 55: 109–31.

STERBA, JAMES P. (1994), 'From Liberty to Welfare', *Ethics*, 104: 64–98.

STURGEON, NICHOLAS (1974), 'Altruism, Solipsism, and the Objectivity of Reasons', *Philosophical Review*, 83: 374–402.

SUMNER, L. W. (1987), *The Moral Foundation of Rights* (Oxford: Clarendon).

WALDRON, JEREMY (1981), 'A Right to do Wrong', *Ethics*, 92: 21–39.

—— (1994), 'Kagan on Requirements: Mill on Sanctions', *Ethics*, 104: 310–24.

WALLACE, R. J. (1990), 'How to Argue about Practical Reason', *Mind*, 99: 267–97.

WATSON, GARY (1975), 'Free Agency', repr. in Watson 1982.

—— (1982), *Free Will*, ed. G. Watson (Oxford: Oxford University Press).

—— (1987), 'Free Action and Free Will', *Mind*, 96: 145–72.

WIGGINS, DAVID (1976), 'Truth, Invention, and the Meaning of Life', repr. in Wiggins 1987.

—— (1987), *Needs, Value, Truth* (Oxford: Blackwell).

WILLIAMS, BERNARD (1973), 'A Critique of Utilitarianism', in J. J. C. Smart and Bernard Williams, *Utilitarianism: For and Against* (Cambridge: Cambridge University Press).

—— (1978), *Descartes* (Harmondsworth: Penguin).

—— (1980), 'Internal and External Reasons', repr. in Williams 1981.

—— (1981), *Moral Luck* (Cambridge: Cambridge University Press).

—— (1985), *Ethics and the Limits of Philosophy* (Cambridge, Mass.: Harvard University Press).

—— (1995), 'Saint-Just's Illusion', in his *Making Sense of Humanity* (Cambridge: Cambridge University Press).

INDEX

agent-neutral values:
  vs. agent-relative values 104–5,
    117–18, 126–9, 131–2, 142
  and the interpretation of action 10–11,
    102–11 *passim*
  and self-governance 12–14, 125–48
agent-relative values:
  vs. agent-neutral values 104–5,
    117–18, 126–9, 131–2, 142
  and cooperation 6–8, 50–9, 77–85
    passim
  and the explanation of action 9–10,
    89–100

Barry, Brian 35 n. 40
Brink, David 8 n. 14, 21 n. 10, 52 n. 7,
  8 n. 53, 87 n. 3, 117 n. 1, 169 n.
  31
Brook, Richard 66 n. 30

Christman, John 138 n. 40
consequentialism:
  act consequentialism 2, 18–26
  decision-theoretic consequentialism
    25–6
  indirect consequentialism 2–3,
    26–33
  individual conscience consequential-
    ism 30–3
  and morality's authority 165–70
    passim
  and social policy 21–5, 66 n. 29, 70 n.
    36, 80 n. 50
  as a form of value monism 10–11,
    12 n. 20, 17 n. 2, 116–17
contractualism:
  Hobbesian contractualism 3–4, 33–6
  Lockean contractualism 3–4, 36–9
  Nagelian contractualism 4, 44–7, 68,
    119 n., 127 n. 19
  Rawlsian contractualism 41–4, 49 n. 2
  Scanlonian contractualism 4, 39–41
  and morality's authority 47 n. 67,
    155–9, 167-8

as a form of value monism 9, 11,
  12 n. 20, 17 n. 2, 87, 117

Dancy, Jonathan 131 n. 31
Daniels, Norman 29 n. 28, 42 n. 57,
  113 n. 45
Darwall, Stephen 95 n.
Davidson, Donald 88–9, 100–15 *passim*,
  118 n. 6, 122, 130, 140, 141 n. 46
desires:
  Davidsonian theory of 88–9, 100–15
    passim
  dispositional analysis of 93–4,
    96–101, 112 n. 41
Dostoevsky, Fyodor 81, 159

externalism:
  about morality 87 n. 3
  about psychological content 90 n. 8

Fodor, Jerry 106 n. 33, 122 n. 12
Fogelin, Robert 122 n. 12
Foot, Philippa 69 n.
forced supererogation 59–62, 65–6, 76 n.
  44
Frankfurt, Harry 12 n. 21, 137–9
Freeman, Samuel 156 n. 4, 163 n. 20
free will:
  Frankfurt's account of 137–9
  vs. self-governance 139–40
Frey, R. G. 31 n. 32

Gauthier, David 15 n., 33 n. 36, 39 n. 49,
  145 n. 55
Gibbard, Allan 36 n. 42, 37 n. 46

Hare, R. M. 31 n. 32
Hobbes, Thomas 3 n. 7, 15 n., 33 n. 35
holism 92 n. 10, 106, 110 n. 40, 120,
  122–3
Hume, David 87 n. 2, 90–2, 93 n. 13
Hurley, S. L. 88 n. 55

impartial beneficence:
    contractualist accounts of 3–4,
        33–47
    initial definition of 1
    intuitive appeal of 16–18
    and self-governance 11–14, 148–54
individual autonomy:
    as a facet of self-governance 74–5,
        140 n. 44
    relation to personal integrity 73–7, 81
    and restrictions 63, 69–77
internalism:
    about morality 8 n. 13, 88 n. 6,
        90 n. 7, 118 n. 7, 131 n. 30, 169 n.
        32
    about psychological content 90 n. 8
    about reason 90–1, 94–7, 99, 111–12
interpretation 10–12, 88, 100–11, 119–25,
        129 n. 24, 130–5

Jackson, Frank 25 n. 20

Kagan, Shelly 1 nn. 1 and 3, 2 n. 4,
        17 n. 1, 24 nn. 16 and 17, 45 n. 64,
        46 n. 65, 57, 61, 158 n. 9,
        169 n. 33
Kamm, Frances Myrna 46 n. 66
Kant, Immanuel 147
Kavka, Gregory 121 n.
Kholberg, Lawrence 48 n.
Korsgaard, Christine 90 n. 8, 94,
        96 n. 16, 100 n. 23, 108 n. 36,
        131 n. 31, 132 n., 147 nn.

Lepore, Ernest 106 n. 33, 122 n. 12
Levi, Isaac 93 n. 12
Lewis, David 109 n.
libertarianism 34 n. 37, 40
Lippert-Rasmussen, Kasper 46 n. 66
Locke, John 3 n. 7, 36 n. 43
Lovibond, Sabina 88 n. 5
Ludwig, Kirk 122 n. 11
Lyons, David 24 nn. 17 and 18

McDowell, John 88 n. 5
Mill, John Stuart 21–5, 27, 29 n. 26,
        70 n. 36
moderated beneficence 45–6, 158, 165–6
Moore, G. E. 114
Morgenbesser, Sydney 93 n. 12
motives:
    Humean theory of 89–94
    vs. reasons 86

Murphy, Liam 40 n. 54, 50 n., 52 n. 8,
        56 n., 57 n. 13, 79 n. 49, 82 n. 54
Myers, R. H. 51 n.

Nagel, Thomas 4, 5 n. 9, 6 n. 11, 9 n. 16,
        10 n. 18, 44–7, 49, 68, 88 n. 4,
        90 n. 8, 91 n., 94, 96 n. 18,
        98 n. 19, 104 n., 105 n. 30,
        117 n. 3, 119 n., 126 n. 17,
        127 n. 19, 128 nn. 21 and 23,
        130 nn., 131, 141 n. 47, 144,
        157–9, 162–5, 167
neutral values, see agent-neutral values

objective commitments 12–13, 137–48
        passim, 151, 159

Parfit, Derek 121 n., 126 n. 17, 127 n. 19
personal integrity:
    as a facet of self-governance 13, 15,
        140 n. 44, 141–54 passim
    and prerogatives 53–5, 82–4
    relation to individual autonomy 73–7,
        81
Pettit, Philip 66 n. 30, 95 n., 160 n.
Plato 136 n., 140 n. 45
prerogatives:
    breadth of 57–9, 61–3, 77
    consequentialist accounts of 2–3,
        18–33
    cooperative rationale for 5–7, 50–5,
        82–4
    initial definition of 1
    intuitive appeal of 16–18
    vs. moderated beneficence 45–7
    Scheffler's formulation of 55–9
    and self-governance 142–8, 164–5
    strength of 55–7, 77–85
principle of charity 106 n. 32

Railton, Peter 25 n. 19, 53 n. 9
Rawls, John 29 n. 28, 41–4, 113, 115,116
reasons:
    contractualist conception of 114–15
    instrumentalist conception of 87–90,
        94–102, 112–13, 156–7
    vs. motives 86
    see also values
reflective equilibrium 29 n. 28, 116
    and radical interpretation 113–15
relative values, see agent-relative values
restrictions:
    breadth of 60–3, 69–75

consequentialist accounts of 2–3,
 18–33
cooperative rationale for 59–63
initial definition of 1–2
intuitive appeal of 16–18
Nagel's account of 45–7
Scheffler's arguments against 63–9
and self-governance 143–8, 164–5
strength of 71 n. 38, 75–7
rights 23–4, 60, 66 n. 29, 70 n. 36
Rousseau, Jean-Jaques 48–9, 140 n. 45

Scanlon, T. M. 4, 39–41, 44 n. 61, 155–7,
 163, 168 n. 27
Scheffler, Samuel 1 n. 3, 2 n. 4, 17 n. 1,
 20 n. 7, 43 n. 59, 45, 55–8,
 59 n. 18, 62–9, 75 n. 43, 77–84,
 142 n. 50, 163 n. 18
secondary principles 24–5, 27, 30
Sidgwick, Henry 128 n. 23
Sosa, David 19 nn.
Smith, Michael 87 n. 3, 93 n. 12, 95 n.,
 96 n. 18, 100 n. 23, 160 n.
special obligations 1 n. 1, 78, 81, 143 n.
 51
Sterba, James P. 39 n. 52
Sturgeon, Nicholas 131 n. 31
Sumner, L. W. 25 n. 19
supererogation 15, 51, 60, 79, 159
 see also forced supererogation

thresholds 26, 64, 73, 75-6, 81

values:
 commensurability of 14,
  152–3
 duality of 7–14, 116–19, 125–37,
  141–2, 152–4
 mutability of 12, 119–25
 objectivity of 10–11, 102–7,
  131–2
 and prerogatives 78 n. 47, 81–5,
  150–2
 relation to reasons 10 n. 18
 universality of 11, 107–8
 see also agent-neutral values; agent-
  relative values
veil of ignorance 42–4

Waldron, Jeremy 23 n. 14, 24 n. 16, 66 n.
 29
Wallace, R. J. 91 n.
Watson, Gary 138 nn.
Wiggins, David 88 n. 5, 141 n. 46, 142 n.
 48
Williams, Bernard 2 n. 5, 14, 52 n. 6,
 53 nn., 87 n. 2, 90 n. 8, 96 n. 18,
 110 n. 38, 117—18, 120–36
 passim, 142 n. 50
Wittgenstein 88 n. 5